Reasoning about Change

The MIT Press Series in Artificial Intelligence
Edited by Patrick Henry Winston and Michael Brady

Reasoning about Change

Time and Causation from the Standpoint
of Artificial Intelligence

Yoav Shoham

The MIT Press
Cambridge, Massachusetts
London, England

PUBLISHER'S NOTE
This format is intended to reduce the cost of publishing certain works in book form and to shorten the gap between editorial preparation and final publication. Detailed editing and composition have been avoided by photographing the text of this book directly from the author's prepared copy.

Illustrations on pages 29, 70, 107, and 141 by Jo Dean.

This book was printed and bound in the United States of America.

Library of Congress Cataloging-in-Publication Data

Shoham, Yoav.
  Reasoning about change.

  (The MIT Press series in artificial intelligence)
  Bibliography: p.
  Includes index.
  1. Artificial intelligence.   2. Reasoning.
3. Time.   4. Causation.   I. Title.   II. Series.
Q335.S487   1988   006.3   87-21360
ISBN 0-262-19269-1

Contents

Series Foreword

Artificial intelligence is the study of intelligence using the ideas and methods of computation. Unfortunately, a definition of intelligence seems impossible at the moment because intelligence appears to be an amalgam of so many information-processing and information-representation abilities.

Of course psychology, philosophy, linguistics, and related disciplines offer various perspectives and methodologies for studying intelligence. For the most part, however, the theories proposed in these fields are too incomplete and too vaguely stated to be realized in computational terms. Something more is needed, even though valuable ideas, relationships, and constraints can be gleaned from traditional studies of what are, after all, impressive existence proofs that intelligence is in fact possible.

Artificial intelligence offers a new perspective and a new methodology. Its central goal is to make computers intelligent, both to make them more useful and to understand the principles that make intelligence possible. That intelligent computers will be extremely useful is obvious. The more profound point is that artificial intelligence aims to understand intelligence using the ideas and methods of computation, thus offering a radically new and different basis for theory formation. Most of the people doing artificial intelligence believe that these theories will apply to any intelligent information processor, whether biological or solid state.

There are side effects that deserve attention, too. Any program that will successfully model even a small part of intelligence will be inherently massive and complex. Consequently, artificial intelligence continually confronts the limits of computer science technology. The problems encountered have been hard enough and interesting enough to seduce artificial intelligence people into working on them with enthusiasm. It is natural, then, that there has been a steady flow of ideas from artificial intelligence to computer science, and the flow shows no sign of abating.

The purpose of this MIT Press Series in Artificial Intelligence is to provide people in many areas, both professionals and students, with timely, detailed information about what is happening on the frontiers in research centers all over the world.

Patrick Henry Winston
Mike Brady

Acknowledgements

This manuscript is a slightly revised version of my Ph.D. dissertation written at the Computer Science Department of Yale University. The Department was an extremely stimulating environment. In addition, modern technology allowed me to interact with a very large number of people from diverse disciplines outside Yale. In the dissertation I acknowledged the support and ideas of thirty seven individuals. Since then I have recalled about ten additional names that should have been included, and, extrapolating, I have no doubt that there are still other names that will come to mind later on. A list of fifty names, and a partial one at that, would be ridiculous. That being the case, let me collectively thank my teachers and colleagues – at Yale, at other US universities (especially at Stanford), in Europe, in Israel and in Japan – and hope to be able to make the individual acknowledgements in more specific forums.

Among those acknowledged will be the members of my thesis committee, Pat Hayes, Mike Fischer, and, most importantly, my advisor, Drew McDermott. In the years to come I will try, undoubtedly without success, to attain Drew's knack for combining broad intuition with mastery of technical details.

I will probably not have another opportunity to publicly acknowledge the support and love of my friends and family during these past few years, especially those of my parents, Leila and Havis, of my sister, Dina, and of Tara Neuwirth, but such personal debts are best left out of public forums in the first place.

Preface

It is hard to think of a research area within Artificial Intelligence (AI) that does not involve reasoning about time in one way or another: medical diagnosis systems try to determine the time at which the virus infected the blood system; circuit debugging programs must reason about the period over which the charge in the capacitor increased; automatic programmers and program synthesizers must deduce that after procedure P is executed the value of variable X is zero; robot programmers must make sure that the robot meets various deadlines when carrying out a set of tasks; logics of knowledge must account for agents' knowledge and beliefs changing as a result of external input and internal reflection; and the list could be continued. An area which seems the least concerned with time is perhaps theorem proving in a domain that is inherently atemporal such as mathematics. Even there, however, when one becomes concerned with so-called meta-level reasoning, time (of the deductive process) is of primary concern.

It is no accident that time plays a central role in AI, since it is such a central notion in our everyday thinking. The image of "time's arrow" is ingrained deep into our perception of the world. Everyone has experienced how some of his/her memories seem to be organized around the axis of time: often semantic cues fail to retrieve an item of memory, and yet that piece of information surfaces easily when one reconstructs events chronologically. For example, when asked to recall amusing events during a month-long hitchhiking trip in France made eight years ago, I can recall only a handful. At the same time, I can a give an almost day-to-day account of that period, and in doing so many more amusing tales come to memory. Our image of "time-flowing-forward" along a single line is quite strong, and notions of time that deviate from it — such as some interpretations of quantum mechanics which perceive time as constantly splitting into the future, or some philosophical treatments of circular time — are counterintuitive to most people.

Almost as central to our intuitive grasping of the world is the concept of *causation*. We view the world as being governed by rules according to which events in the past "cause" others in the future, as if a universal machine existed with abstract levers and gears transferring force to one another. Yet, as central as the concept is to our everyday thinking, philosophers have grappled with the problem of defining causation for centuries.

This book offers a method for representing temporal information and reasoning about it. The emphasis here is threefold:

1. The formulations are required to be both rigorous and natural: they need precise and yet intuitive semantics.

2. The formulations must support specific sorts of inferences. Those inferences should be efficient, and hopefully also natural.

3. The above requirements are not to come at the expense of realistic models of the world. The rules according to which the world operates are complex, and formulations which require one to overidealize it (in order to meet either of the previous requirements, say) are of no interest.

As a by product of these requirements, the formulations suggest a new account of causation, according to which it is a formal concept whose purpose is to accommodate the conflicting demands of reliability and efficiency when predicting the future.

Book Organization

Chapter 1. In this introductory chapter I discuss the particular task with which I am concerned, the *prediction task*, and show two problems that arise in connection with it — the *qualification problem* and the *extended prediction problem* — which are related to the infamous *frame problem*. Since much of this thesis discusses various logical formalisms, I explain the role logic plays in this manuscript. I very briefly introduce the notion of *nonmonotonic logics*, which will play a central role in the solution to the problems just mentioned. I also say a few words on modal logic for the benefit of the readers who happen to have not been exposed to it before.

Chapter 2. A prerequisite for reasoning about change is a language for representing temporal information. In this chapter detailed requirements from such a language are discussed, and two languages are given which meet these requirements, a classical one and a modal one. In connection with these logics I discuss how to distinguish between facts, events, processes, and other similar notions. The two logics are in fact closely related, and in particular I show a translation from the modal logic to the classical one. I then explore the difficulty of deciding whether an arbitrary given formula is valid in the logics.

Chapter 3. Various nonmonotonic logics have been proposed in the recent past, all having strong surface differences. Here I offer a somewhat new, model-theoretic approach to constructing and understanding nonmonotonic logics. This new perspective unifies much of the existing literature on nonmonotonic logics. It also suggests ways of defining radically new nonmonotonic logics, and indeed in the next chapters one such logic is defined.

Chapter 4. Here a solution is offered to the qualification problem mentioned earlier. I first define the logic of *chronological minimization*, a nonmonotonic version of the propositional interval logic defined in Chapter 2. While having some attractive properties, this logic has serious deficiencies as a solution to the problem. To overcome those, the logic is generalized to the logic of *chronological ignorance*, a nonmonotonic modal logic.

In general, the logic of chronological ignorance is quite difficult to reason about. However, I identify a special class of theories in the logic, called *causal theories*, and show that these not only have simple model-theoretic properties (in particular, each causal theory has essentially a unique model), but are also very easy to reason about.

Chapter 5. In this chapter a solution is proposed to the second problem, the extended-prediction problem. The intuitive notion behind the solution is that of *potential histories.* These are ways the world tends to behave, the "natural" course of events. It is shown that this intuitive concept can be captured within the logic of chronological ignorance: while causal theories are not sufficient for this purpose, a somewhat larger class of theories is. These so-called *inertial theories* can on the one hand capture the notion of something taking place "as long as nothing interferes with it," and on the other hand share some of the elegant model-theoretic and computational properties of causal theories.

Chapter 6. The discussion in Chapters 4 and 5 suggests a new account of *caustion,* a concept which plays a central role not only in AI but also in our everyday thinking. Since causation has been the subject of much investigation in philosophy, I briefly survey three of the more influential modern accounts of it within philosophy. I also list some of the properties of causation, a list that brings out some of the difficulties in defining it, and which serves as partial "benchmarks" for any proposed account of the concept. I then explicate my own account of causation, test it against these "benchmarks," and relate it to the three philosophical accounts surveyed earlier. I end the chapter by summarizing what role I think causation can be expected to play in AI, what its potential limitations are, and in the process discuss some of the past work on causal reasoning in AI.

Chapter 7. This summary chapter starts with a short inventory of what this dissertation has accomplished, but most of it is devoted to various limitations of the discussion in chapters 4 and 5, and possible ways to overcome some of these.

Dependence among chapters. The material is organized so that each chapter requires reading the chapter preceding it, but there are some exceptions. The reader who is not interested in the debate over the use of logic, or in a sketchy overview of modal logic, may skip the respective parts of Section 3 in Chapter 1. In Chapter 2 it is sufficient to read Sections 1-3 in order to go on to the next chapter. The other two sections (4 and 5), although very relevant to the chapter, are not needed later on. Chapter 3 is by and large independent of the previous ones, and the reader interested only in nonmonotonic logics can read it in isolation. On the other hand, the reader who wants only as many details of nonmonotonic logic as are needed for the later chapters should skip Section 3. The last major exception to the linear dependence in the text is Chapter 6, in which the general discussion of causation (Sections 1 and 2), which precedes my specific proposal, can be read in relative isolation from anything else. Other parts of Chapter 6 depend on the previous chapters, except for chapter 5. In general, I have tried to indicate in the text itself those parts that are not essential for understanding the remainder of the text.

Reasoning about Change

Chapter 1

Introduction

This book investigates issues in formal reasoning about time. Of course, the passage of time is important only because *changes* are possible. In a world where no changes were possible — no viruses infecting blood systems, no electrical charges changing, no changes in program counters, not even changes in the position of the sun in the sky or the position of the hands on our wrist-watches — not only would there be no computational justification for keeping track of time, but the very concept of time would become meaningless. Not a particularly profound philosophical observation, I nonetheless point it out as a basis for understanding the issues in temporal reasoning. According to it, a theory of time (or, I should say, a theory of *time and change*) must provide the following:

1. A language for describing what is true and what is false over time, what changes and what remains constant.

2. A way of defining and reasoning about rules of "lawful change" in the above language.

By the second requirement I mean something like the following. If you believe in standard laws governing the behavior of physical objects, and if you believe that **ball1** is rolling towards the now-stationary **ball2**, then the rules of lawful change force you to believe that **ball1** will continue to roll and **ball2** will continue to stay put until the impending collision. These particular rules of lawful change are otherwise known as *physics*. I find the term physics appealing and so I will generalize its meaning, calling *any* set of criteria of lawful change "physics." These, however, should be understood most generally: physics, or lawful change criteria, may apply to interpersonal domains ("after insulting b, a invariably feels remorse"), economics ("it is always the case that six months after interests rates go up house prices drop by 20 percent"), the blocks world ("after the action PUTON(a,b) is performed the proposition ON(a,b) holds"), and so on.

Our somewhat vaguely stated goal was to reason about change, but the success or failure of our formulations must be judged relative to a particular class of goals. What specific tasks in temporal reasoning are we aiming at?

One can identify in AI several classes of tasks which require reasoning about time, and their very sketchy characterization is as follows.

1. *Prediction*: Given a description of the world over some period of time, and the set of rules governing change (or physics), predict the way the world will be in some future time. For example, given the current trajectories of two rolling balls, predict their collision.

2. *Explanation*: Given a description of the world over some period of time, and of the physics, produce a description of the world at some earlier time that (together with the physics) accounts for the world being the way it is at the later time. For example, given that you heard a loud noise infer that there must have been a collision between two balls immediately preceding it.

3. *Planning*: Given a description of some desired state of the world over some period of time, and of the physics, produce a sequence of actions that would result in a world fitting that description. For example, to bring about a world in which there was a loud noise at certain point in time, plan to roll two balls towards each other. This is related to the process of explanation, except that here one asks not only "what must be true in order for the world to be a certain way," but also "do I have it in my power to make those things true."

4. *Learning new physics*: Given a description of the world at different times, produce a physics which accounts for regularities in the world.

Although these classes of tasks are obviously related, in AI they have given rise to by and large disjoint fields of research. They vary in complexity, and the prediction task seems to be the easiest, since the other tasks rely on a good solution to it. It turns out, however, that already this easiest task is quite hard, and in fact this entire research effort is aimed at solving it. The remainder of this chapter is devoted to exploring the particular problems associated with predicting the future, and to discussing the methodology that will be adopted in looking for solutions to those problems.

1.1 The prediction task

To see what problems are involved in writing physics which make it possible to predict the future, let us consider a simple case of predicting the behavior of physical objects. Imagine an intelligent robot watching friends play a game of billiards.[1] We join him when there are exactly two balls left on the pool table, and together with the robot we watch them roll towards a collision point as shown in Figure 1.1. We know exactly what is about to happen: the two balls will collide and bounce off appropriately, as shown in Figure 1.2. The question is whether the robot can be expected to know that too, and if so how. How does the robot represent what he sees on the pool table, and what physics does he employ to predict the outcome?

1.1.1 Classical mechanics

Let us first examine what happens if the robot uses classical, or Newtonian, mechanics. Newtonian mechanics keeps track of the values of *quantities*, which are functions on time. These quantities are represented by variables whose values range over some interval of the reals. Examples of quantities are force $f(t)$, acceleration $a(t)$ and mass $m(t)$. The latter is, of course, a constant function in classical mechanics. Typically, the time argument to the functions is omitted, so one writes simply f, a and m. The actual formulation of the physical laws comes in the form of *equations*, which are constraints on values the quantities may assume simultaneously. An example of an equation is $f = m \times a$, which is really shorthand for $\forall t \; f(t) = m(t) \times a(t)$. Two special quantities are spatial location $x(t), y(t), z(t)$ and time itself t, in both cases of which the laws of physics refer only to relative value. The way this is enforced is by using differentials. Time and space appear *only* as differentials, as in $v \, dt = dx$. By convention the formulations include only time derivatives, reflecting the intuition that what physics is about is keeping track of the values of quantities as they change in time, and so the last equation appears as $v = dx/dt$, or (since the only derivatives are time derivatives) simply as $v = x'$. One finds also equations in which time *seems* to appear as an undifferentiated quantity (as in $v = a \times t$), but in these cases the t really stands for "elapsed time," or interval duration, and the equations can be viewed simply as a particular solution of the original differential equations (in this case, $a = dv/dt$), given certain

---

[1] John McCarthy has prepared me for the wrath of some who might be offended by my terminology. It seems that in the following I have confused the vulgar game of billiards with the noble activity of shooting pool, or was it the other way around.

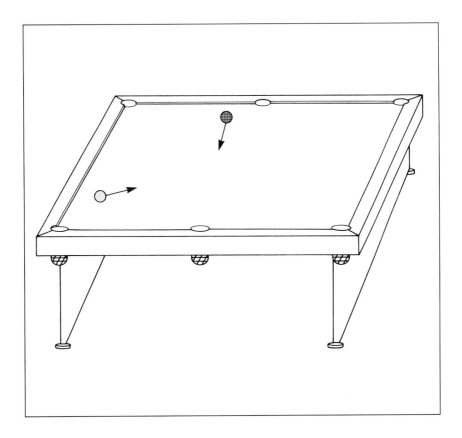

Figure 1.1: First part of the billiards scenario

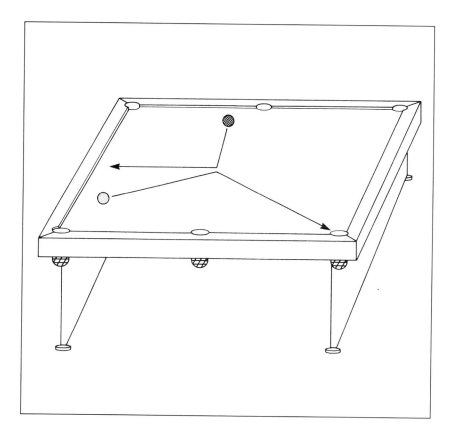

Figure 1.2: The complete billiards scenario

boundary conditions (in this case, $v_0 = 0$ and the fact that the acceleration
is constant). The same applies to equations that seem to mention absolute
spatial values.

To summarize, then, the way Newtonian mechanics talks about temporal information is by having functions of time be its subject matter. These
functions of time participate in sets of differential equations, in which all
derivatives are taken with respect to time. We now come to the question
of how one specifies the initial conditions in a physics problem, and what
permits one to predict from this specification that, say, the two balls will
collide. One would *like* to say that the initial conditions are the position
and velocity of the balls at some time prior to the collision (in order to simplify the analysis, we can assume that the balls are elastic and that they
are of equal mass and size). However, while this description is sufficient
for humans, it is not, strictly speaking, complete, and therefore insufficient
when subjected to formal inference techniques. The problem is that we
have not stated that there are no *other* balls that affect the trajectory of
the two particular balls. Even worse, it does not explicitly state that there
are no holes in the table through which balls might drop, no strong winds
that affect the trajectories of balls, and so on. What then constitutes a
correct description of the scenario?

In [61], Montague offers a formal analysis of Newtonian mechanics. Actually, he talks of *particle mechanics* and *celestial mechanics*. Particle
mechanics consist of Newton's three laws. Celestial mechanics is the specialization of it which specifies that the force between any two particles is
given by the law of gravitation. Montague's interest lies in testing whether
the formal theories have any of several formally defined properties, such as
that of being deterministic. For us what is interesting is the actual encoding
of the theory of particle mechanics (p. 311-318) (adding the gravitational
axiom is a straightforward specialization of the theory that doesn't concern
us immediately). Of that, much is devoted to axiomatizing the properties
of the real numbers and of the integers (p. 312-316). These don't concern
us here directly either since we assume those are well understood (in fact,
even with Montague's axioms we are still left with "nonstandard" models of numbers, and he conditions subsequent theorems on assuming the
standard model). What is important is Montague's encoding of Newton's
laws, which relies on viewing the world as an *n-particle system*. In other
words, the objects in the domain of discourse are exactly n particles, where
n is some fixed integer. The initial conditions are exactly those envisioned
by Laplace[2]: the mass, position and velocity of all the balls at some time
prior to the collision. In general, one must have a finite number of quan-

---

[2]The assertion due to Laplace is that the positions and momenta of all particles in

tites one is interested in, and the initial conditions are a complete listing of their values at some time point. In our domain, this translates to fixing the number of balls, and giving their individual positions and velocities at some point as the initial conditions.

There are some problems with this framework. First, all the initial conditions must refer to the exact same time point. That excludes questions of the form "If city A is 100 miles away from city B, train 1 leaves city A at 1:00 travelling towards city B at 20 mph, and train 2 leaves city B at 2:00 travelling towards city A at 15 mph, when will the two trains meet?," which are so common in textbooks. Second, it seems a little perverse to have to talk about scenarios with different number of balls as if they are unrelated. Is there no way to factor the number of balls out of the formulation? Furthermore, what if there are an infinite number of balls? In that case Montague's formulation does not apply, and for a good reason, as we shall see below when we discuss his encoding of the Newton's second law. Finally, even restricting ourselves to a single situation with a finite number of balls, what if there are very many of them? Do we really have to talk about millions of balls that are millions of miles away? In celestial mechanics these have an effect on the two balls under consideration (though a negligible one), but in the case of billiard balls they only do if they collide with one of the balls. While not a *logical* problem, it certainly poses a practical one.

I will return to these problems shortly, but for the moment let us proceed under the conditions that satisfy Montague's formulation, namely a finite number of balls whose initial conditions are given. In our example, suppose there are exactly five balls (including the two colliding balls), whose position, mass and velocity at some time instant prior to the collision is given. Our remaining task is to justify a modest version of Laplace's claim: given the description of all the balls at the initial time instant, deduce the collision and new trajectories of the two particular balls. To do that, we need to assign precise meaning to the laws of physics. Consider Newton's second law, $f = m \times a$, whose intended meaning is that at any given instant in time, the net force on an object is equal to the product of its mass and acceleration (since we assume uniform mass, we can assume the law $f = a$ and the appropriate adjustment of units). The meaning of the phrase *net force* is the summation of all individual forces acting on the object, and this is where the assumption of a fixed finite number of balls is critical. If there are n balls, the number of individual forces on each ball is $n - 1$, one for each other ball. (Actually, Montague would say that there are n forces,

---

the universe at one time completely determine their positions and momenta at all other times.

thus allowing for "external" forces.) This assumption can only be made
if we have fixed in advance the number of balls. Furthermore, it is easy
to make sense of the notion of summation if there are a finite number of
elements that are being summed. Montague's encoding in logic of the summation operator strongly relies on this finiteness. Things are less obvious
if we allow infinite summation, and in fact it's not clear what it means for
an infinite number of balls to collide. Of course, it makes perfect sense to
speak of an infinite number of balls, only a finite number of which collide at
any moment, but that too is outside the scope of Montague's formulation.
Anyway, since we're making Montague-like assumptions, all that remains
for us is to specify the individual forces that the balls exert on one another.
In Montague's case that force is the law of gravitation. In our case it is
the law of conservation of momentum. Given the law of conservation of
momentum, we can define the force between any two particles as follows.

1. Two balls exert force on each other *only* if they touch.

2. In this case the magnitude of this force is the appropriate function of
   their individual velocities, positions and directions at the time of the
   collision, and the law of conservation of momentum.

Given these assumptions, the laws of physics actually make the right
prediction: they constrain the two balls to collide and bounce off appropriately. This "prediction," however, is purely model theoretic. No attention
was paid to the problem of actually *computing* the point of collision. In fact,
it is very unclear how to perform the computation, since all axioms refer
to time *points*. Somehow we must identify the "interesting" points in time
or space, and interpolate between them by integrating differentials over
time. The problem seems a little circular, though, since the identity of the
interesting points *depends* on the integration. For example, understanding
where the two balls are heading logically precedes the identification of the
collision: if we don't know that the two balls are rolling towards each other,
there is no reason to expect something interesting at the actual collision
point.

How do people solve such physics problems? The inevitable answer
seems to be that they "visualize" the problem, identify a solution in some
mysterious ("analog") way, and only then *validate* the solution through
physics. Much of what goes on in the industry of so-called *qualitative
physics* can be viewed as at attempt to lift that shroud of mystery and
emulate the visualization process on a computer [11]. The solution offered
in qualitative physics is related to another issue addressed by it and which
was ignored here, the fact that precise numerical information (such as the

precise distance between two billiard balls) is unnecessary and unavailable. In qualitative physics it is replaced by qualitative information (such as that whether the distance between the two balls is zero or nonzero, and whether it is increasing, constant or decreasing). A set of such qualititive values gives rise to a qualitative *state*, and, given one such state, one uses the "envisionment" procedure to determine the next state (or set of possible next states).

The details of qualitative physics are not crucial here; all I needed was the principal idea behind the process of envisionment. The envisionment in the billiards domain is simple: it embodies the rule, which is a simple derivative of the physics, that a ball's velocity and travel direction is unchanged during an interval in which it collides with no other ball. But if in this one domain the heuristic for identifying interesting points is simple, in richer domains it is more complex. When we throw a rock we know that the next interesting time point is when its parabolic trajectory is interrupted by our neighbor's window, and when we fix our car's tire we know that the next interesting point is when we next drive over a sharp object. In general it can be arbitrarily hard to identify interesting points from the physics.

To summarize the discussion of classical physics, I have said that if we start out with the complete description of the balls at some point in time, stipulate that those are the only balls that exist, assume that no other potentially influential events take place (no other objects touch the balls, there are no holes in the table, no ball is about to explode, etcetera), adopt a Montague-like description of Newton's kinematic equations, and formulate a dynamic rule about the force exerted between any two balls, then classical physics captures the future behavior of the balls. The most serious drawbacks associated with this approach are:

1. The initial conditions must refer to a unique instant of time. Furthermore, we must give a *complete* description of the initial conditions, which, unless abbreviated, is too costly. So far we have no way of saying "this is all the information that is relevant to the problem."

2. The physics specify which predictions are warranted by the initial conditions, but not how to make them. This information must be supplied from outside the physics.

3. The rules of physics are constraints on the simultaneous values of quantities. This instantaneous flavor of the rules, which makes the formulation elegant and parsimonious, is the reason that predictions about extended periods of time are hard to make.

These shortcomings are actually manifestations of very general problems, ones that transcend the particular framework of classical physics. Before I explicate these general problems, though, let me first give a better feel for them by showing how they are manifested in a different setting, Hayes' *histories* framework.

1.1.2   Histories

In [32] Patrick Hayes suggested a new way of discussing physical scenarios: *histories*.[3] A history is a contiguous chunk of spacetime with which we associate a *type*. Intuitively, the type corresponds to period during which the behavior of the physical object is qualitatively the same. Hayes applied the theory to reasoning about the behavior of liquids. A piece of liquid can exhibit one of several behaviors: free falling, spreading on a surface, being contained in an upward-concave rigid object, entering a container, leaving it, and so on. Each of those is a history-type, and we can write axioms constraining the co-existence of several histories having various types. For example, no two histories may overlap in spacetime. Or, as another example, if there is an entering-history along the rim of a full container then there must also be a leaving (conservation of matter), and so on. The hope is that by creating a rich enough vocabulary of history-types and writing enough restrictions on them we will be able to capture the behavior of the physical objects.

Let us try to reason about our billiards scenario in the histories framework. In our domain of billiards we may want to speak about various kinds of histories: rolling histories, falling histories, parabolic-flight histories, collision histories, strong-wind histories, and probably many others. Let us not worry too much about the precise taxonomy, since the problem will not be lack of expressiveness but rather difficulty of reasoning. For the sake of discussion let us assume two types of histories: ROLLING histories and COLLISION histories, where ROLLING histories describe the rolling of a billiard ball along a straight line. Thus we can represent the scenario involving the two balls by four ROLLING histories, two for each ball, as shown in Figure 1.3: H11 denotes the history of the first ball until the collision and H12 denotes the history of the same ball after the collision, and similarly H21 and H22 denote the histories of the second ball before and after the collision, respectively. We could now write axioms describing the relation between H11, H12, H21 and H22. I won't do that; let us agree that such axioms could be written. The question we are interested in is,

---

[3]This paper actually appeared first in 1978.

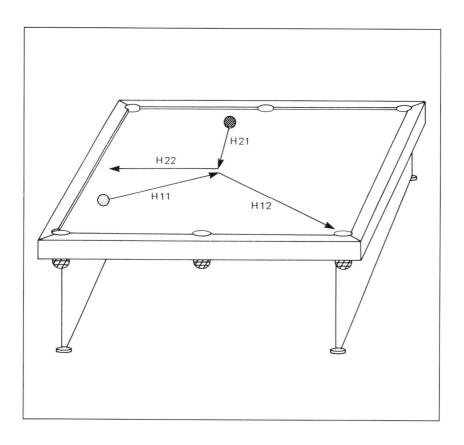

Figure 1.3: Four ROLLING histories

again, how to represent the initial conditions and from this representation
deduce the rest of the scenario.

A natural representation of the initial conditions is by two histories, one
for each ball. Those may be either respective prefixes of H11 and H21,
or else the initial *slices* of those two histories. (A slice is the projection
of a history onto a point in time. This option requires that we be able to
speak about the *velocity* of a history.) Let us consider the first case, shown
graphically in Figure 1.4, in which the initial conditions are prefixes of H11
and H21, say H11' and H21' (the other case would behave similarly.) We
would need axiom(s) that guarantee that the two balls continue rolling. In
other words, we need to predict two new ROLLING histories. What should
those two new histories look like? What should be their spatio-temporal
extent? Surely neither can extend beyond the collision point. Should the
two new histories end exactly at the collision point? If the answer is *no*,
then clearly we are in trouble, since we can iterate this process indefinitely.
We now have two new histories, say H11" and H21". From those we
need to conclude yet two more histories, and so on (see Figure 1.5). It
follows that the two new ROLLING histories H11" and H21" must end
exactly at the collision. What set of axioms could guarantee this property?
Furthermore, suppose we managed to provide axioms that constrain the two
new histories to end at the time of the collision. How could we effectively
compute this time given the axioms?

The key property of each of the two new histories is that it will persist
until it meets another history in spacetime, which in this case happens to
be the other new history. We need to somehow capture the property of
persisting "for as long as possible."

This brings us to another problem. One may say that since we have
only one other history, it is trivial to determine when and where the first
intersection between histories occurs. The problem with that is that we
have not explicitly said that there are no other histories. For example, we
have not explicitly ruled out the existence of a third ball deflecting one
of the two original balls before the collision with the other original ball.
It is tempting to say "ok, the *only* two histories are the ones I told you
about, H11' and H21'." That, however, is simply false, since beside those
two histories we have H11" and H21", the collision history, the two new
ROLLING histories following the collision, and so on. Nor can we say "the
only histories are the two given ones and those that follow from them," at
least not until we define the notion of "following from."

These problems with using the histories framework are closely related
to the problems with using classical mechanics, which were discusses in

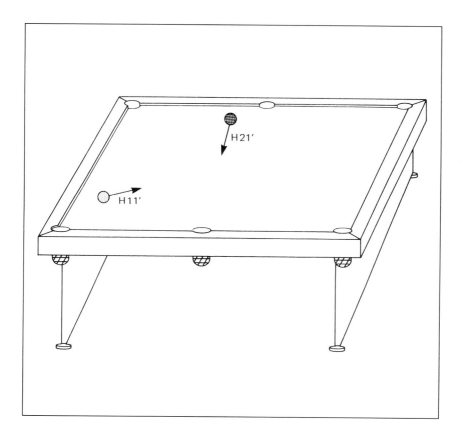

Figure 1.4: Initial conditions of the scenario

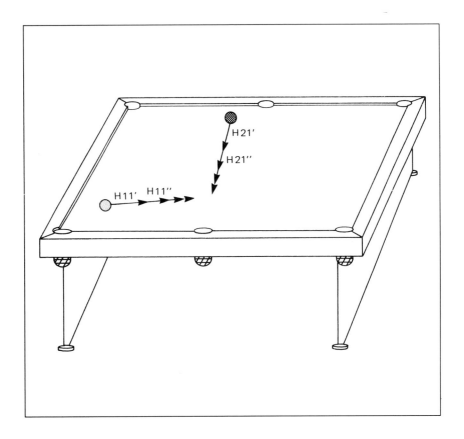

Figure 1.5: An infinite number of histories?

the previous subsection, and to the infamous *frame problem*. The general nature of the problems is discussed in the next section. Two formalism-independent problems are identified, and those explain the particular problems encountered in both classical physics and the histories framework.

1.2   The "qualification," "extended prediction," and "frame" problems

The problems that arise in either classical mechanics or the histories framework are symptomatic of all systems for reasoning about change. The general problem is how to reason *efficiently* about what is true over extended periods of time, and it has to do with certain tradeoffs between risk-avoidance and economy in the process of prediction.

Any rules-of-change (or physics) must support inferences of the form "if *this* is true at time t_1 then *that* is true at time t_2." Since we are interested primarily in predicting the future, a special case of this form will be of particular interest, in which $t_1 \leq t_2$. The crux of the first problem is that the "if" part might get too large to be of practical use. For example, if one wishes to be careful about her predictions, in order to infer that a ball rolling in a certain direction will continue doing so she must verify that there are no strong winds, that no one is about to pick up the ball, that the ball does not consist of condensed explosives that are about to go off in the next instant of time, and we can continue this list, getting arbitrarily ridiculous. Or, to use another example which will be used later on, when one pulls the trigger of a loaded gun one would like to predict that a loud noise will follow, but, strictly speaking, there are a whole lot of other factors that need to be verified: that the gun has a firing pin, that the bullets are made out of lead and not marshmallows, that there is air to carry the sound, and so on.

The alternative is to be less conservative and base the predictions on only very partial information, hoping that those factors which have been ignored will not get in the way. This means that from time to time one must be prepared to make mistakes in her predictions (after all, the ball *might* turn out to be a miniature hand grenade whose fuse has just run out, and someone *might* have tampered with the gun), and be able to recover from them when she does.

I will call this the *qualification problem.*[4] To summarize, it is the problem of trading off the amount of knowledge that is required in order to

---

[4]In [88] I called it the *intra-frame problem*. I then regretted that term, and in [87] I renamed it the *initiation* problem. Later I found that term too inappropriate, and since Matt Ginsberg pointed out the similarity between "my" problem and the problem John McCarthy called the *qualification problem*, I decided to adopt the latter term. Although McCarthy's notion might have been broader than the one presented here, I don't think I'm misusing the terminology too badly.

make inferences on the one hand, and the accuracy of those inferences on the other hand. In the particular context of predicting the future, it is the problem of making sound predictions about the future without taking into account everything about the past. Notice that the problem would disappear if we were willing to dramatically idealize the world: we could take it as a fact that noise always follows the firing of a loaded gun, and simply assume that guns always have firing pins, that there are never vacuum conditions, and so on. The premise of this discussion, however, is that such an overidealization is a nonsolution, since the whole point is for our robots to be able to function in a realistically complex environment.

Severe as it is, the qualification problem is not the only problem that exists, and even if we solved it we would still be in trouble. Briefly, although we would be able to make individual inferences fairly easily, we might be forced to make very many of them. Since we are interested in the prediction task, let me explain the problem in the particular context of predicting the future.

The problem now has to do with the length of time intervals in the future to which the predictions refer (regardless of how much information about the past we require in order to make the predictions), or with the "then" part of the "if-then" inference mentioned earlier. Again, it involves a tradeoff between efficiency and reliability. The most conservative prediction refers to a very short interval of time, in fact an instantaneous one, but that makes it very hard to reason about more lengthy future periods. For example, if on the basis of observing a ball rolling we predict that it will roll just a little bit further, in order to predict that it will roll a long distance we must iterate this process many times (in fact, an infinite number of times). I will call this the *extended prediction* problem.[5]

We have seen the problem arise in classical physics: given (e.g.) the force f at time t, you can only deduce the velocity in the infinitesimal time period following t. In order to deduce the velocity after a finite amount of time you must perform integration over the appropriate interval, but you do not know which interval it is.

The disadvantages of the conservative prediction which refers to only a short time period suggest making predictions about more lengthy intervals. For example, when you hit a billiard ball you predict that it will roll in a straight line until hitting the edge of the table, and when you throw

---

[5](More naming history.) In [88] I called this the *inter-frame* problem. I then regretted that name and, borrowing from Drew McDermott, renamed it the *persistence problem* in [87]. Finally, I realized that persistence was a special case of the general problem, that of predicting occurrences over extended periods of time, and hence the current name.

a ball into the air you predict that it will have a parabolic trajectory. The problem with these more ambitious predictions is again that they are defeasible, since, for example, a neighbor's window might prevent the ball from completing the parabola. Indeed, this is exactly the problem we encountered in the histories framework: we had no coherent criterion for determining the duration of the predicted ROLLING histories.

To summarize, the general extended prediction problem is that, although we might be able to make predictions about short future intervals, we might have to make a whole lot of them before we can predict anything about a substantial part of the future. A special case of this is the *persistence* problem, which is predicting on the basis of the past that a fact will remain unchanged throughout a lengthy future interval (as opposed to the general problem of inferring arbitrary things about such an interval). For example, when we take the billiard ball out of the pocket and place it on a chosen spot on the table, we would like to predict that it will remain in that spot until we hit it.[6]

This problem was noticed a long time ago in the particular context of the *situation calculus*, the formalism introduced by John McCarthy and Patrick Hayes in 1969 [54]. The situation calculus takes as basic the notion of *situations*, which are snapshots of the world at a given moment in time. The result of performing an *action* is the transition from one situation to another.[7] For example, if the action PAINT(HOUSE17,RED) is taken in any situation s_1, the result is a situation s_2 in which the color of HOUSE17 is red. But now consider taking the action REARRANGE-FURNITURE in s_2, which results in a new situation s_3. What is the color of HOUSE17 in s_3? One would like to say that it is still red, since rearranging the furniture does not affect the color of the house, but unfortunately the formalism does not say that. We could add to the formalism the fact that after you rearrange the furniture the color of the house remains unchanged, and this would be what McCarthy and Hayes call a *frame axiom*. The problem is

---

[6](A philosophical aside.) In [59] Drew McDermott notes that most facts in the world are persistent, and luckily so, because otherwise the world would appear very chaotic and unpredictable to us (or, to quote his version of the well-known phrase, the world would become a "blooming buzz"). It seems to me that an alternative view is possible, which relies on a cognitive version of Heisenberg's uncertainty principle. According to this view much of the world is indeed in a state of unfathomable flux, perhaps most of it, and we latch onto the (possibly scarce) time invariants simply because that is all we are capable of doing. The objects and properties of which we talk and think are exactly those out of which we can construct meaningful assertions that are not invalid by the time they are constructed.

[7]For those familiar with dynamic logic, this is precisely the view of the world in a dynamic logic with only deterministic atomic programs and only the composition operator.

that you'd need many such axioms: rearranging the furniture doesn't clean the floors, doesn't change the president of the United States, and the list can be continued infinitely.

(Notice that the problem becomes even worse if one allows concurrent actions, which the situation calculus did not. In this case the frame axioms are simply wrong: someone *might* paint your house while you are busy rearranging your furniture. So we must add an exception to the rule: rearranging furniture results in no change in the color of the house, unless in the meanwhile someone paints the house a different color. But even this isn't quite right, since although someone might paint your house, he might be using a paint that fades away immediately. Therefore we must state an exception to the exception, and so on.)

McCarthy and Hayes called this the *frame problem*.[8] I have had mixed success persuading colleagues that the persistence problem and the frame problem coincide. Since the frame problem was never defined in more detail or generality than it was two paragraphs ago, it seems that the argument is somewhat futile. Certainly philosophers have read into the frame problem even more than the general extended prediction problem (see, e.g., [80]). At any rate, these terminological quibbles are not crucial. What is important is to understand the problems.

The bulk of this thesis is devoted to solving the qualification and extended prediction problems. Solving the qualification problem requires that we show how, based on only very partial information, one can nonetheless make inferences that have some rationale behind them. Similarly, solving the extended prediction problem requires that we exhibit a way of making inferences about significant stretches of time, in a way that is both a sound and efficient. While the details of the proposed solutions are given in later chapters, in the next section I outline the approach taken in searching for solutions.

---

[8]The reference is to animated movies, where consecutive frames usually have identical backgrounds, and differ only in a few local features.

1.3   Methodology

Throughout this manuscript I will be talking about logic, and there has been much controversy over the role of logic in AI research. Let me then first make it clear how I stand on this issue.

1.3.1   On the use of logic in AI

One of the oldest battles in AI is over the use of logic in the field. One can identify two extreme examples of AI researchers. The first are those who spend their lives fiddling with formalisms, worrying about minute technical details, and rarely stopping to worry whether the formalisms are of significant import to AI. On the other extreme one finds those who believe that the only worthy activity in AI is writing programs to handle particular tasks. The second group views the first as consisting of people who use the formalisms as an excuse to avoid thinking about the real problems that need to be solved, just like the drunk who looked for his lost nickel not in the dark where he'd dropped it, but by the lamp-post, where it was easier to see. Some of their arguments against logic are discussed below. The first group views the second as a bunch of self-deluding fools at best, whose programs are trivial and inextensible. Few people fall directly into one extreme or the other, and, although I will be talking in terms of logical systems throughout this manuscript, I don't wish to be associated with the first extreme.

My reasons for using logic are much those that have been offered in the past, for example by Patrick Hayes [31], John McCarthy (in many forums, but in no specific publication of which I can think), and Robert Moore [63]. In particular I will stress the need for maintaining a clear meaning of our theories at all times, which in the context of logic means maintaining model-theoretic semantics. This appeal to mental hygiene was expressed most eloquently by Drew McDermott in [58] (but see [56] for his more recent and somewhat disenchanted view of logic).

Some criticisms of logic are plain silly. For example, the argument "people don't think by making logical inferences, and therefore we shouldn't expect our programs to" is misguided. The claim is not that people think deductively, nor that programs should. However, logic is not all that weird, otherwise it would not have survived as long as it has: even the staunchest opponent of logic could not object to the soundness of, say, *modus ponens*. It is clear that we have the capability of following logical arguments, even ones we could not come up with ourselves. All this means is that we are too limited in our abilities to pursue the consequences of our knowledge, or to arrive at new knowledge only by carefully deriving it from old one. Since our programs have similar limitations with regard to reasoning resources, we can hardly expect them to be less fallible. At the same time that does not mean that our programs shouldn't be able to recognize a good argument when they see one.

For a similar reason I am not impressed with the argument "the domains with which AI deals are inherently messy, and logic is too neat and tidy to be of any use." The argument here is really not against logic in particular but against precision and rigor in general, and it confuses the uncertainty of knowledge with the unclarity of thought. This complaint about logic is the same complaint a lazy pupil has about a severe teacher, namely that the teacher forces him to confront his ignorance. The fact that we use a precise logic doesn't mean that we require that our theories take a stance on every proposition under the sun. The opposite is true: precisely because we are dealing with situations in which information is scant and disorganized, it is doubly important to be clear about what we do and do not know.

While these common arguments against logic and similar other ones do not seem to carry much weight, there are others with which I actually agree. The first one is against the uniqueness of logic as a source of clarity. We use logic because it leaves minimal room for speculation as to the meaning of our theories. The way logic does so is certainly not by merely enforcing a rigid syntax and proof theory; those are almost incidental. Rather, logic is enlightening because it reduces any discussion to the level of naive set theory, at which truth is taken to be self-evident. It is therefore also the case that logic is no better than any other formulation which rests upon universally-agreed-upon foundations. For example, when reasoning about physical objects, some spatial primitives (such as addition of angles modulo 2π) seem as clear and natural as any operations on sets. The argument that these geometric operations can be embedded in set theory is irrelevant; the point is that such an embedding will not add anything to our understanding. Indeed, when some time ago I tried to axiomatize several aspects of the shape of rigid two-dimensional objects, I felt quite foolish: the logical formulation shed no new light on the geometric one, and in fact on its own would be quite opaque (see [35] for a report on "commonsense summer"). So I agree that logic has no sole rights as a source of clarity, but stress that we need to make sure that *some* source of rigor is present. While in theoretical computer science this is common practice, in AI it has been far from the norm.

The second argument against logic, which is still a weak one but nonetheless contains a grain of truth in it, is the drunk-and-lamp-post argument, namely that people using logic spend their time worrying about minute technicalities which have nothing to do with the problems to which the logic is supposed to be applied. I agree that it has sometimes been the case that much too general logics have been proposed for various purposes and developed in some detail, and that instead of demonstrating their utility in concrete and substantial cases their proposers only pointed out intuitively appealing properties of the logics. In those case the logical investigations were justified in part, if only implicitly, on the basis of their mathematical ingenuity and elegance, rather than any new light they shed on some fundamental problem. Our lesson should be to always keep the motivating problem in sight, and to make sure that any logical investigation we undertake is directly relevant to solving that problem.

There is a related argument against logic, a much stronger one, which is related also to the first argument which I dismissed. There I said that people can appreciate logical arguments even though they employ nonlogical techniques in their own reasoning, something of a Chomskian competence/performance distinction. That raises the question of what part of the reasoning process the logical analysis constitutes. The critics of logic, even if they concede that the logical analysis of things makes sense, might say that it is still an insignificant part of thinking, and that since deduction is not the primary inference mechanism we should concentrate instead on other mechanisms of reasoning. This argument appears in both a moderate form and an extreme form, depending on the proposed alternative processes. The moderate proposal is to replace logical analyses by less rigid symbolic processes, such as induction or abduction (or "plausible explanantion"). The extreme form is to dismiss the premise that the basis for reasoning must be symbolic processing, but that instead it should be a biological-like mechanism simulating neural activity (i.e., the various connectionist paradigms [84]).

This last argument deserves serious consideration, and is, at least in its moderate form, very reasonable. In fact, I agree with the claim that it is misguided to develop a logical representation that is not geared towards some particular class of tasks. There may be logical analyses that are devoid of a computational component but that are nonetheless illuminating (perhaps because they give insight into the underlying ontology), but they are rare. The bulk of this thesis concerns the question of how one makes efficient inferences within an inherently intractable logic. The ultimate test of our logics is whether or not they can be used to reason efficiently about a significant class of problems that have to do with the passage of time. I intend to show that they can be, in a way that closely matches a method people have invented for their own reasoning about those same problems. Furthermore, the reasoning in the logic is not done by manipulating axioms and deriving sentences using inference rules. In general there is an over-emphasis in AI on axiomatic systems, even though the real importance of logic is its model theory. When we consider efficient inferencing in our logics we will reason directly about the models of our theories, dissociating the logic from any particular proof theory.

Even the extreme form of the argument against a symbolic basis for the reasoning process contains a grain of truth in it, although I strongly disagree with the conclusion that logical investigations are misguided. The argument for connectionism is ultimately irrefutable, since we have an existence proof in the form of the human (or for that matter, animal) brain. The only problem with the connectionist schemes is that they haven't worked. They never seem to perform any task having the complexity of, say, temporal reasoning. That doesn't mean that they will not get more sophisticated in time, but the burden of the proof that connectionism will eventually work lies, at this time, with its proponents. My guess is that the connectionist schemes cannot but improve in time, but that as the mechanisms get more complex we will need more sophisticated ways of programming them and especially for discussing their behavior. We will end up inventing some high level description of the machine's behavior, just like higher-level computer languages replaced machine language, and just as people invented constructs such as logic to help put some order in their otherwise convoluted and unstructured process of thinking.

Still, as I have said, there is a grain of truth in the argument in favor of "neural representations." One of the main problems with logic is its "brittleness." By that I mean not only the practical impossibility of performing perfect logical inferences, but the limitations of the very notion of a precisely defined concept. The difficulty in defining concepts via necessary and sufficient conditions is well known, witness Wittgenstein's discussion of the blurred boundaries of the concept of 'game' [102], and Rosch and Mervis's experiments on 'family resemblance' between concepts and 'prototypicality' [83]. The basic claim is that concepts are not well defined, but instead are more or less similar to one another. For example, consider a robot having to reason on the basis of his perceptions of the world, and assume that he has very detailed information on dogs. Suddenly he sees a smallish, friendly-looking, hair-covered, tail-wagging creature with sad round eyes, which gives the impression of starving for both food and companionship. Should he invoke his dog-rules in the case? The thing is different from any dog he'd ever seen before, but still is very dog-like. It would be nice if logic allowed one to make variable-strength inferences, so that the strength of the inference about this particular creature would depend on how dog-like it was.[9]

There are some logics that support a limited form of graded inferences, such as Zadeh's *fuzzy logic* [103] and Nilsson's *probabilistic logic* [67]. Perhaps those are sufficient to escape the brittleness of logic; it is hard to tell, given the limited experience with them. However, the neural representations offer an attractive alternative, in which not only the inferences are not clear-cut, but even the concepts are not. The idea is to associate a concept with a pattern of activity, with slight perturbations of that pattern corresponding to slight deviations from the original "concept." In fact, logical operations too can be encoded as patterns of activity, and, again, slight deviations from those patterns will result in slightly-less-than-logical inferences. Thus logical thinking can be viewed as merely the end of a spectrum, the other end being something like stream-of-consciousness thinking, complete with creative remindings and random nonsequiturs. If this picture is at all correct (if such an underspecified description can be said to be 'correct' or 'incorrect'), it still does not mean than logical analysis is worthless. It does follow, however, that at some point logical analysis should be embedded in the underlying neural machinery, and thus integrated with the less analytical modes of that machine. Such investigations lie far outside the scope of this dissertation.

Let me then summarize my position on logic. I will be using it as a way of lending clarity to my formulations. There may be other ways, but I have chosen logic, which on the one hand enjoys uncontested solid foundations, and on the other hand turns out to be useful for my purposes. Logic is not a solution to any problem, it is only a setting in which a clear solution can be given. Furthermore, I accept the fact that it is up to me to convince the reader that the logics are of any use. The proof should consist of the logics themselves that must have clear syntax and semantics and must be intuitively appealing (at least to the reader that is not inherently allergic to logic), but more crucially the proof must include of a method of using the logics naturally and efficiently for the purpose for which they were designed.

---

[9]The general need for fuzzy concepts was impressed on me by M. Minsky. Lest the particular example seem far-fetched, let me recount the story of my acquaintance, who brought back from Mexico a stray dog. He'd had him for several months when the dog became sick and had to be taken to the veterinarian. It was there that my friend was gently informed that his pet was in fact an unusually large rodent.

1.3.2   Nonmonotonic logics

Both the qualification problem and the extended prediction problem involve a tradeoff between reliability and precision in making predictions. The general idea behind the solutions to them is to indeed take the shortcuts and ignore much of the information that is potentially relevant, and thus pay the price of having to retract some of the conclusions in the face of contradicting evidence. The trick will be to keep this price down to a minimum.

First we need to provide a coherent criterion for making defeasible inferences. If one appeals to classical logic all one gets in return is cold silence, since there the notion of defeasible conclusions is meaningless. Some point out to this as confirmation that practical inferences are not logical. The fact of the matter is, however, that defeasible inferences can be shown to rest on very logical (if nonclassical) foundations, which brings us to nonmonotonic logics.

In classical logic anything that follows from a set of facts follows also from an enlarged set of facts. In other words, if $A \models C$ then $A \wedge B \models C$. In this sense it is said that classical logic is *monotonic*. This is true of propositional calculus and first-order predicate logic, and for that matter also of higher-order predicate logic and modal logic. *Nonmonotonic logics* are those which do not have this this property.

Defeasible inferences are inherently nonmonotonic. For example, from the fact that a ball is rolling in a certain way we infer that it will continue to do so, but if we add the fact that there is another ball directly in its path we change our prediction. This is why defeasible inferences cannot be represented in the classical logics. It also suggests that nonmonotonic logics may be more suitable.

The solutions I will propose to the problems indeed rely on nonmonotonic logic, but I will not adopt any of the existing proposals (e.g., McCarthy's *circumscription* [53], Reiter's *default logic* [81], McDermott and Doyle's *nonmonotonic logic I* [60], McDermott's *nonmonotonic logic II* [57], or Clark's *predicate completion* [10]). Instead, I will suggest a somewhat new, model-theoretic approach to constructing and understanding nonmonotonic logics. It turns out that none of the logics mentioned above capture the inferences in which we are interested, but that the new approach suggests other nonmonotonic logics that do. I will discuss the general approach to nonmonotonic logics in Chapter 3, and the particular nonmonotonic logic of *chronological ignorance* in the chapters following it.

1.3.3   A few words on modal logic

I have assumed that the reader is familiar with the basics of propositional calculus (PC) and first-order predicate calculus (FOPC), and will continue to assume that throughout the manuscript. I will be making substantial use also of modal logic, and undoubtedly most readers are familiar with that too. Still, I suspect that at least some of the readers are not, and I don't wish to lose them at this early point. Fortunately, the transition from classical logic to the modal one (assuming the now-standard Kripke semantics) is easy to explain, which I will now do. The reader who has even a basic understanding of modal logic should skip this subsection.

Consider a classical formula, either propositional or first-order. In order to explain its meaning we speak of *interpretations*, which in the PC case means a truth assignment for each of the propositional symbols, and in the FOPC case means the denotation of all constant-, function- and relation-symbols. A *Kripke structure*, which in modal logic is the analog of an interpretation and which was proposed by S. Kripke in [42], is the result of simply multiplying the above image.

More specifically, a Kripke structure consists of *worlds* (or *possible worlds*), each of which is a classical interpretation. The interpretations in distinct worlds can be quite different: a formula may be true in one world but not in another. If the worlds are PC interpretations then we have a *propositional modal logic*, and if they are FO interpretations then we get a *first-order modal logic*. In either case the worlds are connected by directed links: any two worlds may be connected in one direction, in both directions, or in neither. This relation between worlds is sometimes called the *accessibility relation*, sometimes the *reachability relation*, and sometimes the *alternativeness relation*. Different restrictions on this relation result in different modal systems. If it is reflexive then the Kripke structure is said to be a T-structure. If it is both reflexive and transitive then it is said to be an S_4-structure. If it is in addition symmetric then it is an S_5-structure (and it turns out that a relation that is reflexive, transitive and symmetric is really an equivalence relation).[10] Other modal systems are similarly defined.

If in classical logic the question is whether or not a formula is satisfied by an interpretation, in modal logic the question is whether or not a formula is satisfied by a Kripke structure *in a particular world*, since, as was just said, truth varies among worlds. The fact that φ is true in a Kripke structure K at a world w is denoted by $K, w \models \varphi$.

---

[10]For those familiar with these systems, I am not referring to *axiomatic* T, S_4 and S_5, but only to the structure of the possible worlds.

The reason modal logic is interesting is that we allow statements that are interpreted in one world to refer to other worlds, those that are accessible from it (that is, that are related to it by the accessibility relation). If φ is any formula, then the formula $\Box\varphi$ (pronounced "box φ" or "necessarily φ") is true in W_1 iff φ is true in *all* worlds that are accessible from W_1. Similarly, the formula $\Diamond\varphi$ (pronounced "diamond φ" or "possibly φ") is true in W_1 iff φ is true in *some* world that is accessible from W_1. It is easy to see that $\Diamond\varphi$ is equivalent to $\neg\Box\neg\varphi$.

Thorough introductions to modal logic are the books by Hughes and Cresswell [36] and by Chellas [9].

The historical reasons for modal logic were the wish of philosophers to distinguish between "necessary truth" and "contingent truth," and the $\Box$ and $\Diamond$ notation preceded the formal model-theoretic interpretation of Kripke. Given the formal semantics, however, one can attach any intuitive meaning to the possible worlds that is consistent with their formal definition. Several such meanings have been used in the past, and in fact I will make use of two different ones myself.

One common use of modal logic is in logics of time. In this particular application possible worlds are typically identified with *time points*, and the accessibility relation with the temporal precedence (to be precise, it is usually assumed that the "world" t_2 is accessible from the "world" t_1 iff $t_1 \leq t_2$). Since the $\leq$ relation is both reflexive and transitive one gets an S_4-system. For example, the formula $\neg\textbf{rain} \supset \Box\neg\textbf{rain}$ means that "if it's not raining now then it never will." I too will be speaking about a modal temporal logic, but with one further twist: worlds will be equated with time *intervals* rather than time points, and therefore also different modal operators will be used.

Another application of modal logic, which has gained much popularity lately and which is related to another use that I will make of modal logic, is as a logic of knowledge. This application, which has its roots in the work of Hintikka [34], was used by Moore to reason about intelligent agents [62], and more recently by Halpern, Moses, Fischer, Immerman and many others to reason about distributed computation (see, e.g., [26]). In this application the set of possible worlds is equated with the set of all the ways the world could have been which are compatible with what an agent knows in a given world. An agent is said to know a proposition in a particular world if the proposition is true in all worlds that are accessible from that world. Here the symbol $\Box$ is often replaced by the symbol K, and so the fact that an agent knows φ is represented by the formula Kφ. In the particular context of distributed computation, worlds are the *global histories* of the computation, or the sequence of states each processor went through. For each processor p with a given *local history* h (that is, the sequence of states p itself went through), the set of possible worlds are the set of global histories in which the local history of p is also h, that is, all global histories that are "indistinguishable" as far as p is concerned.

The most important thing to notice about modal logic is that it is unnecessary from the technical point of view. Any modal logic can be replaced by a first-order one, in which the "possible worlds", whatever they denote, are simply made into objects in the language, the accessibility relation becomes a relation symbol, and $\Box$ and $\Diamond$ become quantifiers. Taking propositional modal temporal logic as a case in point, one can replace (e.g.) the modal formula

$$\neg\texttt{rain} \supset \Box\neg\texttt{rain}$$

by the first-order formula

$$\neg\ \texttt{rain}(\texttt{t}_1) \supset \forall\ \texttt{t}_2\ (\texttt{t}_1 \leq \texttt{t}_2 \supset \neg\ \texttt{rain}(\texttt{t}_2)).$$

The reason it is sometimes convenient to use the modal logic is because it is concise and elegant, as the example just given shows. Furthermore, modal logic gives us the opportunity to accord a certain type of individuals, those that correspond to the possible worlds, a special status, so that they are understood implicitly without need for explicit mention.

From the definitions it follows that, just like classical logic, modal logic is monotonic. Here too we can define nonmonotonic versions of the logic, in a way that is entirely analogous to the way we construct nonmonotonic versions of classical logic. Again, the details of the construction are discussed in Chapter 3.

1.3.4   Typography and notational conventions

I will use `this sort of font` to represent logical formulas. Thus, for example, the time point symbol will be $\texttt{t}$ whereas the time point itself will be t. Similarly, I will distinguish between the relation-symbol $\preceq$ and the actual relation $\leq$, although in a context in which a fixed interpretation of time is assumed, I will use $\leq$ also as a relation symbol.

As far as logical formulas go, I will distinguish between constants and variables. In the propositional case, I will use lower-case font to express propositional symbols, as in p, q, p_1 and `navigate`. In the first-order case I will use upper-case letters for constant-, function- and relation-symbols, reserving lower-case letters for variables, as in $\forall$ v (v>1980 $\supset$ PRESIDENT(v,USA,REAGAN)).

I will also be using the standard connectives ($\lor$, $\land$, $\neg$, $\supset$, $\equiv$) and quantifiers ($\forall$, $\exists$).

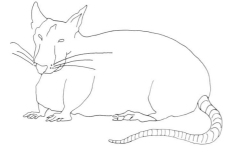

Chapter 2

Logics of Time Intervals

In the introductory chapter it was said that a prerequisite for reasoning about change is a language for representing temporal information. This chapter is devoted to developing such a language, and is organized as follows.

The first section discusses general choices that need to be made when deciding on a temporal representation, and the particular decisions I have made in this connection.

The second section introduces a logic of time intervals that is essentially a classical logic, giving both the propositional and first-order versions of it. The section also compares this logic to previous formalisms in AI, the one due to James Allen and the other to Drew McDermott.

In the third section I consider some ontological questions. What is the relation among what have been at different times called facts, properties, events, processes, occurrences, and other such animals? Are these distinct entities, or are they all derived from some basic construct? The usual answer, at least in AI, has been that they are distinct concepts that are related in various ways (for example by *causal connection*, a concept to which I will return in a later chapter). I will argue differently, and suggest that all these different concepts actually originate from the single notion of a *temporal proposition*.

These first three sections are the "required" part of the chapter, since later chapters depend on them. The last two sections are the "optional" reading.

Section 4 introduces a new, modal logic of time intervals, and includes a survey of previous interval-based modal logics (both in computer science and philosophy).

Section 5 is devoted to expressiveness and complexity issues, and is very brief. It is shown that the modal logic can be embedded in the classical one, and it is argued informally that the classical logic is in fact strictly more expressive. The complexity of the validity problem for the modal logic is also discussed. The main results that are mentioned are that the validity problem for the modal logic is generally undecidable, although how badly so depends on specific assumptions that are made about the structure of time.

Actually, I believe that the general satisfiability and validity problems are the wrong ones from the standpoint of AI, and give my reasons at the end of the section. I therefore also believe that the undecidability results should not discourage us. Decidability is discussed primarily because it is a central notion in theoretical computer science and certain philosophical circles, and discussion of the new logic would be incomplete without it. But since in my opinion we should be looking at other, more constrained issues (as I do in later chapters), the discussion in Section 5 is fairly brief, and the main results are given without most of the details (those appear in publications that are cited in the section itself).

Much of the work described in this chapter was carried out jointly with Joe Halpern. Sections 4 and 5 are completely the product of our joint effort, but the other sections too have benefitted greatly from his input.

2.1   Making initial choices

Suppose we want to represent the information that a particular house, HOUSE17, was red at time t. Several questions arise in this connection.

2.1.1   Over what do we interpret assertions?

The first issue to resolve is what t represents: is it a time *point*, a time *interval*, or perhaps a more complex temporal entity? Perhaps there are different kinds of assertions, some of which are interpreted over time points, some of which over time intervals, some of which over collections of disjoint intervals, and so on?

In theoretical computer science one finds both kinds of answers. The original formulations of modal temporal logic by A. Pnueli [75] and dynamic logic by V. Pratt [78] were committed to interpreting assertions over time points. Later several generalizations of these systems appeared (Nisihmura [68], Parikh [69]) which introduced both "point assertions" and "interval assertions". More recently there has been a move in theoretical computer science towards more uniform interval-based logics (e.g., Harel, Kozen and Parikh [29], Halpern, Manna and Moszkowski [24], Moszkowski [65]), in which assertions are interpreted *only* over intervals. These interval-based logics will be discussed in more detail later in this chapter, when I introduce a new modal logic of time intervals. These two trends in theoretical computer science have their origins in formal philosophy. For a thorough introduction to temporal logic that contrasts the two approaches very clearly the reader is referred to van Benthem's [98].

In AI too one finds systems of all three kinds: point-based, interval-based, and mixed. Early formalisms such as the McCarthy and Hayes' situation calculus [54] only allowed statements about what was true at a particular time point (or, in the terminology of situation calculus, a particular situation). Later formalisms allowed statements referring to time intervals (e.g., McDermott [59] and Hayes [32]), some actually ruling out statements that refer to time points (e.g., Allen [2]). I will discuss AI formalisms, especially those of McDermott and Allen, in more detail later in the chapter.

The situations that we would like to reason about require reasoning about time intervals. The assertions "the robot executed the NAVIGATE routine", "the temperature rose by five degrees", and "I jogged to the ocean and back", may be true over time intervals but at no time instant. I will therefore interpret assertions over intervals. Furthermore, I will not have *other* assertions which will be interpreted over time points. Instead, I will allow interpreting assertions over intervals of zero duration.

2.1.2 What are the primitive temporal objects?

Another question arises which is related to, but quite distinct from, the previous one. It is the question of what we take to be the basic temporal element in our ontology of time. One can conceive of other possibilities, but the two major contenders are *points* and *intervals*. Since we are interpreting assertions over intervals we clearly want them (the intervals) in the ontology, but that leaves us with at least two options.

Intervals can be considered primitive objects which are related in various ways: "I_1 is *completely before* I_2", "I_1 *abuts* I_2, "I_1 *overlaps* I_2", etcetera. If this alternative is adopted and one still wants to talk about time points without introducing them as primitive, one must define them by legal operations on intervals, for example the intersection of some infinite set of intervals (see, e.g., [3]).

Alternatively, one can take points as the only primitive kind of objects, the only relation between between two points (other than identity) being "P_1 *precedes* P_2". In this case an interval is thought of simply as an ordered pair of points (its begin-point and end-point) such that the first either precedes or is equal to the second (and thus a point P is identified with the interval $\langle P, P \rangle$).

All the interval-based work in theoretical computer science (which, as promised, will be surveyed later in the chapter) takes points as primitive. This is mostly true also in AI, the most outstanding exception of which I am aware being J. Allen's formalism [2]. In interval-based logics in philosphy (and later I will discuss them, too, briefly) one encounters both approaches [8,37,82].

Proponents of the first alternative, that of treating intervals as primitive, cite the intuitive appeal of intervals and the artificial nature of points. After all, people never experience anything that is durationless. A point is merely a mathematical abstraction that has no manifestation in our life.

I will nevertheless opt for the second alternative, that of taking points as primitive and defining intervals in terms of those. Clearly any property of intervals can be expressed as a property of their end points, and in fact we will see that the point-based formulations are more concise as well as more intuitive.

2.1.3   Is there a relation between the truth of an assertion over an interval and its truth over parts of that interval?

A question one is often asked is whether the intervals are "open" or "closed," that is, whether the intervals contain their end points. The answer is that the question is meaningless. If an interval is defined to be an ordered pair of points, not a set of points, then it makes no sense to ask if P_1 is an element of $\langle P_1, P_2 \rangle$. Perhaps this is a slight misuse of terminology on my part, since traditionally in mathemtics an interval is indeed defined to be a set of points. In fact, my view of an interval allows the set of points that lie between the endpoints of an interval not to be mutually comparable (in other words, in general I allow time not only to branch, but also to meet again after branching).

It is nice to have this most general formulation, but in most cases will want to assume specific temporal structures (such as that of the integers), in which it makes sense to view an interval as a totally ordered set of points. In that case, it is really not important whether one views the intervals as open or closed. What *is* important, however, is whether there is a relation between the truth value of an assertion over an interval to its truth value over parts of that interval. When we say that HOUSE17 was red over the interval $\langle 1,4 \rangle$, that seems to entail that it was red over the interval $\langle 2,3 \rangle$, the interval $\langle 2,2 \rangle$, and all other subintervals of $\langle 1,4 \rangle$. The first question is whether or not that is indeed a correct inference: does truth transport from intervals to their subintervals? Another question is, suppose we indeed allow the conclusion that HOUSE17 was red over all subintervals of $\langle 1,4 \rangle$, is it red also over the intervals $\langle 1,1 \rangle$ and $\langle 4,4 \rangle$?

In the philosophical literature a similar question that arises is whether *homogeneity* is assumed. An assertion is homogenous if the following is true: for any interval $\langle P_1, P_2 \rangle$, the assertion holds over $\langle P_1, P_2 \rangle$ iff it holds over every subinterval of $\langle P_1, P_2 \rangle$ [82]). In theoretical computer science the issue that comes up is that of *locality*: an interval logic is local if an assertion holds over $\langle P_1, P_2 \rangle$ iff it holds over P_1 (or, equivalently, over the interval $\langle P_1, P_1 \rangle$).

While transporting truth from intervals to subintervals seems appropriate for assertions such as "HOUSE17 is red", it seems less adequate for "I ran more than five miles" or "the robot executed the NAVIGATE routine from start to finish". The common approach has been to say that these are different kinds of entities: the first assertion is a "fact" or a "property", and the others are "events", or something similar to that. My approach will be different. I will start with a single entity, a temporal proposition, and will refrain from making any *a priori* association between the truth of an assertion over an interval to its truth value over parts of that interval. That will enable us to not make distinctions between facts, events, etcetera when we have no need for such distinctions (and that will turn out to be the case when we discuss causation later on). For some purposes we *will* want to make these distinctions, and many more besides. In Section 3 of this chapter I show how we can categorize temporal propositions in a way that subsumes the fact/event dichotomy and other similar fixed categorization schemes.

2.1.4 Is time discrete or continuous? Linear or branching? And so on

As far as temporal ontology goes, I have so far committed myself only to treating points as our primitive objects, and having them be related by $<$, the precedence relation. I have not yet placed any restriction on $<$. Presumably, we will always want to assume that time is acyclic (that is, that it is a partial order), although some would dispute even this assumption (for treatment of cyclic time see, e.g., [79,98]). The status of other properties (all of which are, by the way, independent of whether we interpret proposition over points or intervals) is even more controversial. Do time points form a *discrete* structure, so that between any two points there are a finite number of points? This leads to another question: is time *unbounded*? That is, does every point have a later point and an earlier point? Perhaps only a later point? If time is not discrete, is it *dense*? That is, is it the case that between any two points there lies a third one? If so, is time *complete*? That is, if a series of points is bounded from above by another point, does there exist a point that is the least upper bound of that series? (This is the property that distinguishes the reals from the rationals; both are dense, but while the reals are complete the rationals are not.) Independently of the above questions, we can ask whether time is branching or linear. Perhaps it branches only into the future? If it branches both ways, do we allow two branches that diverge into the future to meet later on in the more distant future?

Again, these are not questions to which there are correct and incorrect answers. We are the ones constructing the logic, and we can decide one way or another, depending on the applications we have in mind. In most of the literature in theoretical computer science one finds discrete time (the only exception of which I am aware is [5]). This makes perfect sense in the context of computer programs and digital devices, where one can collapse continuous processes into their two end points (for example, the point before the interpreter executes a command and the point after the execution is completed). In philosophy there has not been a commitment to the discrete view of time; indeed, Burgess [8] specifically assumes density. In AI, the early formalisms which viewed time as discrete (most notably the situation calculus [54]) have been replaced, or at least complemented, by continuous models [32,59,2].

Assumptions about other properties of time also vary considerably. For example, philosophers have considered both branching and linear structures of time [79,98]. Following them, so have theoretical computer scientists (see, e.g., [16,74]). Most AI formalisms assume linear time, although there have been some exceptions, such as McDermott's logic [59].

My approach will be to delay commitment on most of these matters, although I will usually want to view time as having the structure of the real numbers, and almost always as being linear (I will capture the property of ignorance, or indeterminacy, through other means, as we shall see in the Chapter 4). We certainly would not want to always assume discreteness, since some of the occurrences of interest to us are inherently continuous, such as the temperature gently rising or a bucket gradually filling with water until it overflows. Sometimes, however, we will want to assume other structures of time (usually that of the integers), either because it happens to be an appropriate abstraction, or in order to simplify the discussion. The important thing is to be aware of our assumptions about time and of their significance when making inferences, either when writing axiomatic systems (though that is not the main thrust of the work described here), or when reasoning directly about the possible models of our theories.

2.1.5   What logical form?

We have agreed to interpret assertions over time intervals and that time intervals are defined in terms of time points. We now have to choose the actual method for associating an assertion with an ordered pair of points. Suppose we want to represent the assertion "HOUSE17 was red over the interval $\langle 1,4 \rangle$". We have several options available to us.

First, we can simply include time as an argument (or, in this case, two arguments) to a predicate: COLOR(1,4,HOUSE17,RED). This option, however, is not acceptable from our standpoint, although there is nothing technically wrong with it. The problem is that if time is represented as an argument (or several arguments) to predicates, then there is nothing general you can say about the temporal aspect of assertions. For example, you cannot say that "effects cannot precede their causes"; at most you can say that about specific causes and effects. Furthermore, without further restrictions, there is nothing to disallow formulas in which there are many time arguments, or none at all. For example, there is nothing to disallow the formula COLOR(HOUSE,CAT,MOUSE,RED), although there is no intuitive meaning that we can attach to that formula. Indeed, this first option accords no special status to time — neither conceptual nor notational — which goes against the very spirit of our enterprise.

We will want to seperate the atemporal component of assertions (such as "HOUSE17 is red") from their temporal component (the time interval). Following McDermott's practice in [59], we will adopt the terminology of formal philosophers and call the atemporal component of the assertion a *proposition type*.

One way to associate a proposition type with an interval is both the proposition-type and the interval-symbol appear to be arguments to some global "predicate": TRUE(1,4,COLOR(HOUSE,RED)). This second option has been, in one guise or another, widely accepted in AI. It requires that one be careful about the logical status of COLOR(HOUSE17,RED), about what consitute well-formed formulas, and about the meaning of these formulas. There are basically two possible approaches. the first is to really "reify" the propositions (or, as John McCarthy once proposed, "thingify" them), so that COLOR(HOUSE17,RED) is just a term in the language. The alternative to keep both the propositional nature of proposition-types and the classical nature of the logic as a whole. I will discuss this in more detail in the next section.

Another way to associate a proposition type with an interval is by taking the modal route, not mentioning time at all, but instead complicating the interpretation of our formulas. If in classical logic a formula φ is either true in an interpretation M (written $M \models \varphi$) or false in it, now a formula would be either true in M at a given interval I (written $M, I \models \varphi$) or false there. In our example we would have $M, \langle 1, 4 \rangle \models$ COLOR(HOUSE17,RED).

This third option, which has been favored in formal philosophy and theoretical computer science, has for the most part been ignored in AI until very recently.

The three options mentioned above can be thought of as having linguistic analogues. The first option can be thought of as representing the assertion "the house was red at the interval $\langle 1,4 \rangle$," the second as representing "it was true at $\langle 1,4 \rangle$ that the house was red," and the third as standing for "the assertion 'the house was red' was true at $\langle 1,4 \rangle$". The remainder of this chapter is devoted to pursuing the last two options.

2.2   A classical logic of time intervals

In the previous section it was mentioned that logics featuring "reified" assertions, assertions that appear to be arguments of some "predicate" such as TRUE, are common in AI. By way of motivating a new logic that has that same general appearance, let me briefly review what are probably the two most influential temporal formalisms in AI nowadays: those of James Allen and Drew McDermott.

2.2.1   Allen's and McDermott's formalisms

In [2], Allen develops a temporal logic in which time intervals are not only that to which assertions refer, but also the only primitive objects in the temporal ontology. For Allen, the basic entities that are associated with time are *properties*, *events* and *processes*.

The fact that a property holds for an interval is denoted by the formula HOLD(p,i), where p is a *property type* and i is an interval. A property is true for an interval iff it holds for every subinterval. (As mentioned in the previous section, this is what philosophers call the quality of *homogeneity.*) Actually, Allen requires a stronger axiom; more on his Axiom H.2 in a moment. Three examples of properties are that a particular object is green, elongated and tasty. A property need not be monadic in nature: another example of a property is that the distance between two robots does not exceed the range of their radios.

The fact that an event occurred over an interval is denoted by the formula OCCUR(e,i), where e is an *event type*. In contrast with properties, an event cannot occur over two intervals one of which contains the other. An example Allen gives of an event type is CHANGE-POS(ball,pos1,pos2). Finally, *processes* are a hybrid case, which are intended to be typified by the sentence "I am walking"; it is (according to Allen) true of an interval if it occurred in a "substantial" number of subintervals. In fact Allen has to make do with the following definition: a process occurred over an interval iff it occurred over *some* subinterval. The fact that a process p took place over interval i is denoted by the formula OCCURRING(p,i).

Allen's interests go far beyond the mere representation of temporal information, and include weighty topics such as actions, causation, intentions and planning. Let us however halt here and see to what degree we can attach a meaning to the assertion in Allen's logic.

What defines the meaning of HOLD(p,i)? For that matter, what is
the set of all well-formed properties? If we have a property of the form
COLOR(HOUSE,RED), which Allen allows, what is the criterion by which
we allow the property COLOR(ROOF(HOUSE),RED) but not the property
ROOF(HOUSE)? In ordinary logic the former would be a wff and the latter
a term, but that distinction is lost in Allen's logic. Also, Allen introduces
connective-like functions:

> To allow properties to name complex logical expressions, there
> is a set of functions AND, OR, NOT, ALL, and EXISTS, that
> correspond to the logical operators ... (p.130)

So, apparently, one can apply functions to properties and obtain new properties. Are these all the functions one can apply? Furthermore, the ALL and
EXISTS functions imply that properties contain variable-like entities; what
does *that* imply about the structure of well-formed properties? In short,
the set of properties look suspiciously like the set of first-order formulas.
If that is the case, then not only have we not given precise syntax and semantics for the new language, but in fact we have given up the off-the-shelf
first-order predicate calculus (FOPC) and the associated model theory.

The reason Allen goes to all this trouble is because he tries to accommodate both his wish to grant time a special status and his desire to retain
the expressiveness of FOPC, all that without resorting to a logic which he
views as more complex:

> Note that if we had introduced HOLD as a modal operator we
> would not need to introduce properties into our ontology. We
> have not followed this route, however, since it seems more com-
> plicated in the later development of occurrences.

What I will do is offer an alternative way of achieving these simultaneous
goals, one that does not obscure the first-order nature of our assertions.

This is also a good point at which to illustrate the advantages of having
points, rather than intervals, as the basic temporal element. Consider, for
example, Allen's Axiom H.2 (p.130),

$$\text{HOLD(p,i)} \equiv \forall\ \text{i'} \in \text{i}\ \exists\ \text{i''} \in \text{i'}\ \text{HOLD(p,i'')}$$

(where $\in$ denotes the 'subinterval' relation). This strange looking formula
states that a property holds over an interval iff for any subinterval there

exists a subsubinterval over which that property holds. This would be greatly simplified if we allowed points into the ontology; what the formula is really meant to capture is that a property holds over an interval iff it holds at all points during the interval. The axiom H.2 is not only less natural, but actually allows some very weird models which I am sure Allen does not intend for it (such as models in which time has the structure of the reals, and a property holds over an interval just in case it holds over all its subintervals whose end points are rational).

This awkwardness is propagated onwards. For example, Theorem H.7 (p.131) reads:

$$\text{HOLD}(\text{OR}(p,q),i) \equiv$$
$$\forall\; i' {\in} i\; \exists\; i'' {\in} i'\; (\text{HOLD}(p,i'')\; \vee\; \text{HOLD}(q,i'')).$$

Again, if we had points at our disposal, we would replace this theorem by another one stating simply that OR(p,q) holds over an interval iff at any point in the interval either p holds or q does.

McDermott's construction is similar to Allen's in that his building blocks are *fact types* and *event types*. Unlike Allen, however, he introduces time points (or states) as primitive. The formula[1] T(t,p) means that the fact type p holds at time t. Note that unlike Allen's properties which are interpreted over intervals, facts are interpreted over points. The formula TT(t1,t2,p) is merely an abbreviation for the formula $\forall\; t\; (t1{\leq}t{\leq}t2 \supset T(t,p))$. Finally, the formula OCC(t1,t2,e) means that event type e occurred over the interval $\langle t_1,t_2\rangle$.

McDermott starts out by giving precise semantics to the sentences. The construction is set theoretic: the meaning of a fact type is simply a set of time points, and the meaning of an event type is a set of pairs of time points. McDermott treats T(t,p) as merely an abbreviation for $t \in p$, TT(t1,t2,p) as an abbreviation for $[t1..t2] \subset p$, and OCC(t1,t2,e) as an abbreviation for $\langle t1,t2\rangle \in e$. McDermott's semantics are essentially those of propositional modal logic, although he introduces them differently

---

[1]I'm using standard notation rather than McDermott's LISP-like notation for the sake of uniformity.

by using set-theoretic notions in the language itself in a way that makes the semantics explicit.

In fact, the logic I that will introduce bears a strong resemblance to McDermott's logic. The propositional version is merely a syntactic variant of it, and the first-order version is its direct generalization. The idea is that if one wishes to include function symbols and variables in fact-types and event-types (as McDermott does: CLEARTOP(x), WATER-VOL(TANK1)), then the semantics need some beefing up. Doing that will on the one hand make clear the meaning of those assertions that have a coherent one (such as T(t,CLEARTOP(x))), and on the other hand expose those assertions that do not have a clear meaning (such as the ones containing McDermott's causal predicates, PCAUSE and ECAUSE, or Allen's ones, ECAUSE and ACAUSE).

In the next subsection I present the propositional version of a classical interval logic, and in the subsection following that I present the full first-order one. Already in the propositional case we will encounter constant symbols, variables, a relation symbol and quantifiers. I nonetheless call it the propositional case since the constant symbols will denote only time points, the variables will range only over time points, and the only relation symbol will be $\preceq$, denoting temporal precedence.

2.2.2   The propositional case

We want to associate an atemporal assertion, such as "the house is red," with a time interval. The most straightforward way of doing that is to simply form an interval/assertion pair, which is precisely what we will do. Each primitive formula will be a pair $\langle i,p \rangle$, where i is an interval symbol and p is a primitive propositional symbol. Since we have agreed to treat time points, rather than time intervals, as basic, an interval symbol i is really a pair $\langle t_1,t_2 \rangle$, where the t_i's are time-point symbols. For notational convenience I will follow McDermott's and Allen's lead, and replace the formula $\langle \langle t_1,t_2 \rangle,p \rangle$ by the more appealing TRUE(t_1,t_2,p).[2]

The precise syntax and semantics are given below.

Syntax

Given P: a set of primitive propositions, TC: a set of time point symbols, TV: a set of (temporal) variables, U: TC∪TV, and $\preceq$: a binary relation

---

[2]I suspect that formal logicians would prefer the convention $p[\![t_1,t_2]\!]$, which would remove the potential danger of having an innocent reader take TRUE to be modal operator. I stick to the AI tradition out of blind loyalty.

symbol, the set of well-formed formulas (wffs) is defined inductively as follows:

1. If $u_1 \in U$ and $u_2 \in U$ then $u_1 = u_2$ and $u_1 \preceq u_2$ are wffs.

2. If $u_1 \in U$, $u_2 \in U$ and $p \in P$ then TRUE(u_1, u_2, p) is a wff.

3. If φ_1 and φ_2 are wffs then so are $\varphi_1 \wedge \varphi_2$ and $\neg \varphi_1$.

4. If φ is a wff and $v \in TV$ then $\forall v \; \varphi$ is a wff.

We assume the usual definitions of $\vee$, $\supset$, $\equiv$, $\exists$ and so on. We can also use the following syntactic sugar: TRUE(u_1, u_2, $\varphi_1 \wedge \varphi_2$) is shorthand for TRUE($u_1$, u_2, φ_1) $\wedge$ TRUE(u_1, u_2, φ_2), TRUE(u_1, u_2, $\neg\varphi$) is shorthand for $\neg$TRUE(u_1, u_2, φ)[3], and so on.

Semantics

An *interpretation* is a a tuple $\langle TW, \leq, M \rangle$, where TW is a nonempty universe of time points, $\leq$ is a binary relation on TW, $M = \langle M1, M2 \rangle$ is a meaning function $M1$:   TC $\rightarrow$ TW and $M2$:   P $\rightarrow$ $2^{TW \times TW}$.

We require that $\langle w_1, w_2 \rangle \in M2(p)$ iff $\langle w_2, w_1 \rangle \in M2(p)$. This convention, suggested by Johan van Benthem, makes explicit the intuition that a pair of time points denotes a single interval. Alternatively, we could omit this requirement, and simply pay no attention to the truth value of formulas TRUE(t_1, t_2, p) such that $M1(t_1) \not\leq M1(t_2)$.

A *variable assignment* is a function VA: TV $\rightarrow$ TW. An interpretation $S = \langle \; TW, \leq, \langle M1, M2 \rangle \rangle$ satisfies a wff φ under the variable assignment VA (written $S \models \varphi[VA]$) given the following inductively defined conditions (in the following, for any $u \in U$, $VAL(u)$ is defined to be $M1(u)$ if $u \in$ TC, and $VA(u)$ if $u \in$ TV):

- $S \models (u_1 = u_2)[VA]$ iff $VAL(u_1) = VAL(u_2)$.

- $S \models (u_1 \preceq u_2)[VA]$ iff $VAL(u_1) \leq VAL(u_2)$.

- $S \models$ TRUE(u_1, u_2, p)$[VA]$ iff $\langle VAL(u_1), VAL(u_2) \rangle \in M2(p)$.

- $S \models (\varphi_1 \wedge \varphi_2)[VA]$ iff $S \models \varphi_1[VA]$ and $S \models \varphi_2[VA]$.

---

[3]One may prefer a different interpretation of TRUE(u_1, u_2, $\neg\varphi$); more on "strong negation" in Section 2.3.

- $S \models \neg\varphi[VA]$ iff $S \not\models \varphi[VA]$.

- $S \models (\forall \mathsf{v}\ \varphi)[VA]$ iff $S \models \varphi[VA\,']$ for all $VA\,'$ that agree with VA everywhere except possibly on v.

An interpretation S is a *model* for a wff φ (written $S \models \varphi$) if $S \models \varphi[VA]$ for *all* variable assignments VA. A *sentence* is a wff containing no free variables. Clearly, if a sentence φ is satisfied by an interpretation S under some variable assignment then φ is satisfied by S under *any* variable assignment, and therefore S is a model for φ. A wff is *satisfiable* if it has a model. A wff φ is *valid* (written $\models \varphi$) if its negation is not satisfiable.

2.2.3 The first-order case

The propositional nature of the logic presented in the previous section restricts one to basic assertions that are "structureless": the assertion "HOUSE17 is red" collapses into a single propositional letter p, and so on. We cannot say something about all houses. We cannot say that if you paint a roof of a house with a certain color then the entire house becomes of that color (because paint drips). We will therefore now generalize the logic to a full first-order one. The construction is straightforward for the most part; the few subtleties that exist will be pointed out as they arise.

Syntax

Given:

TC : a set of time point symbols,

C : a set of constant symbols that is disjoint from TC,

TV : a set of temporal variables,

V : a set of variables that is disjoint from TV,

TF : a set of temporal function symbols (typical ones being the arithmetic operators), each associated with a fixed arity,

F : a set of function symbols that is disjoint from TF, each associated with a fixed arity, and

R : a set of relation symbols, each with a fixed arity,

The set of *temporal terms* is defined inductively as follows:

1. All members of TC are temporal terms.

2. All members of TV are temporal terms.

3. if $\mathtt{trm}_1, \ldots, \mathtt{trm}_n$ are temporal terms, and $\mathtt{f} \in \mathtt{TF}$ is an n-ary function symbol, then $\mathtt{f}(\mathtt{trm}_1, \ldots, \mathtt{trm}_n)$ is a temporal term.

The set of *nontemporal terms* is defined in exactly the same way, with TC replaced by C, TV replaced by V, and TF replaced by F.

The set of well-formed formulas (wffs) is defined inductively as follows:

1. If $\mathtt{trm}_a$ and $\mathtt{trm}_b$ are temporal terms, then $\mathtt{trm}_a = \mathtt{trm}_b$ and $\mathtt{trm}_a \preceq \mathtt{trm}_b$ are wffs.

2. If $\mathtt{trm}_a$ and $\mathtt{trm}_b$ are temporal terms, $\mathtt{trm}_1, \ldots, \mathtt{trm}_n$ are nontemporal terms, and $\mathtt{r} \in \mathtt{R}$ an n-ary relation symbol, then $\mathtt{TRUE}(\mathtt{trm}_a, \mathtt{trm}_b, \mathtt{r}(\mathtt{trm}_1, \ldots, \mathtt{trm}_n))$ is a wff.

3. If φ_1 and φ_2 are wffs then so are $\varphi_1 \wedge \varphi_2$ and and $\neg \varphi_1$.

4. If φ is a wff and $\mathtt{z} \in \mathtt{TV} \cup \mathtt{V}$ is a variable, then $\forall \mathtt{z} \; \varphi$ is a wff.

Again, we assume the usual definitions of $\vee$, $\supset$, $\equiv$, $\exists$, and so on. Below are some examples of sentences (or wffs with no free variables):

$\mathtt{TRUE}(\mathtt{t}_1, \mathtt{t}_2, \mathtt{COLOR}(\mathtt{HOUSE17}, \mathtt{RED}))$

$\exists \mathtt{u} \; \mathtt{TRUE}(\mathtt{t}_3, \mathtt{t}_4, \mathtt{ON}(\mathtt{u}, \mathtt{B}))$

$\forall \; \mathtt{v} \; (1776 \preceq \mathtt{v} \wedge \mathtt{v} \preceq 1986 \supset$
$\qquad\qquad \mathtt{TRUE}(\mathtt{v}, \mathtt{v}, \mathtt{GENDER}(\mathtt{PRESIDENT}(\mathtt{USA}), \mathtt{MALE})))$

$\forall \mathtt{v}_1, \mathtt{u} \; \exists \mathtt{v}_2 \; (\mathtt{v}_1 \prec \mathtt{v}_2 \wedge \mathtt{v}_2 \leq \mathtt{v}_1 + 30_{min} \wedge$
$\qquad\qquad ((\mathtt{TRUE}(\mathtt{v}_1, \mathtt{v}_1, \mathtt{SOLID}(\mathtt{u})) \wedge \mathtt{TRUE}(\mathtt{v}_1, \mathtt{v}_2, \mathtt{HEATING}(\mathtt{u})))$
$\qquad\qquad \supset \mathtt{TRUE}(\mathtt{v}_2, \mathtt{v}_2, \mathtt{LIQUID}(\mathtt{u})) \;)$

Notice that in the third example the term PRESIDENT(USA) contains the function symbol PRESIDENT that depends implicitly on time (in addition to its dependence on the explicit argument). Such functions, which were called *fluents* by McCarthy and Hayes in [54], will therefore be interpreted in a way that takes time into account. In fact, the interpretation of all function symbols will be time dependent; of course, the value of a function along the time dimension may be constant. The same applies to the interpretation of relation symbols. Constant symbols, on the other hand, will be interpreted in a time-independent fashion. For example, the symbol USA will denote the same object at all times. In other words, we will assume that constant symbols are what philosophers have called *rigid designators* [42].

The respective intended meanings of the sentences above are that HOUSE17 is red from t_1 to t_2, that there's something on B from t_3 to t_4, that at no time between 1776 and today has the USA had a woman president, and that if you heat a solid object then it melts within half an hour. Next we guarantee that these indeed *are* the meanings.

Semantics

An *interpretation* is a tuple $S = \langle TW, \leq, W, TFN, FN, RL, M \rangle$, where

TW is a nonempty universe of time points,

$\leq$ is a binary relation on TW,

W is a nonempty universe of individuals that is disjoint from TW,

TFN is a set of total functions in $\bigcup_k (TW^k \rightarrow TW)$,

FN is a set of total functions in $\bigcup_k (W^k \rightarrow W)$,

RL is a set of relations over W, and

$M = \langle M1, M2, M3, M4, M5 \rangle$ is a meaning function as follows. *M1: TC* $\rightarrow TW$, *M2: $C \rightarrow W$*, *M3: $TF \rightarrow TFN$*, *M4: $TW \times TW \times F \rightarrow FN$*, and *M5: $TW \times TW \times R \rightarrow RL$*.

    (Again, we require that $M4$ and $M5$ be symmetric in the first two arguments; that is, $M4(w_1, w_2, f) = M4(w_2, w_1, f)$ and similarly for $M5$. Alternatively, we could ignore the truth value of formulas over "reversed" interval, that is, over pairs $\langle w_1, w_2 \rangle$ s.t. $w_1 \not\leq w_2$.)

A *variable assignment* is a function $VA = \langle VAT, VAV \rangle$, such that *VAT:* TV $\rightarrow TW$ and *VAV:* V $\rightarrow W$.
M and VA induce a time-dependent meaning MVA on arbitrary terms in the following way.

We first define the meaning of arbitrary temporal terms. That meaning is the same regardless of when the terms are interpreted: the terms 1.1.2000 and $(12{:}00 + 12_{min})$ each denote a single, unambiguous absolute time. The precise meaning of temporal terms is as follows. If $tv \in TV$ then $MVA(\texttt{tv})$ = $VAT(\texttt{tv})$. If $tc \in TC$ then $MVA(\texttt{tc})$ = $M1(\texttt{tc})$. If $f \in TF$ and $\texttt{trm}$ = $\texttt{f}(\texttt{trm}_1, \ldots, \texttt{trm}_n)$ is a temporal term, then $MVA(\texttt{trm})$ = $M3(\texttt{f})$ $(MVA(\texttt{trm}_1), \ldots, MVA(\texttt{trm}_n))$.

The meaning of arbitrary nontemporal terms is slightly trickier since it is time-dependent: the meaning of $\texttt{PRESIDENT(USA)}$ depends on the time of interpretation. We therefore make the following definition. If $v \in V$, then for all $w_1, w_2 \in TW$, $MVA(w_1, w_2, \texttt{v})$ = $VAV(v)$. If $c \in C$ then $MVA(w_1, w_2, \texttt{c})$ = $M2(c)$. The temporal dependence of the interpretation enters in the following definition: if $f \in F$ and $\texttt{trm}$ = $\texttt{f}(\texttt{trm}_1, \ldots, \texttt{trm}_n)$ is a nontemporal term, then
$$MVA(w_1, w_2, \texttt{trm}) =$$
$$M4(w_1, w_2, \texttt{f}) \ (MVA(w_1, w_2, \texttt{trm}_1), \ldots, MVA(w_1, w_2, \texttt{trm}_n)).$$

The interpretation S and the variable assignment VA satisfy a wff φ (written $S \models \varphi[VA]$) under the following inductively defined conditions.

- $S \models \texttt{trm}_1 = \texttt{trm}_2[VA]$ iff $MVA(\texttt{trm}_1) = MVA(\texttt{trm}_2)$.

- $S \models \texttt{trm}_1 \preceq \texttt{trm}_2[VA]$ iff $MVA(\texttt{trm}_1) \leq MVA(\texttt{trm}_2)$.

- $S \models \texttt{TRUE}(\texttt{trm}_a, \texttt{trm}_b, \texttt{r}(\texttt{trm}_1, \ldots, \texttt{trm}_n))[VA]$ iff
  $\langle MVA(MVA(\texttt{trm}_a), MVA(\texttt{trm}_b), \texttt{trm}_1), \ldots$
  $\ldots, MVA(MVA(\texttt{trm}_a), MVA(\texttt{trm}_b)), \texttt{trm}_n) \rangle$
  $\in M5(MVA(\texttt{trm}_a), MVA(\texttt{trm}_b), \texttt{r})$.

- $S \models (\varphi_1 \wedge \varphi_2)[VA]$ iff $S \models \varphi_1[VA]$ and $S \models \varphi_2[VA]$.

- $S \models (\neg\varphi)[VA]$ iff $S \not\models \varphi[VA]$.

- $S \models (\forall \texttt{z} \ \varphi)[VA]$ iff $S \models \varphi[VA']$ for all VA' that agree with VA everywhere except possibly on $\texttt{z}$.

The next few definitions are identical to those made in the propositional case. An interpretation S is a *model* for a wff φ (written $S \models \varphi$) if $S \models \varphi[VA]$ for *all* variable assignments VA. A *sentence* is a wff containing no free variables. Again, it is clear that if a sentence φ is satisfied by an interpretation S under some variable assignment then φ is satisfied by S under *any* variable assignment, and therefore that S is a model for φ. A wff is *satisfiable* if it has a model. A wff φ is *valid* (written $\models \varphi$) if its negation is not satisfiable.

2.3 Ontology: facts, properties, events, and other animals

We now have a temporal logic on our hands which enjoys both clear syntax and precise semantics, and yet one might feel a little disappointed. When all is said and done, all we are left with are *temporal propositions*, which associate a *proposition type* with a time interval. These temporal propositions are rather bland entities that enjoy none of the glamour of some more exotic objects.

For example, we have already seen that Allen introduces three distinct entities: *properties, events,* and *processes* [2]. Similarly, McDermott introduces *facts* and *events* [59]. Of course, even for Allen and McDermott, the meaning of these terms is quite narrower than their everyday usage suggests (for example, one loses the implicit importance that we attach to events and that gives rise to the adjective 'eventful'). Nevertheless, these terms have much intuitive appeal, and in this section I will try to recapture some of that lost sparkle. I will provide the means for distinguishing between fact-like (or property-like) proposition types, event-like proposition types, and so on. In fact I will be able to construct a categorization of proposition types that is richer and more flexible than the fact/event dichotomy or the property/event/process trichotomy. For example, the assertions "I ran more than two miles" and "I ran less than two miles" do not fit into either of those two categorization schemes; they will into the new one.

The way we will distinguish between different kinds of propositions is by specifying how the truth of the proposition over one interval is related to its truth over other intervals. I have already mentioned that philosophers talk about *homogeneity* [82]: a homogeneous proposition is true of an interval iff it is true over all its proper subintervals (with or without the end points, depending on the definition). But this is exactly what characterizes "facts" or "properties"! And what characterizes event types, if not the fact that the same event cannot occur over two overlapping intervals, or over two intervals one of which contains the other, or some similar constraint? In this way we can characterize other proposition types. The following definitions are not meant to be exhaustive or even obligatory – they primarily illustrate the power we have at our disposal.

The following discussion applies to both the propositional and first-order versions of the classsical logic. For the propositional version interpret a proposition-type to mean a primitive propositional symbol. For the first-order case interpret a proposition-type to be a relation symbol with the approporiate number of arguments.

Definition 2.1 *A proposition-type* x *is* downward-hereditary *(written* ↓x*) if, whenever it holds over an interval, it holds over all of its subintervals, possibly excluding the two end points.*

In the interval logic given in the previous section, ↓x is captured by the axiom

$$\forall\ t_1, t_3, t_4, t_2$$
$$t_1 \leq t_3 \leq t_4 \leq t_2\ \land$$
$$t_1 \neq t_4\ \land\ t_3 \neq t_2\ \land$$
$$\text{TRUE}(t_1, t_2, x)$$
$$\supset\ \text{TRUE}(t_3, t_4, x)$$

Example: "The robot travelled less than two miles" is downward-hereditary.

Definition 2.2 *A proposition-type* x *is* upward-hereditary *(written* ↑x*) if, whenever it holds for all proper subintervals of some nonpoint interval (except possibly at its end points), it also holds over the nonpoint interval itself.*

In the classical logic ↑x is captured by the axiom

$$\forall\ t_1, t_2$$
$$t_1 < t_2\ \land$$
$$(\forall\ t_3, t_4$$
$$t_1 \leq t_3 \leq t_4 \leq t_2\ \land$$
$$(t_1 \neq t_3\ \lor\ t_2 \neq t_4)\ \land$$
$$t_1 \neq t_4\ \land\ t_3 \neq t_2$$
$$\supset\ \text{TRUE}(t_3, t_4, x))$$
$$\supset\ \text{TRUE}(t_1, t_2, x)$$

Example: "The robot travelled at a speed of two miles per hour" is upward-hereditary.

(From here on I only give the intuitive definitions of the properties of proposition-types, omitting the axioms capturing those properties.)

We can define two variations on ↓ and ↑, the downward versions being weaker and the upward versions being stronger.

Definition 2.3 *A proposition-type* x *is* point-downward-hereditary *(written* $\downarrow_p$x*) if, whenever it holds over an interval, it holds at all of its internal points.*

Definition 2.4 *A proposition-type* x *is* point-upward-hereditary *(written* $\uparrow^p$x*) if, whenever it holds at all internal points of some nonpoint interval, it holds also over the nonpoint interval itself.*

Definition 2.5 *A proposition-type* x *is* interval-downward-hereditary *(written* $\downarrow_i$x*) if, whenever it holds over a interval, it holds over all of its nonpoint-subintervals.*

Definition 2.6 *A proposition-type* x *is* interval-upward-hereditary *(written* $\uparrow^i$x*) if, whenever it holds over all nonpoint subintervals of some nonpoint interval, it holds also over the nonpoint interval itself.*

Examples: "The robot changed location" is $\downarrow_i$ but not $\downarrow_p$. Similarly, "The robot did not change location" is $\uparrow^i$ but not $\uparrow^p$.

Definition 2.7 *A proposition-type is* liquid *(written* $\updownarrow$x*) if it is both upward-hereditary and downward-hereditary.*

Example: "The robot's arm was in the GRASPING state" is liquid.

We make similar definitions for *point-point-liquid* proposition types $\updownarrow_p^p$, *interval-interval-liquid* ones $\updownarrow_i^i$, *point-interval-liquid* ones $\updownarrow_p^i$ and *interval-point-liquid* proposition types $\updownarrow_i^p$. Note that these are not all independent qualities. For example, it is easy to verify the validity of $\updownarrow_p^p$x $\supset$ $\updownarrow$x.

Observation: point-point-liquid proposition-types coincide with Allen's properties and McDermott's facts. Liquid proposition-types coincide with philosophers' homogenous propositions.

Definition 2.8 *A proposition-type is* concatenable *if whenever it holds over two consecutive intervals it holds also over their union.*

Example: "The robot started and ended at the same place" and "The robot travelled an even number of miles" are concatenable.

Definition 2.9 *A proposition-type is* gestalt *if it never holds over two intervals one of which properly contains the other.*

Example: "Exactly six minutes passed" is gestalt.

Definition 2.10 *A proposition-type is* solid *if it never holds over two properly overlapping intervals.*

Example: "The robot executed the NAVIGATE procedure (from start to finish)" is solid.

Observation: Allen's and McDermott's events correspond either to gestalt propositions, or to solid ones, or to both.

One can devise further categories of proposition types, but let me halt here. At this point it can already be shown that the ability to make fine-grained distinctions of this sort can shed light on otherwise somewhat mysterious theorems. Consider Allen's definition of negation: NOT(p) holds over an interval if p does not hold for any subinterval.[4] For Allen, NOT can be applied only to properties, and not (for example) to events. He then asks what is the meaning of the operator NOT(NOT(...)), and gives a somewhat unintuitive proof that NOTs cancel out. In the new logic we are in a position to perform a broader analysis, by subjecting arbitrary proposition types to strong negation. We will use the same definition as Allen does. To be precise, we will say that NOT(x) holds over an interval if a) x does not hold for that interval, and b) x does not hold over any of its subinterval, except perhaps at the end points. Doing that, we can prove the following much stronger statements. All proofs are completely straightforward and are omitted.

Lemma 2.1
TRUE(t_1,t_2,NOT(NOT(x))) $\equiv \forall$ t (t_1<t<t_2 $\supset$ TRUE(t,t,x))

Corollary 2.2
$\downarrow_p$x $\equiv \forall$ t_1,t_2 (TRUE(t_1,t_2,x) $\supset$ TRUE(t_1,t_2,NOT(NOT(x))))

Corollary 2.3
$\uparrow_p$x $\equiv \forall$ t_1,t_2 (TRUE(t_1,t_2,NOT(NOT(x))) $\supset$ TRUE(t_1,t_2,x))

Corollary 2.4
$\updownarrow_p^p$x $\equiv \forall$ t_1,t_2 (TRUE(t_1,t_2,x) $\equiv$ TRUE(t_1,t_2,NOT(NOT(x))))

---

[4]This is what philosophers call *strong negation* [37]. I think this is the wrong notion to adopt, since it can easily be defined in terms of weak negation, but I use it here in order to demonstrate the utility of the new categorization.

Since Allen's properties coincide with $\updownarrow_p^p$-propositions, the last corollary explains why NOTs cancel out in his system.

To summarize this section, I propose that rather than introduce facts, events, properties and so on as separate objects, we should start with the primitive notion of a temporal proposition. We can then devise categorizations of proposition types, relying on the relation between the truth of the proposition over one interval and its truth over others.

The advantages of this approach are twofold. First, we are not compelled to make any distinction when we have no need for it. For example, we when say that "x causes y", the x and y may be facts, events, or something else. If we wish to provide a general account of causal reasoning we need an umbrella term for these x and y, which we now have. Second, when we *do* need to categorize temporal propositions, we have the ability to do so in as fine a grain as we wish to, unconstrained by any fixed categorization. I showed one such categorization of temporal propositions which by far transcends in expressiveness those that have appeared in the literature, and which as a side effect renders very intuitive an otherwise somewhat mysterious theorem.

2.4   A modal logic of time intervals

(A reminder.) The material in both this section and the next one is
not needed in later chapters. The reader who is not interested in modal
temporal logics and in decidability should feel free to skip ahead to the
next chapter.[5]

The second logic of time intervals I introduce is a modal one. For a
thorough introduction to modal logic see [36] or [9]. A brief discussion
of modal logic and its application to temporal logic appears also in the
introductory chapter. The idea is to associate an interval with an assertion
not through the syntax but through the semantics: a formula will make
no mention of time, but will be interpreted independently over different
time intervals. This "temporal indexicality" of assertions make implicit
the notion of *the current interval*: it is the interval relative to which the
assertion is interpreted. In point-based modal temporal logic implicit is
the notion of *now*, the current time instant.

Of course, we will still want to be able to relate time points to one
another (otherwise it is pointless to mention them in the first place, no
pun intended). In the classical logic this is done through the $\preceq$ relation.
Since in the modal version we make no explicit mention of time we cannot
make use of $\preceq$; instead, we introduce modal operators.

In point-based modal temporal logics the basic modal operator is $\Diamond$
(pronounced either "diamond" or "possibly"). In most constructions it is
the direct analogue of the $\preceq$ relation: $M, t \models \Diamond\varphi$ iff there is some point t'
such that $t \leq t'$ and such that $M, t' \models \varphi$. $\Box$ (pronounced either "box" or
"necessarily") is the dual to $\Diamond$, and is defined by $\Box\varphi \equiv \neg\Diamond\neg\varphi$. The first
widely known application of this kind of logic to reasoning about programs
was suggested by A. Pnueli [75]. In fact, in most applications in theoretical
computer science, where discrete time is usually assumed, further modal
operators are employed, such as $\bigcirc$ for "at the next time instant." Other
constructions are possible too, where for example $\Diamond$ stands not for "at
some later point" but "at some point — either later, or earlier, or right
now." For a thorough survey of point-based temporal logics by formal
philosophers see van Benthem's [98].

---

[5]The details of the modal logic presented in this section, as well as its translation
into the classical logic and the complexity results discussed in the next section, describe
work carried out jointly with Joe Halpern.

In an interval-based temporal logic the situation is slightly more complex. Whereas the only relation between two distinct points is *after* (and its inverse *before*), we now have in addition *abutting, during, beginning, ending, overlapping,* and so on. We will therefore need more modal operators. As we shall see, it will be sufficient to introduce three very natural pairs of operators in order to capture all twelve possible relations between two distinct intervals.

I will begin, however, with a brief survey of the relevant literature on interval-based modal logics in computer science and philosophy.

2.4.1   Related work: interval-based modal logics of time

Although most of the work on modal temporal logic has been point-based, recent years have seen a growing interest in interval-based modal logics. As usual, the initial idea of dealing with intervals goes back to the philosophers (e.g., [27], and more recently [37,82,8,98]). In computer science, there has recently been work on *process logic* [77,69,29], where intervals (or "paths") represent pieces of computation, and even more recently work on *interval temporal logic* [66,24].

I will survey that work in this section, although, as it will turn out, none of it quite meets our needs, either because of built-in assumptions about time, or because of choices of modal operators that are insufficient for our purposes. In general, the one property all the interval-based logics have in common is that they interpret propositions over intervals of time. They differ among themselves, however, on several counts.

The first distinction is the ontological one mentioned in the first section of this chapter: are intervals primitive objects in the logic, or are they defined in terms of points, and *those* are the only primitive objects? In philosophy one finds logics of both kinds. For example, in the logic of Burgess [8] intervals are defined by their end points, whereas in the logics of Humberstone [37] and Roper [82] intervals are primitive objects related by the $\subset$ (*subinterval*) and $<$ (*completely before*) relations. In computer science all interval-based modal logics construct intervals out of points.

Another distinction between various logics was mentioned earlier and stems from the commitment to a particular underlying temporal structure. With no exception, all interval-based modal temporal logics in computer science have been committed to the discrete and linear view of time (see details below). This has not been the case in philosophy. Burgess explicitly assumes a dense and linear order. Roper assumes linearity, but apparently nothing beyond that.

Another source of difference between the modal logics is the choice of tense operators. In computer science, the strong commitment to a discrete and linear order dictated fairly standard modal operators (see details below). In philosophy there has been less uniformity. For example, the only operator discussed by Humberstone is F, standing for "in some interval after the current interval". The one other operator mentioned by Humberstone as a subject for future research is R, standing for "in some interval *immediately* after the current interval." Roper uses two other modal operators, which are also adopted by Burgess: G (for "in all intervals beginning during the current interval"), and H (for "in all intervals ending in the current interval").

For a more detailed discussion of temporal logics in philosophy, both point-based and interval-based, see [98]. Let me now discuss particular interval-based logics in computer science. SOAPL is a fairly complex logic introduced by Parikh [69]. It has two kinds of formulas: those interpreted over states and those interpreted over "paths", or sequences of states. Parikh proved that validity in the logic is (nonelementarily) decidable, but did not provide a complete deductive system. Nishimura's logic [68] is an attempt to merge temporal logic with dynamic logic. He showed his logic to be as expressive as SOAPL. His logic too is rather complex, and maintains the distinction between "state" formulas and "path" formulas.

At roughly the same time Pratt introduced process logic, in which formulas are interpreted over paths and in which two new modal operators were introduced (*during* and *preserves*) [77]. Later Harel, Kozen and Parikh refined the formulation [29]. They introduced two new modal operators (in addition to the ones introduced by dynamic logic): f (*first*) and suf (roughly, *until*). More precisely,

$s_1, \ldots, s_n \models f\ p$ iff $s_1 \models p$, and

$s_1, \ldots, s_n \models p$ suf q iff, for some j, $s_j, \ldots, s_n \models q$, and for all i such that $1 \leq i < j$, $s_i, \ldots, s_n \models p$.

Harel et al. show that satisfiability in the resulting logic is decidable (although not necessarily elementarily so), and give a complete axiomatization for it. Those results depend on assuming that a proposition is true over an interval iff it is true at the first time point of that interval; that is, assuming locality. This property is captured in process logic by the axiom schema p ≡ f p. The assumption of locality is really at odds with the reason for our interest in a logic of intervals, since, as Harel et. al. themselves put it, "every path formula ultimately expresses properties of *states*." They mention the fact that without the axiom p ≡ f p there are path properties that cannot be expressed, and leave open the question of decidability in the absence of this axiom of locality. Later Streett settled this question by showing that global propositional process logic is Π_1^1-complete [95]. In some informal sense, the new logic that will be proposed can be viewed as extending point-based modal temporal logic in a way that is analogous to the way global process logic extends dynamic logic.

Interval temporal logic [24,66] is also an extension of temporal logic in which formulas are interpreted over paths. The two modal operators considered there are ○ (*next*) and ; (*chop*). The meaning of these operators is given by:

$s_1, \ldots, s_n \models$ (p;q) iff $s_1, \ldots, s_i \models$ p and $s_i, \ldots, s_n \models$ q for some i.

$s_1, \ldots, s_n \models$ ○ p iff $s_2, \ldots, s_n \models$ p.

Thus, the ○ operator strongly commits ITL to the discrete view of time. In [24] it is shown that satisfiability for ITL is undecidable, and that if locality is assumed then satisfiability is decidable but nonelementary. The ITL extension of temporal logic is different from ours in two ways. First, in our logic we are not committed to viewing time as discrete. Second, even if we assume discreteness of time in our logic, the two logics are not comparable in their expressive power. On the one hand our logic cannot emulate the *chop* operator of ITL, and on the other hand we provide means of referring to intervals *outside* the reference interval, which ITL does not.

Finally, [86] offers another interval-based temporal logic. Schwartz, Melliar-Smith and Vogt augment modal temporal logic by constructs referring to intervals explicitly: if p is a wff then so is [I]p, where I is an interval designator. For example, the formula [(x=y)⇒(y=16)]□(x>z) is intended to mean that x is greater than z throughout the interval beginning at the first time x equals y and ending at the first time after that when y equals 16. Intervals are assumed to consist of linearly ordered and discrete time points, and again locality is assumed. In [73] it is shown that satisfiability for this logic is nonelementarily decidable.

2.4.2 Informal syntax and semantics of the new modal logic

Let me start with an informal description of the new logic. I restrict the discussion to the propositional case; the first-order version will be dicussed later very briefly.

Formulas are interpreted over intervals. Well-formed formulas are those of propositional calculus, augmented by the several modal operators. There are twelve possible relations between two distinct intervals: *immediately after, later, earlier, during,* and so on (see [2]). Fortunately we do not need twelve modal operators, since the twelve relations are not independent of one another. It turns out that it is sufficient to define three pairs of operators as follows:

$\langle A \rangle$: at some interval beginning immediately after the end of the current one

$\langle B \rangle$: at some interval during the current one, beginning when the current one begins

$\langle E \rangle$: at some interval during the current one, ending when the current one ends

$\langle \overline{A} \rangle$: at some interval ending immediately before the beginning of the current one

$\langle \overline{B} \rangle$: at some interval of which the current one is a beginning

$\langle \overline{E} \rangle$: at some interval of which the current one is an end

Pictorially, the modal operators pick out intervals as shown in Figure 2.1.

We define the dual operators as usual: $[X]\varphi \equiv \neg\langle X \rangle\neg\varphi$ (where X is A, B, E, $\overline{A}$, $\overline{B}$ or $\overline{E}$).

Using these operators we can define the rest:

$\langle L \rangle = \langle A \rangle\langle A \rangle$: at some later interval

$\langle D \rangle = \langle B \rangle\langle E \rangle$: at some interval during the current one

$\langle O \rangle = \langle E \rangle\langle \overline{B} \rangle$: at some "future overlapping" interval (see figure 2.2)

$\langle \overline{L} \rangle = \langle \overline{A} \rangle\langle \overline{A} \rangle$: at some earlier interval

$\langle \overline{D} \rangle = \langle \overline{B} \rangle\langle \overline{E} \rangle$: at some interval completely overlapping the current one

$\langle \overline{O} \rangle = \langle B \rangle\langle \overline{E} \rangle$: at some "past overlapping" interval (see figure 2.2)

Pictorially, these operators select intervals as shown in Figure 2.2.

As was said earlier, I allow point intervals in the logic. Also, I assume that both the B and E operators refer to *strict* subintervals. Given this assumption, it follows that the formula [B]false, where false $=_{def}$ p $\wedge$

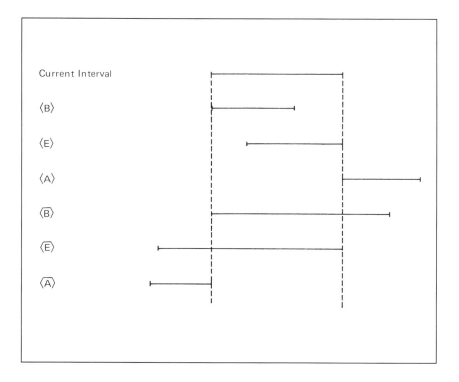

Figure 2.1: The six basic modal operators

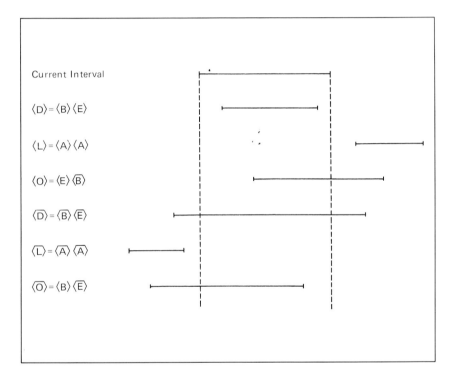

Figure 2.2: Derived modal operators

¬p, holds only of point intervals. We can use this observation to define a "beginning point" modal operator [[BP]], where [[BP]] φ says that φ holds at the beginning point of the interval:

[[BP]] φ ≡ (φ∧ [B]false) ∨ ⟨B⟩(φ∧ [B]false)

By analogy, it is easy to define the "end point" modal operator:

[[EP]] φ ≡ (φ∧ [B]false) ∨ ⟨E⟩(φ∧ [B]false)

Notice that both "point" operators are their own duals: [[BP]] φ ≡ ¬[[BP]] ¬φ, and similarly for [[EP]]. That is why, rather than have the two [ ] and ⟨ ⟩ operators that would be identical for the point operators, I have chosen the single [[ ]] notation.

2.4.3   Expressing assertions in the logic

Since this new logic is quite different from ones used in AI in the past, let me briefly show how one can use the logic to express situations of interest in two popular areas of AI, both heavily involved in reasoning about time. In neither case do I intend to shed new light on the particular area; I only draw on the two in order to give a feeling for the logic. In both examples it is assumed that the structure of time is linear.

Qualitative physics

The area of AI known as qualitative physics is concerned with reasoning about relatively simple physical situations, using only rough and qualitative information, in much the same way as people do in everyday life [11]. Typical problems are predicting the outcome of placing a kettle on a burner, reasoning about liquids flowing between containers, and reasoning about collisions between moving objects. Although reasoning about time is clearly central to qualitative physics, the actual work that has been done makes no use of temporal formalisms (again, see [11]).

Consider representing the sentence "if you open the tap then, unless someone punctures the canteen, the canteen will eventually be filled." In our logic this assertion is represented by the formula

open-tap ⊃ ⟨A⟩(¬⟨D⟩puncture ⊃ [[EP]]filled)

Automatic planning

Another area of AI heavily involved in temporal reasoning is automatic
planning, where a (usually simulated) robot must reason about carrying out
outstanding tasks, managing available resources, meeting various deadlines
and interacting with other agents. In this area there has been some use
of temporal formalisms, most notably by McDermott [59] and Allen [2].
Here we demonstrate that our modal logic too is suitable for representing
planning situations of the sort that have been discussed in the literature.

As an example that is slightly more complex than the qualitative physics
one, consider the statement "if the robot executes the `charge-battery`
routine then at the beginning of the *following* execution of the `navigate`
routine its batteries will be fully charged."

Our logics, both the classical one and this modal one, are intended as
very basic vehicles for representing temporal information. If AI has taught
us anything, it is that intelligent information processing relies on a detailed
and finely-structured knowledge representation. I will now demonstrate
how more sophisticated definitions can be built on top of our "assembly
language" logic. In the previous section I categorized proposition types,
showing how we can arrive at coherent definitions of, and distinctions between, what are usually called *events, facts, properties, processes* and the
like. In particular, I defined the notion of *solid proposition types*. A proposition type was said to be solid if no two properly overlapping distinct
intervals ever satisfied it. For example, "The robot executed the `navigate`
routine (from start to finish)" is a solid proposition. It is easy to define the
notion in the modal logic; we simply assume the following axiom schema:

$$\texttt{solid}(\varphi) =_{def}$$
$$\varphi \supset \neg\langle B\rangle\varphi \wedge \neg\langle E\rangle\varphi \wedge \neg\langle D\rangle\varphi \wedge \neg\langle O\rangle\varphi \wedge \neg\langle \overline{B}\rangle\varphi \wedge \neg\langle \overline{E}\rangle\varphi \wedge \neg\langle \overline{D}\rangle\varphi \wedge \neg\langle \overline{O}\rangle\varphi$$

Assertions of the form "the next time that" are very common, and so it
will be useful to define a new binary modal operator. For a solid proposition
φ, $\boxed{\text{NTT}}(\varphi,\vartheta)$ will mean that ϑ holds in the first interval which satisfies φ
and which begins after the current interval:

$$\boxed{\text{NTT}}(\varphi,\vartheta) =_{def} \texttt{solid}(\varphi) \wedge [A]([D]\neg\varphi \supset [A]((\varphi \wedge \neg\langle B\rangle\varphi \wedge \neg\langle D\rangle\varphi) \supset \vartheta))$$

Given this definition, the assertion about the robot is simply

$$\texttt{charge-battery} \supset \boxed{\text{NTT}}(\texttt{navigate}, [\![\text{BP}]\!]\,\texttt{battery-full})$$

2.4.4 Formal syntax and semantics

Syntax

Given Φ_0 a set of atomic propositions, the set of all wffs is defined inductively as follows. All atomic propositions are wffs. If φ_1 and φ_2 are wffs then so are $\neg\varphi_1$, $\varphi_1 \wedge \varphi_2$, $\langle A \rangle \varphi_1$, $\langle B \rangle \varphi_1$, $\langle E \rangle \varphi_1$, $\langle \overline{A} \rangle \varphi_1$, $\langle \overline{B} \rangle \varphi_1$ and $\langle \overline{E} \rangle \varphi_1$. We use the standard abbreviations: $\vee$, $\supset$, and so on.

Semantics

An *interpretation* is a pair $\langle S, V \rangle$. S is a *temporal structure* $\langle T, \leq \rangle$, where T is a set of time points and $\leq$ is a partial order on T. V is a *meaning function* $V : \Phi_0 \rightarrow 2^I$, where $I = \{\langle t_1, t_2 \rangle : t_1 \leq t_2)\}$. The only assumptions I will make about $\leq$ is that it has "linear intervals," which means that for any two points t_1 and t_2 such that $t_1 \leq t_2$, the set of points $\{t : t_1 \leq t \leq t_2\}$ is totally ordered. In other words, if $t_1 \leq t_3$, $t_1 \leq t_4$, $t_3 \leq t_2$ and $t_4 \leq t_2$, then either $t_3 \leq t_4$ or $t_4 \leq t_3$. Note that given this assumption, the set of points induce a forest-like structure w.r.t. $\leq$ (a forest is a collection of trees). Actually, no part of the discussion in this paper depends on the assumption. I make it simply because it fits our intuition about the nature of time. In particular, given the assumption about the linearity of intervals, one can intuitively think of the pair $\langle t_1, t_2 \rangle$ as the closed interval of points between t_1 and t_2. To investigate the logic in its full generality, I have not imposed any further assumptions on the nature of time, such as linearity or continuity. Of course, we can easily do so. In fact, as will be shown in the next section, some of these assumptions can essentially be expressed by formulas in the logic.

We interpret wffs over pairs $\langle t_1, t_2 \rangle$ such that $t_1, t_2 \in T$ and $t_1 \leq t_2$. In any interpretation $\mathbf{M}$ and with respect to any interval $\langle t_1, t_2 \rangle$, each formula φ is either true (written $\mathbf{M}, \langle t_1, t_2 \rangle \models \varphi$) or false (written $\mathbf{M}, \langle t_1, t_2 \rangle \not\models \varphi$). When clear from the context, the interpretation $\mathbf{M}$ may be omitted, and so in those cases we write simply $\langle t_1, t_2 \rangle \models \varphi$ and $\langle t_1, t_2 \rangle \not\models \varphi$.

The truth value of any wff in $M = \langle \langle T, \leq \rangle, V \rangle$ is determined by the semantic rules given below. For convenience, we define the strict version of $\leq$: $t_1 < t_2 \equiv t_1 \leq t_2 \wedge t_2 \not\leq t_1$.

1. For all $\varphi \in \Phi_0$, $\langle t_1, t_2 \rangle \models \varphi$ iff $\langle t_1, t_2 \rangle \in V(\varphi)$

2. $\langle t_1, t_2 \rangle \models \neg\varphi$ iff $\langle t_1, t_2 \rangle \not\models \varphi$

3. $\langle t_1, t_2 \rangle \models \varphi_1 \wedge \varphi_2$ iff $\langle t_1, t_2 \rangle \models \varphi_1$ and $\langle t_1, t_2 \rangle \models \varphi_2$

4. $\langle t_1, t_2 \rangle \models \langle A \rangle \varphi$ iff there exists t_3 s.t. $t_2 < t_3$ and $\langle t_2, t_3 \rangle \models \varphi$

5. $\langle t_1, t_2 \rangle \models \langle B \rangle \varphi$ iff there exists t_3 s.t. $t_1 \leq t_3$, $t_3 < t_2$ and $\langle t_1, t_3 \rangle \models \varphi$

6. $\langle t_1, t_2 \rangle \models \langle E \rangle \varphi$ iff there exists t_3 s.t. $t_1 < t_3$, $t_3 \leq t_2$ and $\langle t_3, t_2 \rangle \models \varphi$

7. $\langle t_1, t_2 \rangle \models \langle \overline{A} \rangle \varphi$ iff there exists t_3 s.t. $t_3 < t_1$ and $\langle t_3, t_1 \rangle \models \varphi$

8. $\langle t_1, t_2 \rangle \models \langle \overline{B} \rangle \varphi$ iff there exists t_3 s.t. $t_2 < t_3$ and $\langle t_1, t_3 \rangle \models \varphi$

9. $\langle t_1, t_2 \rangle \models \langle \overline{E} \rangle \varphi$ iff there exists t_3 s.t. $t_3 < t_1$ and $\langle t_3, t_2 \rangle \models \varphi$

A wff φ is said to be *satisfiable* relative to a class of temporal structures $\mathcal{A}$ if, in some interpretation $\langle \langle T, < \rangle, V \rangle$ such that $\langle T, < \rangle \in \mathcal{A}$, we have $\langle t_1, t_2 \rangle \models \varphi$ for some $t_1, t_2 \in T$. A wff is satisfiable relative to a temporal structure if it is satisfiable relative to the singleton consisting of that structure. φ is *valid* relative to $\mathcal{A}$ if $\neg \varphi$ is not satisfiable relative to $\mathcal{A}$.

2.4.5   A first-order modal logic?

I have so far given only the propositional version of the modal logic of time intervals. As in the propositional case of the classical logic, here too that limits us to "holistic" assertions, so that the assertion "HOUSE17 is red" collapses into a single letter p, and so that there is nothing we can say about the color of *all* houses from which we could infer the color of HOUSE17. This is too limiting, and in order to make the logic of any practical use we would need the first-order version.

I will not, however, provide the first-order version, and there are two reasons for that. First, it is an easy exercise, given the way we generalized the propositional version of the classical logic to its first-order version. Second, from the next chapter onwards I will be using the classical logic rather that the modal one. The reason for that is that, as we are about to see, the two logics (the classical and the modal) are intimately related. In particular, any assertion in the modal logic can be transformed very easily into an equivalent first-order one.

One may wonder, if that is the case, why did I bother introducing the modal logic in the first place? Here too the answer is twofold. First, it is very concise and elegant. This conciseness is shared by all modal logics, including point-based modal temporal logic, which is one reason the latter has become so popular. The compact nature of the logic makes it a good framework in which to devise complete axiomatizations. This in itself is not the focus of our particular work. Nevertheless, a related benefit of the simplicity of the modal logic *will* come in handy, which brings us to the second use of the modal logic: the ease of determining how difficult it to reason in the logic. More specifically, I will briefly look into the question of how hard it is to determine whether a given formula is valid for the logic. Since the modal logic can be translated into the classical one, any *lower bound* we find for the modal logic is inherited by the classical one. In the next section I indeed discuss such lower bounds. All the proofs can be translated into the classical logic, but the result would be much clumsier.

2.5   Expressiveness and complexity of the two interval logics

I have presented two logics of time intervals. For the classical logic I gave
both the propositional version and the first-order one. For the modal logic I
gave only the propositional version, although it would not be hard to define
the first-order version too. It was said several times that the two logics are
closely related. I now make that relation explicit. I will show that any
sentence in the modal logic can be translated into an equivalent sentence
in the classical logic. As a result we will have that the classical logic is
at least as expressive as the modal one. In fact, I will argue (somewhat
informally) that it is *strictly* more expressive. As another result we will
have that any *lower bounds* we show for deciding validity or satisfiability in
the modal logic is inherited by the classical logic. I discuss the complexity
of the validity problem at the end of this section.

2.5.1   Translating from the modal logic to the classical one

It is well known that any modal logic with standard Kripke semantics
can be translated into an equivalent classical logic. The idea is to add
new constant symbols to represent the possible worlds, and (one or more)
new relation symbols to represent the (one or more) accessibility relations
between the possible worlds. In our case this would mean adding constant
symbols to represent time intervals, and six new relation symbols, one for
each modal operator.

This is not quite what we have in our classical logic. On the one hand
we have in it time-point symbols rather that time-interval symbols, and
on the other hand we have the single $\preceq$ relation rather than six different
ones. We will nevertheless be able to translate from the modal logic into
our classical one. The following procedure is one way of doing so (it similar
to a procedure suggested to us privately by Johan van Benthem).

The translation is straightforward. We use the variable symbols t_1, t_2,
..., which will designate time points. Intuitively, where in the modal logic
we would say that a proposition p was satisfied by the interval $\langle t_1, t_2 \rangle$ in a
certain interpretation, in the first-order logic we will say that the formula
TRUE(t_1,t_2,p) is true under the appropriate interpretation.

Each modal formula φ is translated into a first-order formula φ_t with two free variables: t_1 and t_2. The translation is as follows (we use $t_1 \prec t_2$ to abbreviate $t_1 \preceq t_2 \land \neg t_2 \preceq t_1$):

1. If p is a primitive proposition then $p_t = t_1 \preceq t_2 \land \text{TRUE}(t_1, t_2, p)$

2. $(\neg\varphi)_t = t_1 \preceq t_2 \land \neg(\varphi_t)$

3. $(\varphi \land \varphi')_t = \varphi_t \land \varphi'_t$

4. $(\langle B \rangle \varphi)_t = \exists\, t_3\ (t_1 \preceq t_3 \land t_3 \prec t_2 \land \varphi_t[t_3/t_2])$.
   By $\varphi_t[t_3/t_2]$) we mean φ_t, with all free occurrences of t_2 replaced by t_3.

5. $(\langle A \rangle \varphi)_t = \exists\, t_3\ (t_1 \preceq t_2 \land t_2 \prec t_3 \land \varphi_t[t_2/t_1, t_3/t_2])$.

6. ...and similarly for the other modal operators.

φ and φ_t are "equivalent" in the sense that, roughly speaking, if the one is valid then so is the other. Actually this needs to be made more precise. As we shall see in the next subsection, when we speak of the validity and satisfiability problems in the modal logic we do so with respect to certain assumptions about time. For example, some assertions that are valid for discrete time are not valid for dense time, and vice versa. When we speak of the validity (or satisfiability) in the classical logic we do not have that freedom: time points are individuals in our domain, and it is up to us to constrain them through our axioms to have the right properties. With no axioms whatsoever, there is nothing to exclude a model for φ_t in which time is, for example, cyclic. Furthermore, even if time has the right properties, we need to exclude the possibility that $t_2 \prec t_1$.

Fortunately, we can achieve all that in FOPC. For example, to ensure that time is acyclic we simply add the condition $\forall\, t_1, t_2\ (t_1 \preceq t_2 \land t_1 \preceq t_2 \supset t_1 = t_2)$. Other properties can be expressed similarly. Let the formula time-properties express all those restrictions we care to impose on the structure of time. It is the case then that the modal formula φ and the classical formula time-properties $\land\ \exists\, t_1, t_2\ (t_1 \preceq t_2 \land \varphi_t)$ are equi-satisfiable. Similarly, the modal φ and the classical time-properties $\supset \forall\, t_1, t_2\ (t_1 \preceq t_2 \supset \varphi_t)$ are equi-valid.

2.5.2   The classical logic is strictly more expressive

The translation from the modal logic to the classical logic means the classical logic is at least as expressive as the modal one. A natural question

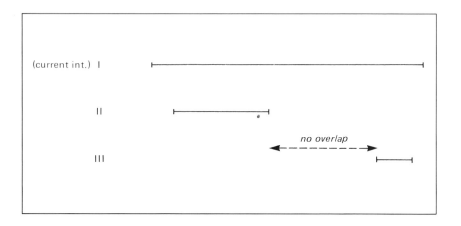

Figure 2.3: Three time intervals

to ask is whether the reverse process is possible: can each classical formula be translated into an equivalent modal one?

The answer is, I believe, no, but I will only argue for it informally here. Intuitively, the modal operators allow us to express the relation between any *two* intervals, but many relations between three or more intervals are not expressible. For example, there is no way to capture the relation between the intervals dscribed graphically in Figure 2.3. This relation arises, for example, in the context of the assertion "Whenever the robot executes the NAVIGATE routine, at the beginning of the execution it first walks around in circles for while, and then at some later point during the execution it runs out of electricity and needs assistance". Assuming the fact-type NAVIGATE stands for complete execution of the NAVIGATE routine (interval I), the fact-type CIRCLES stands for the robot walking around in circles (interval II), and the fact-type THIRSTY stands for the robot running out of electricity (interval III), the statement is easy to represent in the propositional version of the classical logic:

$\forall$ $t_1 \prec t_2$
  NAVIGATE $\supset$
  $\exists$ $t_1 \prec t_3 \prec t_4 \preceq t_5 \prec t_2$
    TRUE(t_3, t_4, CIRCLES) $\wedge$ TRUE(t_5, t_5, THIRSTY)

In the modal logic there is no way to express this relation between

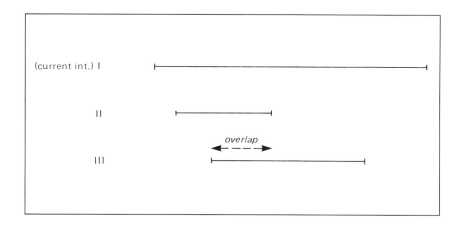

Figure 2.4: Another three time intervals

the three intervals, the ones satisfying NAVIGATE, CIRCLES and THIRSTY. There is another modal operator, a binary one, which has appeared in the literature and which could help in this particular example. It is the ; operator (pronounced "chop") which was introduced in process logic and used for example in ITL [66]. p ; q is true of an interval if the interval can be decomposed into two consecutive intervals, the first satisfying p and the second satisfying q. This would certainly take care of the robot example just given – the assertion would be simply NAVIGATE ⊃ TRUE ; CIRCLES ; TRUE ; THIRSTY ; TRUE.[6] There are other assertions, however, that cannot be handled by the ; operator. For example, we can complicate the structure described in Figure 2.3 so that intervals II and III overlap rather than being disjoint (see Figure 2.4). This structure arises, for example, from the statement "whenever the robot executes the TRAVEL-FROM-NY-TO-LA routine, after a while its engine starts heating. Shortly after it starts heating the robot may not drive at more than 5 mph for fear of burning the engine. The engine starts cooling after some time (because the fan is finally activated), but it takes a while before it is cool enough to bring the robot up to full speed. Afterwards the robot may travel at top speed until it finishes executing the TRAVEL-FROM-NY-TO-LA routine."

This complex statement cannot be represented using only ; and the

---

[6]Since ; is associative, the above formula is unambiguous. TRUE is defined to be p ∨ ¬p.

other six modal operators. If if we consider statements that refer to four or more intervals, it is even easier to construct statements that are not representable even in the augmented modal logic.

This lack of expressiveness can and should be made more precise. It is certainly not self-evident what the limitations of any given set of modal operators are. Since it is not a central issue here, I have not attempted a rigorous proof of the claims about the limited expressiveness of our modal logic, with or without ;, although that is something well worth doing. Before doing that one would have to properly define the problem: what it means for an assertion to be expressible by a set of modal operators, and what set of assertions are being considered.

There are several open questions that are waiting to be settled, once this is done. One such question is whether there exists a finite set of modal operators which make the modal logic as expressive as the classical one. I conjecture that for any set of modal operators describing exactly the relation between any n intervals there is a relation between $n + 1$ intervals that is not expressible by that set.

This raises another interesting open theoretical question. Clearly for any fixed n we can devise a finite set of modal operators that are sufficient to express any statement referring to n or less intervals. The question is how large this set of operators needs to be. The obvious upper-bound is exponential in the number intervals. Can one do any better?

2.5.3   Complexity of the validity problem

From the perspective of AI, no logic, no matter how clear and elegant its semantics may be, is of any interest unless it can be used to reason about domains of interest; this point was emphasized already in Chapter 1. Our temporal logics are no exception, and the following chapters are devoted to showing how inferences can be made efficiently in our logics (or, to be precise, in another logic that is based on them). The question is what we mean by the words "making inferences efficiently".

In this subsection I briefly look into one particular interpretation of this phrase, an interpretation that is commonly adopted by theoretical computer scientists. According to it we ask how hard it is to determine whether an arbitrary given formula is *valid* in the logic. A related question is how hard it is to decide whether an arbitrary given formula is *satisfiable* in the model. This latter question is equivalent to deciding whether an arbitrary given formula is *not* valid (since a formula is satisfiable just in case its negation is not valid). In all cases we are interested in the *worst case* (and see discussion of this below): a procedure that decided 99% of the formulas correctly but made incorrect judgments on the remaining 1% would not be acceptable. Nor would a procedure that made correct judgements only on formulas whose written form is less than three miles long. A similar criterion applies when evaluating the *efficiency* of a decision procedure: a procedure that decided the validity of 99% of the formulas in linear time but required double exponential time for the remainder would be considered double exponential in time.

We would certainly be delighted to lay our hands on an efficient procedure for deciding validity. At the very least it could serve as a proof-checker. For example, if we came up with a plan φ_1 to achieve the goal φ_2 in the context φ_3, we could verify its correctess by deciding the validity of the formula $\varphi_1 \wedge \varphi_3 \supset \varphi_2$. Other applications of such a decision procedure are equally obvious.

The precise complexity of the validity problem depends critically on assumptions we make about the underlying structure of time. The bottom line, however, is the following:

For no interesting models of time can we hope to have any decision procedure, let alone an efficient one. For some of them we cannot even hope to have a complete axiomatization.

Complete discussion of this issue is beyond the scope of this dissertation. For detailed lower and upper bounds the reader is referred to [25]. The detailed lower bounds are summarized in Appendix A.

I started out this section by saying that a logic is useful only to the extent that it permits effective inferences. I have now said that if we want to make any realistic assumption about the nature of time then we must give up hope of arriving at a decision procedure for our logics. Does that mean that our logics are useless and should be abandoned?

I think that the answer is no, and that the problem is that deciding general validity is *not* the problem we are facing. Our logics are very natural in that the formal meaning of the symbols appearing in them directly mirrors their intuitive meaning. Writing statements in the logics will force our inferences to be *sound*; rather than a mere rewriting of symbols by our program we will now have a derivation of logical sentences which is justified on semantical grounds. The fact that we cannot have a uniform

procedure for automatically making all inferences should come as a shock
to no one in AI. It is widely acknowledged today that any successful planner must have detailed knowledge of the domain in which it is to operate,
and that therefore a good planner in one domain may be useless in another.
For the same reasons it seems a little naive to aim for a general-purpose,
domain-independent decision procedure, and instead we should lower our
sights considerably. One can describe arbitarily complex situations in the
logic, and it is not our goal to be able to make arbitrarily complex inferences. In fact, we would like the inferences to be as simple as possible, and
thus the "worst case" criterion is clearly the wrong one for our purposes.
People have very definite ideas about the nature of time, although they
never see all the consequences of their assumptions. We do not expect our
programs to be any better; human-level performance on their part will be
quite satisfactory.

Furthermore, we need not content ourselves with only "heuristic" methods for making inferences in the logics, ones that do not permit rigorous
analysis (although that too would be an entirely reasonable approach to
take). Although the general decision problem is too hard, we can identify
special classes of formulas, which on the one hand are expressive enough
to capture situations of interest, and on the other hand can be reasoned
about more easily than in the general case. This is in fact precisely what
I do in the next chapters.

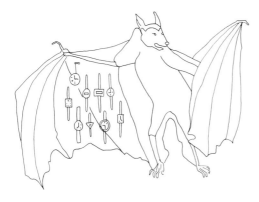

Chapter 3

Nonmonotonic Logics

In the introductory chapter it was explained why a temporal logic alone does not yield an effective method for reasoning about change. In particular, two problems were shown to arise — the qualification problem and the extended prediction problem — and it was said that solutions to them will involve nonmonotonic logics, those logics which permit "jumping to conclusions," or assigning sentences "default truth values," or reaching conclusions which rely in part on the "absence of evidence to the contrary."

I will not adopt any of the existing nonmonotonic logics (e.g., McCarthy's *circumscription* [53], Reiter's *default logic* [81], McDermott and Doyle's *nonmonotonic logic I* [60], McDermott's *nonmonotonic logic II* [57], or Clark's *predicate completion* [10]). Instead, in this chapter I will suggest a somewhat new, model-theoretic approach to constructing and understanding nonmonotonic logics. Although a complete analysis is yet to be carried out, it appears that despite its simplicity, the proposed framework both unifies and generalizes many of the existing nonmonotonic formalisms. In particular, it turns out that none of the particular logics mentioned above capture the temporal inferences in which we are interested, but that the general framework suggests other specific logics that do.

The intuition behind my approach is the following. The meaning of a formula in classical logic is the set of interpretations that satisfy it, or its set of *models* (where "interpretation" means truth assignment for PC, a first-order interpretation for FOPC, and a ⟨Kripke interpretation, world⟩-pair for modal logic). One gets a nonmonotonic logic by changing the rules of the game, and accepting only a subset of those models, those that are "preferable" in a certain respect (these preferred models are sometimes

called "minimal models," a term introduced by McCarthy in connection
with circumscription). The reason this transition makes the logic nonmonotonic is as follows. In classical logic $A \models C$ if C is true in all models
of A. Since all models of $A \wedge B$ are also models of A, it follows that
$A \wedge B \models C$, and hence that the logic is monotonic. In the new scheme we
have that $A \models C$ if C is true in all *preferred* models of A, but $A \wedge B$ may
have preferred models that are not preferred models of A. In fact, the class
of preferred models of $A \wedge B$ and the class of preferred models of A may
be completely disjoint!

Many different preference criteria are possible, all resulting in different
nonmonotonic logics. The trick is to identify the preference criterion that
is appropriate for a given purpose. It turns out that the preference criteria
that are implicitly adopted by any of the nonmonotonic systems mentioned
above are wrong as far as the qualification and extended prediction problems go.

Fortunately, another preference criterion can be identified that is exactly right for these two problems, and the following chapters discuss it at
some length. In the remainder of this chapter I look at the general case
of nonmonotonic logics in more detail. I first provide new definitions of
nonmonotonic logic and of notions such as nonmonotonic satisfiability and
nonmonotonic entailment. I then discuss the intuitive idea behind nonmonotonic inferences, and in the process address the question of whether
it is meaningful to distinguish, as has been suggested, between nonmonotonic inferences that are *default inferences* and those that are *autoepistemic
inferences*. In the last section I briefly show how previous nonmonotonic
systems fit in with the new definitions.

3.1 Formal construction of nonmonotonic logics

This first section is devoted to defining the notion of nonmonotonic logics in the most general sense. At the time this work was carried out I was unaware of related work done previously by Bossu and Siegel [6], otherwise I would have made an effort to use their terminology where possible. I compare my treatment of nonmonotonic logic to theirs in the comparison section at the end of this chapter.

The discussion in this section will be most general, and when I talk of a "standard logic" I allow in principle any logic with the usual compositional, model-theoretic semantics. Rather than give a precise definition of this condition, however, let me in the following assume that by a "standard logic" one means the propositional calculus or first-order predicate logic, either classical or modal (i.e., one of four logics[1]); extension to other cases (such as higher-order logic) will be obvious. In order to have the following discussion apply uniformly to the classical and modal logics, let me misuse the terminology slightly by calling anything which goes to the left of the $\models$ an *interpretation*. In the classical cases this is what is indeed usually called an interpretation. In the modal cases it is a pair ⟨Kripke structure,world⟩.

The transition to nonmonotonic logic puts into question notions that are well understood in logic, such as satisfaction, entailment, satisfiability, validity, and proof theory. To see what these might mean in the context of nonmonotonic logic, it will be helpful to make some precise definitions. We first recall some definitions in the standard case.

Definition 3.1 (Reminder)
Let $\mathcal{L}$ be a standard logic, and A and B two sentences in $\mathcal{L}$.

> *The fact that an interpretation M satisfies A is denoted by $M \models A$. In this case we say that M is a <u>model</u> of A.*

> *A is <u>satisfiable</u> if A has a model.*

> *A is <u>valid</u> if A is satisfied by all interpretations. Clearly A is satisfiable iff $\neg A$ is not valid.*

---

[1]For the sake of discussion, let us assume that whenever a modal system is mentioned, one means an S_5 system. The reader will see that nothing will depend on this assumption, however.

A _entails_ B _(written_ $A \models B$ _) if_ B _is satisfied by all models of_ A, _or,_
equivalently, if all models of A _are also models of_ B.

From these definitions, the deduction theorem follows very easily (this is
further misuse of terminology on my part, since the deduction theorem
really refers to deducibility and not to entailment, but I know of no name
for the following true fact):

Theorem 3.1 (Reminder)
Let $\mathcal{L}$ _be a standard logic, and_ A, B _and_ C _sentences in_ $\mathcal{L}$. _Then_ $A \wedge B \models C$
iff $A \models B \supset C$.

Nonmonotonic logics are the result of associating with a standard logic
a preference relation on models. More specifically, we make the following
definitions. Let $\mathcal{L}$ be a standard logic and A a sentence in it, and let $\sqsubset$ be
a strict partial order on interpretations for $\mathcal{L}$. Intuitively, $M_1 \sqsubset M_2$ will
mean that the interpretation M_2 is _preferred over_ the interpretation M_1.
$\mathcal{L}$ and $\sqsubset$ define a new logic $\mathcal{L}_{\sqsubset}$. I will call such logics _preference logics._
The syntax of $\mathcal{L}_{\sqsubset}$ is identical to that of $\mathcal{L}$. The semantics of $\mathcal{L}_{\sqsubset}$ are as
follows.

Definition 3.2 _An interpretation_ M _preferentially satisfies_ A _(written_
$M \models_{\sqsubset} A$ _) if_ $M \models A$, _and if there is no other interpretation_ M' _such that_
$M \sqsubset M'$ _and_ $M' \models A$. _In this case we say that_ M _is a preferred model_ _of_
A.

Clearly, if $M \models_{\sqsubset} A$ then also $M \models A$. Next I define the notions of
satisfiability and validity in $\mathcal{L}_{\sqsubset}$. These can be defined in more than one
way, none of them entirely satisfactory. The definition of satisfiability is
the more intuitive of the two.

Definition 3.3 A _is preferentially satisfiable_ _if there exists an_ M _such that_
$M \models_{\sqsubset} A$.

Clearly, all preferentially satisfiable formulas are also satisfiable, though
the converse is not necessarily true. In fact, there may exist formulas φ
such that neither φ nor $\neg\varphi$ are satisfiable. The definition of preferential
validity is even less intuitive. In fact, I have no intuition at all on what
preferential validity should mean. Since that is the case, I will define it
simply as the dual relation to preferential satisfiability:

Definition 3.4 *A is preferentially valid (written $\models_{\sqsubset} A$) iff $\neg A$ is not preferentially satisfiable.*

Lemma 3.2 *A is preferentially valid if for any M, either*

1. *$M \models A$, or else*

2. *there is an M' such that $M \sqsubset M'$ and $M' \not\models A$.*

(The proof follows immediately from the definitions.) Again, it is easy to see that all valid formulas are also preferentially valid, although the converse is not true. Indeed, preferential validity has some strange properties. For example, depending on $\sqsubset$, both a formula and its negation can be preferentially valid. Or, as a more concrete example, for $\sqsubset$ that is *unbounded* (that is, if for any M there is an M' such that $M \sqsubset M'$), if φ is valid then, not only is φ preferentially valid, but so is $\neg\varphi$.

Perhaps it makes no sense to define the notion of validity in this general context. There are, however, restricted cases where the above definition of preferential validity is very well behaved:

Definition 3.5 *A partial order $\sqsubset$ on models is said to be <u>bounded</u> if there does not exist an infinite sequence of models $M_1, M_2, M_3 \ldots$ such that $M_1 \sqsubset M_2 \sqsubset M_3 \sqsubset \ldots$*

Theorem 3.3 *Let $\mathcal{L}$ be a preferential logic, $\sqsubset$ a bounded partial order on its models, and A a formula in $\mathcal{L}$ (and therefore also in $\mathcal{L}_{\sqsubset}$). Then A is satisfiable in $\mathcal{L}$ iff A is preferentially satisfiable in $\mathcal{L}_{\sqsubset}$.*

Proof:

$\Leftarrow:$ Trivial.

$\Rightarrow:$ Suppose $M_0 \models A$. Define an A-sequence to be any sequence of models
$\langle M_0, M_1, M_2, \ldots \rangle$ such that for every element M_i in the sequence, a) $M_i \models A$, and b) if there exists an M_{i+1} in the A-sequence then $M_i \sqsubset M_{i+1}$. Clearly at least one A-sequence exists, the sequence $\langle M_0 \rangle$. From the boundedness of $\sqsubset$ it follows that no infinite A-sequences exist. Therefore there is at least one maximal A-sequence $\langle M_0, M_1, M_2, \ldots, M_n \rangle$, one that cannot be extended to a longer one. Then by definition $M_n \models_{\sqsubset} A$. ∎

Corollary 3.4 *Under the same conditions, A is valid in $\mathcal{L}$ iff A is preferentially valid in $\mathcal{L}_\sqsubset$.*

Observation. $\mathcal{L}$ can be viewed as a special case of $\mathcal{L}_\phi$, where ϕ is the empty relation. Note that ϕ is bounded.

As was said before, despite these well-behaved properties, preferential satisfiability and validity are somewhat strange notions. Fortunately, neither is central to understanding nonmonotonic reasoning. What is crucial is the notion of preferential entailment, and that has a very intuitive definition:

Definition 3.6 *A <u>preferentially entails</u> B (written $A \models_\sqsubset B$) if for any M, if $M \models_\sqsubset A$ then $M \models B$, or, equivalently, if the models of B (preferred and otherwise) are a superset of the preferred models of A.*

Definition 3.7 *$\mathcal{L}_\sqsubset$ is monotonic if for all $A,B,C \in \mathcal{L}$, if $A \models_\sqsubset C$ then also $A \wedge B \models_\sqsubset C$.*

Observation. The above definition is equivalent to saying that a logic is monotonic if all preferred models of $A \wedge B$ are also preferred models of A. Again viewing $\mathcal{L}$ as the special case $\mathcal{L}_\phi$, we note that $\mathcal{L}_\phi$ is monotonic.

Observation. If $\mathcal{L}$ is a preferential logic, it may contain sentences A and B such that both $A \models_\sqsubset B$ and $A \models_\sqsubset \neg B$. Furthermore, A need not be inconsistent for this to be the case – it is sufficient that it have no preferred models. Indeed, in preferential logic the role played by preferential satisfiability is exactly analogous to that played by satisfiability in standard logics, witness the following easy lemma:

Lemma 3.5 *Let $\mathcal{L}_\sqsubset$ be a preferential logic, and A a sentence in it. Then A is preferentially satisfiable iff there does not exists a sentence B in $\mathcal{L}_\sqsubset$ such that both $A \models_\sqsubset B$ and $A \models_\sqsubset \neg B$.*

It is interesting to see what happens to the deduction theorem in light of the new definition of entailment. It turns out that while the theorem is false in general, a weaker version of it still holds, in which the 'iff' is changed to an 'if'. First we give a lemma whose truth follows trivially from the definitions.

Lemma 3.6 *Let $\mathcal{L}_\sqsubset$ be a preferential logic, A and B two sentences in it, and M a model. Then if $M \models B$ and $M \models_\sqsubset A$, then $M \models_\sqsubset A \wedge B$.*

Theorem 3.7 *Let $\mathcal{L}_\sqsubset$ be a preferential logic, and A, B and C three sentences in it. Then, if $A \wedge B \models_\sqsubset C$, then also $A \models_\sqsubset B \supset C$.*

Proof:

1. $A \wedge B \models_\sqsubset C$ (assumption).

2. $A \not\models_\sqsubset B \supset C$ (assumption).

3. There exists an M_0 such that $M_0 \models_\sqsubset A$, but $M_0 \not\models B \supset C$ (from 2).

4. $M_0 \models_\sqsubset A$, $M_0 \models B$, and $M_0 \not\models C$ (from 3).

5. $M_0 \not\models_\sqsubset A \wedge B$ (from 1).

6. If $M_0 \models_\sqsubset A$ and $M_0 \models B$ then $M_0 \models_\sqsubset A \wedge B$ (Lemma 3.6).

7. Contradiction (from 4,5 and 6). ■

The converse to this theorem does not hold: if $A \models_\sqsubset B \supset C$ then it does not necessarily follow that $A \wedge B \models_\sqsubset C$. It is not hard to construct a counterexample, for example one in which C is identically false, $A \wedge B$ is *not* identically false, and B is false in all preferred models of A. In fact, it is easy to show that if the converse to the theorem holds then the logic is necessarily monotonic:

Theorem 3.8 *Let $\mathcal{L}_\sqsubset$ be a preferential logic. Then the following two statements are equivalent:*

1. *For all $A,B,C \in \mathcal{L}_\sqsubset$, if $A \models_\sqsubset B \supset C$ then also $A \wedge B \models_\sqsubset C$.*

2. *$\mathcal{L}_\sqsubset$ is monotonic.*

Proof:
The $(2 \Rightarrow 1)$ direction is trivial. For the $(1 \Rightarrow 2)$ direction, assume that $A \models_\sqsubset C$. Therefore by definition $A \models_\sqsubset B \supset C$ for any B. Then by the assumption in the statement of the theorem $A \wedge B \models_\sqsubset C$. ■

Notice that so far the discussion has been entirely model-theoretic, and I have made no mention of syntactical considerations (such as proof theory). Indeed, many of the notions that are quite clear in monotonic logic, such as complete axiomatization, cease to make sense in the context of nonmonotonic logic. The whole motivation behind nonmonotonic logics is the desire to be able to "jump to conclusions," inferring new facts not only from what is already known but also from what is not known. This seems to imply that traditional inference rules, which are rules for deriving new sentences from old ones, are inadequate.

What is the alternative? I'm not at all sure that there is one. The natural approach is to replace derivation rules in which the l.h.s. refers only to previously derived sentences with rule whose l.h.s. refers also to sentences *not* previously derived. Indeed, this is close to what both Reiter and McDermott do in their systems (see last section in this chapter). But it turns out that referring merely to sentences that were not explicitly derived is insufficient, and one ends up with rules of the form "if α has been derived, and if β is consistent with what has been derived, then derive γ." However, rules that demand checking consistency no longer have the computational advantages of traditional inference rules.

Perhaps something else is possible, along the lines of what are known as systems for *truth maintenance* (or *belief maintenance*, or *reason maintenance* or *data dependencies*) [15,50,55,14], in which the entities manipulated by programs are not sentences, but rather beliefs and records of justifications for each belief. For these programs to be elevated to the level of a proof procedures, however, much more needs to be said about the meaning of the justifications, about consistency, about soundness and completeness, and so on.

I do not pursue this line of enquiry here. The main point to remember is that such syntactical considerations are entirely secondary. What is important is to have clear semantics, which determine what sentences follow from one another. Reasoning about sentences can then proceed without any proof theory, and indeed that is what I will do in the following chapters.

3.2 The meaning and utility of nonmonotonic inferences

My treatment of nonmonotonic logics so far has been purely technical. This section is devoted to discussing the intuitive meaning behind nonmonotonic inferences. I will try to clarify some of the confusion arising from the apparent connection between probabilistic information and nonmonotonic inferences, and in the process argue against the suggestion that there are two fundamentally different sorts of nonmonotonic inferences.

The distinction I am alluding to was suggested by Robert Moore in [64]. He contrasts *default inferences*, which are based on some statistical facts (e.g., that most birds can fly), with *autoepistemic inferences*, which are based on the lack of some particular knowledge. Says Moore,

> Consider my reason for believing that I do not have an older brother. It is surely not that one of my parents once casually remarked, "you know, you don't have any older brothers," nor have I pieced it together by carefully sifting other evidence. I simply believe that if I had an older brother I would surely know about it ... This is quite different from a default inference based on the belief, say, that most MIT graduates are oldest sons ...

On the face of it this distinction is quite appealing (certainly I was convinced for a while), but upon closer examination it seems to break down completely.

To begin with, one may note that Moore applies his own logic, labelled an autoepistemic one, to the flying birds example, which he himself characterizes as a default case.[2] Furthermore, consider Moore's own older-brother example. If one accepts the statement "if I had an older brother then I'd know it," surely one must also accept the statement "if I *didn't* have an older brother then I'd know it." Yet if we adopt this latter sentence rather than the first one, the opposite inference will follow, namely that I have an older brother. On what basis does one prefer the first sentence to the second one, if at all? Notice that if you adopt *both* sentences, then you end up with two distinct preferred models – one in which you have an older brother and know it, and another in which you don't have an older brother and know it – which isn't much help.

---

[2] A fact pointed out to me by Ray Perrault.

Let me suggest a different distinction than the one made by Moore, and argue on behalf of what might be called *the ostrich principle*, or, the *what-you-don't-know-won't-hurt-you* principle. According to it, rather than distinguish between different kinds of default inferences, one should distinguish between the *meaning* of sentences on the one hand, and the (extra logical) *reason* for adopting that meaning on the other. The meaning, I argue, can be viewed epistemically. The reason for adopting that meaning is computational economy, which often relies on statistical information.

Consider the flying birds example. The *meaning* of "birds fly by default" is that if I don't know that a particular bird cannot fly, then it can. The computational *reason* for adopting this meaning is that now whenever a bird can indeed fly, we need not mention the fact explicitly – either in external communication with other reasoners, or in "internal communication," i.e., thought – it will follow automatically. Of course, if we happen to be talking about a penguin, we had better add the knowledge that penguins cannot fly, or else we will make wrong inferences. In the long run, however, we win: the overwhelming percentage of birds about which we are likely to speak can indeed fly, and so on average this default rule saves us work. If this gain seems small, consider a realistic situation in which we apply thousands and thousands of such rules.

Can we identify a similar rationale behind the rule "by default, I do not have an older brother"? It is less obvious here, which is why the two cases seem superficially different. Yet such motivation must exists or else one wouldn't prefer this rule to the opposite one.[3]

I am not at all arguing that one makes φ true by default just in case φ is true most of the time. As I have said, the flipside of making a default assumption is the danger of making faulty inferences. For example, if a bird is being discussed and its type is unknown, we will infer that it can fly even though it might turn out to be a penguin. If this seems harmless, think of making the default inference "people you'll meet on the street will not stab you in the back" in a city in which only 5% of the population are back stabbers. In this case the relatively small chance of being badly hurt seems to outweigh the computational resources needed to reason about individual people on the street, and the discomfort of wearing a steel-plated

---

[3]After being convinced of its conclusion, Drew McDermott, half in jest, suggested the following counting argument. The average couple has two children, so the speaker has a 50% chance of being the younger one, in which case there is a 50% chance that the older sibling is male. Thus in 75% of the cases the speaker does not have an older brother, which is not quite as overwhelming as the percentage of flying birds, but still is higher than 50%.

vest. Notice that if the 5% dropped to 0.00000000005%, we'd take off the armor and stop looking darkly at passers by. Indeed, that is exactly how we treat the possibility of a nuclear war. Clearly, one must maximize his expected utility when selecting a nonmonotonic theory. I offer no general guidelines for making such a selection (although when I discuss a particular nonmonotonic logic in the next chapters, I also identify the circumstances under which it is advantageous to adopt it). All I am suggesting here is to separate the two issues, that of defining the meanings of nonmonotonic logics, and that of selecting one.

Notice. The remainder of this section, in which two more arguments are offered in support of the proposed meaning/utility distinction, assumes acquaintance with McCarthy's *circumscription*, and with modal logics of minimal knowledge. The reader who is not familiar with those may wish to read the relevant subsections of the next section before finishing this one.

The reader may still be bothered by the fact that circumscription involves only classical sentences, and it is not clear how epistemic notions enter into it. It is not hard, however, to convert circumscription into a logic of minimal knowledge. The basic idea is instead of circumscribing a formula $\varphi(x)$, to add the axiom $\forall x \; \varphi(x) \supset \Box\varphi(x)$. (For example, in the flying birds case we add the axiom $\forall x \; \text{CANFLY}(x) \supset \Box\text{CANFLY}(x)$.) Since we prefer models in which as few propositional formulas as possible are known, the effect is to have φ true of as few x's as possible. The natural reading of the axiom $\varphi \supset \Box\varphi$ is indeed "if φ were true then I'd know it." However, if we take the contrapositive form of the axiom, we get the familiar "default rule": $\Diamond\neg\varphi \supset \neg\varphi$, or "if it is possible that φ is false then it is."

As a final clincher in the argument for the meaning/utility distinction, let me show how this distinction resolves the Lottery Paradox, discussed, for example, in [57]. The paradox is as follows:

A lottery is held with 1 million participants. The odds of any particular individual's winning are so low that we infer by default that he won't. Yet if we repeat this inference for each of the 1 million participants, the result will contradict our knowledge that at least one person must win.

In the logic of minimal knowledge we describe the situation by

$$[\text{WIN}(P_1) \lor \text{WIN}(P_2) \lor \ldots \lor \text{WIN}(P_{1,000,000})] \land$$
$$\forall x \; \text{WIN}(x) \supset \Box\text{WIN}(x)$$

The most ignorant models are ones in which one of the million people wins and we know that he won it, but the identity of that person varies among models. We are therefore not justified in concluding that any particular individual will not win, since there are models in which he does. True, those models are vastly outnumbered by those in which he does not win, but nonmonotonic logics do not let us express the property of a proposition being true in "most" models. This once again shows that such probabilistic information plays a role in choosing the meaning but not in defining it.

So in the above formulation we cannot conclude that a particular individual will not win, nor should we want to. If one claims that such a conclusion *is* one that corresponds to default reasoning people use, one must agree to the conclusion that no rational person would ever buy lottery tickets, a prediction that obviously isn't borne out in reality.[4] However, the above formulation is not as useless as it might appear. We can still make inferences involving the possibility of people winning, in which rather than condition an inference on their not winning, we condition it on the *possibility* of their not winning. For example, we may add the sentence

$$\Diamond\neg\texttt{WIN(ME)} \supset \neg\texttt{SHOULD-RESIGN-JOB(ME)}$$

The rationale here is again statistical. Although there is a model in which I win the lottery and therefore needn't bother teaching a course on AI, it would be foolish for me to resign on that basis.

---

[4]The argument that indeed no rational person should, given that in all lotteries the expected winning amount is negative, is irrelevant. The example would still hold if some bored millionaire organized the lottery, charging each participant one dollar and giving the winner one million and one dollars.

3.3   A look at past nonmonotonic logics

I have so far refrained from discussing any details of previous nonmonotonic formalisms. I have done so deliberately in order to present the concept of nonmonotonic logic to the reader in what I believe is its "pure form," and in a way which does not obscure the essence of the concept by inessential considerations. Nevertheless, my formulation was strongly influenced by previous nonmonotonic systems, some of which I have already mentioned. In fact, while it is clear how some previous systems are special cases of the general framework just presented, the connection to others is not completely understood at the moment. In this section I will very briefly survey some of the better known formulations, and indicate how they fit in with the general scheme which I defined above.

(A Reminder.) The following chapters do not depend on this section. Those readers who have no intrinsic interest in past nonmonotonic logics may skip to the beginning of the next chapter.

3.3.1   Circumscription

The formalism which is closest in spirit to the definitions given in the previous section is the logic of *circumscription*. It is actually a family of logics, starting with John McCarthy's original formulation in [52], and continuing with later formulations by McCarthy himself [51] and more recently by Vladimir Lifschitz [46,47].

The property common to all versions of circumscription is the existence of a *circumscription axiom*. It is essentially a second-order axiom that is assumed to implicitly accompany any first-order theory (by a theory I mean a collection of sentences). In McCarthy's original formulation, the circumscription axiom (and I am using Lifschitz' recent reconstruction of it) was:

$$A(P) \; \wedge \; \forall p \; \neg(A(p) \; \wedge \; p{<}P)$$

where p is a predicate variable with free variables x, and p<P stands for

$$\forall x(px \supset Px) \; \wedge \; \neg\forall x(Px \supset px)$$

Intuitively, what this means is that if x are the free variables of a wff P, then the effect of circumscribing P in a theory A is to limit the instances of x which satisfy P to only those that are necessary in light of A. For example, the result of circumscribing CANFLY(x) in {∀b (BIRD(b) ⊃ CANFLY(b)), BIRD(POLLY)} has the effect that the *only* object that can fly is POLLY.[5]

Notice that this is exactly a way of preferring some models to others. The sentence ∀b (BIRD(b) ⊃ CANFLY(b)) ∧ BIRD(POLLY) has many models, but circumscribing CANFLY is a way of preferring models in which only POLLY can fly.

In the terminology used earlier, circumscribing P(x) defines a preference criterion according to which $M_1 \sqsubseteq M_2$ if

1. For all x, M_1 and M_2 agree on the interpretation of function symbols and all relation symbols other than P,

2. for all x, if $M_2 \models P(x)$ then also $M_1 \models P(x)$, and

3. there exists a y such that $M_1 \models P(y)$ but $M_2 \not\models P(y)$.

Thus the original version of circumscription is simply a special case of nonmonotonic logic, as I defined it earlier. The same is true of the more sophisticated versions of circumscription which have appeared since then. For example, the axiom of *parameterized circumscription* is the following generalization of original axiom (again, I am using Lifschitz' reconstruction of it):

$$A(P,Z) \land \forall pz \ \neg(A(p,z) \land p<P)$$

where Z is a tuple of predicates or function symbols. Here, the preference criterion embodied in the axiom requires minimizing the extension of P, possibly by varying the denotation of the symbols appearing in Z. In other words, according to this new criterion, $M_1 \sqsubseteq M_2$ if

1. M_1 and M_2 agree on the interpretation of all function symbols and all relation symbols other than P and those appearing in Z,

2. for all x, if $M_2 \models P(x)$ then also $M_1 \models P(x)$, and

---

[5]One has to be careful here. The inference that the only object that can fly is POLLY is certainly the intended one, but, as shown by Etherington, Mercer and Reiter in [18], the original formulation did not have this property. The discussion here refers to the formulation which allows varying some predicates in the process of minimizing others.

3. there exists a y such that $M_1 \models P(y)$ but $M_2 \not\models P(y)$.

Several other circumscription schemes have been suggested, such as *joint circumscription* and *prioritized circumscription*. Most recently, Vladimir Lifschitz has suggested a family of circumscription axioms called *pointwise circumscription* [47]. Without going into the details, these new schemes allow one to express preference criteria that were not expressible in previous circumsciption schemes.

To avoid giving the wrong impression, it must be said that the notion of preferred models was implicit in McCarthy's work from the start. In fact, in his original paper he gave precisely the first minimality criterion that was stated above, although in subsequent publications the model-theoretic discussion seemed to play a diminishing role. Other researchers too have addressed the model theory of nonmonotonic logics, such as Lifschitz in [47] and Etherington in [17].

My formulation can be viewed as a suggestion to generalize McCarthy's approach in three ways:

I.   Start with any standard logic, not necessarily FOPC. For example, I will base my formulations on a standard modal logic.

II. Allow any partial order on interpretations, not only the one implied by a particular circumscription axiom. For example, I will suggest a preference criterion that relies on temporal precedence.

III. Shift the emphasis to the semantics, stressing the partial order on models and not the particular way of defining that partial order. The various circumscription axioms, either McCarthy's original ones or Lifschitz's more recent ones, are one way of doing so, and they are most elegant. It remains to be seen whether that particular way of expressing the preference criterion on models, using a second-order axiom, has additional advantages. In my own formulations I will choose other means of defining preference criteria.

3.3.2   Bossu and Siegel

I mentioned earlier that, unaware of Bossu and Siegel's work reported in [6], I rediscovered some of their ideas and renamed some of their terms, and by now I am too fond of my definitions to let go of them. I will now compare the two formulations. The summary of the relation between the two treatments is that the they share the basic semantical approach, although there are some minor technical differences between the two, but that Bossu and Siegel thoroughly investigated what turns out to be a very special case of my general formulation. In a little more detail the connection is as follows.

The main part common to both Bossu and Siegel's treatment and my own is the model-theoretic approach, which posits a partial order on interpretations. There are some minor differences in the precise definitions. For example, whereas I defined φ to be preferentially satisfiable (or, in their terminology, *minimally modelable*) if φ has a preferred model, Bossu and Siegel require in addition that *any* nonpreferred model of φ have a better model than it which is preferred. Or, as another example, they explicitly reject the definition I chose for preferential entailment (which they call *subimplication* and denote by $\models$), since if φ is not preferentially satisfiable (i.e., it has no maximally preferred models) then it entails both ϑ and $\neg\vartheta$. I don't view that as a disadvantage, since preferential satisfiability plays a role that is completely analogous to satisfiability. Thus by the same argument one should object to the regular notion of entailment, since inconsistent (i.e., unsatisfiable) theories entail both ϑ and $\neg\vartheta$.

These are fairly minor differences, and they are overwhelmed by the similarity in the semantical approach to nonmonotonic logics. There is, however, a big difference between the two treatments, and that is in their generality. Whereas I allow starting with arbitrary standard logics as a basis (see comment at the beginning of this section), Bossue and Siegel require starting with FOPC. More crucially, whereas I allow *any* partial order on interpretations, Bossu and Siegel assume one fixed such partial order. As they themselves say,

> The difference between [John McCarthy's] definition and ours is that McCarthy 'minimizes' on some literals only, whereas we 'minimize' on every literal.

Circumscription was discussed in the previous subsection. As we have seen, in the simplest version of the logic, preferred models are those in which $P_1(x_1)$, ..., $P_n(x_n)$ are true for as few x_i's as possible, where the P_i's are predicate symbols specified separately, and x_i are the arguments to P_i. What Bossu and Siegel do is fix the P_i's to be all the predicate symbols that appear in the theory that is being modeled.

Bossu and Siegel seem to imply that from their perspective, that of maintaining certain kinds of data bases, there is justification for choosing this particular partial order on interpretations. Be that as it may, this preference criterion is definitely *not* useful for solving the problems in temporal reasoning which motivated me to discuss nonmonotonic logic in the first place, and indeed in the next chapter I will introduce a radically different one.

3.3.3 NML, autoepistemic logic and minimal knowledge

It would be natural to discuss next Reiter's *default logic* [81], which since its publication has gained as much popularity as circumscription. However, the embedding of default logic in the "preferred models" setting will require talking about a modal logic, which at first might seem a bit radical. Let me then first address various nonmonotonic systems that are modal to begin with.

Along with circumscription and default logic, a series of somewhat more ambitious logics has appeared in the literature, which tried to represent in the logic itself notions such as consistency, belief or knowledge. The first construction was *Nonmonotonic Logic I* by Drew McDermott and Jon Doyle [60]. Problems in the logic later prompted McDermott to propose *Nonmonotonic Logic II* [57]. Later, drawing on previous work by Stalnaker [94] and Konolige [41], Robert Moore proposed an alternative, epistemic view of McDermott's logic, and a reformulation of it called *Autoepistemic Logic* [64]. Moore's formulation was changed slightly and further investigated by Halpern and Moses in [23] (they prefer to talk of self-knowledge rather than self-belief, which is what underlies the difference between the two logics). In the following I will refer directly to Halpern and Moses' formulation.

The formulas of their logic are simply those of modal logic, with $\Box$ serving as the necessity operator.[6] The intuitive interpretation of the modal operator is epistemic, and so $\Box\varphi$ reads "φ is known."[7]

---

[6]They actually use the operator K, but I adopt $\Box$ since later I will want to use the $\Diamond$ operator, and there is no widely accepted convention as to the dual of K. Moore uses L rather than K, and suggests that the M operator in NML II be viewed as the dual to L.

[7]Recall the application of modal logic to reasoning about knowledge, which was mentioned in the introductory chapter. Halpern and Moses choose the model in which the agent has total introspective capabilities, which is the S_5 system (I am ignoring the extension to many knowers here).

The question Halpern and Moses consider, which is also the one considered explicitly by Moore and implicitly by McDermott, is what it means for a theory to be a "complete" description of what is known. Moore views the theory as a data base, so that if an assertion is not in the database and does not follow from it deductively, then the assertion is not known. Similarly, Halpern and Moses ask what it means to say "I know α" and imply that that is *all* I know. So, if the data base contains the assertions p and q (or, if $\alpha = p \wedge q$), then all the base facts (those containing no modal operator) that are known are p, q, and their tautological consequences. In addition many nonbase facts are known, such as the fact $\neg\Box r$. Notice that this is a nonmotonic property: if r is added to the data base then $\Box r$ is true, and therefore $\neg\Box r$ is no longer known.

Halpern and Moses conclude that the statement "all I know is α" is meaningful only under certain conditions. They actually give four different conditions for it to be meaningful, and show all four to be equivalent. For the first one, they borrow from Moore (and, through him, from Stalnaker) the notion of a *stable set*. A collection of formulas T is called *stable* if it has the following properties:

1. T contains all instances of tautologies.

2. If $p \in T$ and $p \supset q \in T$ then $q \in T$.

3. $p \in T$ iff $\Box p \in T$.

4. $p \notin T$ iff $\neg\Box p \in T$.

Let us call the subset of a stable set T consisting of all the base formulas (again, those containing no modal operator) the *kernel* of T (although this is not a definition that any of the above authors make).

According to Halpern and Moses' first definition, the statement "all I know is α" is meaningful only if there is stable set T containing α whose kernel is T', such that for any stable set $S \neq T$ with kernel S', T' is a proper subset of S'. In that case T is exactly all that is known.

The same definition can be couched in terms of preferred models. In fact, the following definition of preferred models is almost identical to one of the other three offered by Moses and Halpern. Let us define a preference criterion on Kripke interpretations according to which $M_1 \sqsubset M_2$ if

1. for all base wffs φ, if $M_2 \models \Box\varphi$ then also $M_1 \models \Box\varphi$, and

2. there exists a base wff φ such that $M_1 \models \Box\varphi$ but $M_2 \not\models \Box\varphi$.

Let us also say that M_1 and M_2 are *equiignorant* if for all base wffs φ, $M_1 \models \Box\varphi$ iff $M_2 \models \Box\varphi$.

We are now in a position to couch the analysis of "all I know is α" in our terms (I assume that α is a single formula). "All I know is α" is meaningful just in case all preferred models of $\Box\alpha$ are equiignorant, and in that case all I know is all that is known in those preferred models. I think this second definition is more intuitive than the first one.

3.3.4 Default logic

The nonmonotonic logic cited most often, perhaps other than circumscription, is Raymond Reiter's *default logic* [81]. It is also the logic that is the least natural to fit into the general framework of preference logics. In fact, as we shall see, I will be able to capture only variants of Reiter's original logic in this framework.

A default theory is a pair $\langle W,D \rangle$, where W is a set of ordinary sentences, and D is a set of *default rules*. Default rules are inference rules which have the form

$$\alpha{:}M\beta_1, \ldots, M\beta_n \,/\, \gamma$$

In fact, Reiter allows for default rule schemes, so α, β_i and γ may have and share free variables. Informally, such an inference rule reads "if you know α, and for all i β_i is consistent with all you know, then infer γ – but in the future make sure that the β_i's remain a consistent assumption." An example of a default rule is :M($\neg$CANFLY(x)) / $\neg$CANFLY(x), whose informal meaning is that for any object, if it is consistent to assume that it cannot fly, assume so.

More precisely, Reiter defines the notion of an *extension*. Intuitively, an extension is reached by adding as many of the default inferences as possible, but making sure that when a default inference is made, the assumptions on which it is based are never violated. Reiter provides several equivalent formal definitions of an extension, possibly the most intuitive one being the following (it is restricted to the case of closed wffs):

Let E be a set of closed wffs, and let $\Delta = \langle W, D \rangle$ be a closed default theory. Define $E_0 = W$, and for all $i \geq 0$

$$E_{i+1} = Th(E_i) \cup \{\gamma : (\alpha:M\beta_1, \ldots, M\beta_n \,/\, \gamma) \in D,\ \alpha \in E_i,\ \text{and for}$$
$$\text{all } i,\ \neg\beta_i \notin E\}$$

where $Th(X)$ are all the monotonic consequences of X (note the occurrence of E in the definition of E_{i+1}). E is an *extension* of Δ if

$$E = \cup_{i=0}^{\infty} E_i$$

For example, the (open) default theory

```
W = {BIRD(POLLY),BIRD(x)⊃CANFLY(x),PROFESSOR(MCCARTHY)},
    D = {:M(¬CANFLY(x)) / ¬CANFLY(x)}
```

has a single extension, which includes the sentence ¬CANFLY(MCCARTHY). In general, a default theory may have many extensions or none at all.

The general motivation behind the definition seems clear, but not all of the actual details are as obviously motivated. For example, in [48] Lukaszewicz suggests an alternative definition of an extension, which leads to a very different default logic. It is hard to choose among such alternatives without a model-theory for the logic, since in its absence all one has to go by is a gut-level feeling. In fact, at the end of this subsection I will propose a slight variation on the definition of E_{i+1}. To the "naked eye" the two formulations will be, I think, equally attractive, but the modified version will have some nice theoretical properties.

In light of the discussion in the previous subsection, the reader will not be surprised to learn that I propose translating any default theory into a modal one, interpreting the modal operator epistemically, and identifying an appropriate preference criterion on Kripke structures.

To simplify the discussion, in the following I will discuss only default theories in which default rules contain a single default assumption (that is, all rules have the form $\alpha:M(\beta) \,/\, \gamma$). A default theory $\langle W,D \rangle$ will be translated into the modal theory

$$\{\Box w : w \in W\} \cup \{\Box\alpha \wedge \Diamond\beta \supset \Box\gamma : (\alpha:M(\beta)/\gamma) \in D\}$$

For example, consider the first example given in [81]:

$$W = \{B \supset \neg A \wedge \neg C\} \, , \, D = \{:M(A)/A, :M(B)/B, :M(C)/C\}$$

This default theory is translated into the modal theory:

$$\{\Box(B \supset \neg A \wedge \neg C), \Diamond A \supset \Box A, \Diamond B \supset \Box B, \Diamond C \supset \Box C\}$$

The default theory has two extensions: $Th(W \cup \{A,C\})$ and $Th(W \cup \{B\})$. The modal theory has many models, including those in which much more is known than only A and C, or B. However, we will identify a definition of "preferred models" according to which in all preferred models either $Th(\{B\})$ are all the propositional sentences that are known, or else $Th(\{A,C\})$ are.

Define the *biases* of a default theory $\langle W, D \rangle$ to be $\{\beta: (\alpha:M(\beta) \,/\, \gamma) \in D\}$. For each default theory with a set of biases S, we define a preference criterion $\sqsubseteq_S$ on models. Let M_1 and M_2 be two models, and $S_i = \{s: s \in S$ and $M_i \models \Diamond s\}$, $(i = 1, 2)$. Then $M_1 \sqsubseteq_S M_2$ if

1. $S_1 \overset{\subseteq}{\neq} S_2$, or

2. $S_1 = S_2$, and $\{\varphi: M_2 \models \Box\varphi\} \overset{\subseteq}{\neq} \{\varphi: M_1 \models \Box\varphi\}$.

Intuitively, we prefer models with minimal sets of biases whose negation is known (the set of "violated biases"), and among those we prefer models in which as little as possible is known (that is, among those we assume the preference criterion which was discussed in the previous subsection). One can verify that this two-layered preference criterion allows only models in which all that is known is B and its tautological consequences, or else all that are known are A, C and their tautological consequences.

As was said earlier, this preference criterion does not reflect Reiter's original formulation. Consider, for example, the second example given in [81]:

$$W = \phi \, , \, D = \{:M(C)/\neg D, :M(D)/\neg E, :M(E)/\neg F\}$$

In Reiter's system this theory has a unique extension, $Th(\{\neg D, \neg F\})$, but if we translate this theory to the modal one and assume the preference criterion just defined, we end up with two classes of minimal models: those in which $\neg D$ and $\neg F$ are known and $\neg E$ is not (which correspond to the "correct" extension), but also those in which $\neg E$ is known and $\neg D$ and $\neg F$ are not. It turns out that in Lukaszewicz' formulation the latter *is* a legal extension, which suggests that indeed the preference criterion captures his modification of Reiter's system (as I have said, I will not give a formal proof of this connection).

Intuitively, the reason $Th(\{\neg E\})$ is not an extension in Reiter's system is because there is nothing to "block" the application of the default rule $(:M(C)/\neg D)$; the application of a default rule cannot be blocked by the rule's own consequence. Therefore $\neg D$ is always in the extension, precluding the possibility of ever applying the second default rule. This suggests a modification of the previous preference criterion, a modification which takes into account the fact that sets of default rules may "dominate" one another. For example, $\{:M(C)/\neg D\}$ dominates $\{:M(D)/\neg E\}$, since the consequent $\neg D$ implies the dissatisfaction of the precondition $: M(D)$, and nothing in the second set implies the dissatisfaction of the precondition $: M(C)$. As another example, neither of the two sets $\{:M(C)/\neg D\}$ and $\{:M(D)/\neg C\}$ dominates the other, since each implies the dissatisfaction of the preconditions in the other set.

The complete preference criterion is as follows. Let M_1 and M_2 be two models of W such that $S_i = \{s\colon s \in S$ and $M_i \models \Diamond s\}$, $(i = 1, 2)$. According the new criterion, $M_1 \sqsubset_S M_2$ if

1. $S_1 \overset{\subseteq}{\neq} S_2$, or

2. $S_1 = S_2$, and $\{\varphi\colon M_2 \models \Box\varphi\} \overset{\subseteq}{\neq} \{\varphi\colon M_1 \models \Box\varphi\}$, or

3. S_1 and S_2 are noncomparable (neither one contains the other), and

   (a) there exist $S_2' \subset S_2$ and $S_1' \subset S_1$ such that

      i. $W \cup \{\Box\gamma\colon (\alpha{:}M(\beta)/\gamma){\in}D,\ \beta \in S_2',$ and $M_2 \models \alpha\} \models \Box\neg\beta_1$, for some $\beta_1 \in S_1'$, and such that

      ii. there does not exist a $\beta_2 \in S_2'$ such that $W \cup \{\Box\gamma\colon (\alpha{:}M(\beta)/\gamma){\in}D,\ \beta \in S_1',$ and $M_1 \models \alpha\} \models \Box\neg\beta_2$, and

   (b) there do not exist $S_2' \subset S_2$ and $S_1' \subset S_1$ where the roles are reversed, that is, such that

      i. $W \cup \{\Box\gamma\colon (\alpha{:}M(\beta)/\gamma){\in}D,\ \beta \in S_1',$ and $M_1 \models \alpha\} \models \Box\neg\beta_2$, for some $\beta_2 \in S_2'$, and such that

      ii. there does not exist a $\beta_1 \in S_1'$ such that $W \cup \{\Box\gamma\colon (\alpha{:}M(\beta)/\gamma){\in}D,\ \beta \in S_2',$ and $M_2 \models \alpha\} \models \Box\neg\beta_1$.

According to this new criterion, the modal theory corresponding to the default theory in the second example has one class of models, those in which all that is known are $\neg D$, $\neg F$ and their tautological consequences.

As was mentioned earlier, even this preference criterion does not correspond exactly to Reiter's system. The difference manifests itself in the context of the well-known default theory

$$W = \phi, \; D = \{:M(A)/\neg A\}$$

In Reiter's system this theory has no extension. The corresponding modal theory is

$$\Diamond A \supset \Box \neg A$$

or, equivalently,

$$\Diamond A \supset \neg \Diamond A$$

This formula does have a class of preferred models, those in which all that is known are $\neg A$ and its tautological consequences. Intuitively, the difference reflects the difference between the procedural and denotational interpretations: "if A is consistent then infer $\neg A$" seems paradoxical, but "if you do not know $\neg A$ then you know $\neg A$" makes perfect sense: it means "you know $\neg A$" (recall the propositional tautology $(A \supset \neg A) \equiv \neg A$).

Is it possible to modify the preference criterion further to adhere to Reiter's definition? I don't know, though there are some indications that the answer is negative. Let me, however, raise the question of whether Reiter's particular definition, which is most ingenious technically, is well-motivated. On what basis should we adopt his formulation, and not the one just given, or for that matter the previous one (which, as I conjectured, corresponds to Lukaszewicz' formulation)? In fact, it is possible to modify Reiter's definition to fit the last preference criterion, rather than vice versa. The modification needed is in the definition of E_{i+1} (again, for simplicity I assume that all rules contain a single assumption):

$$E_{i+1} = Th(E_i) \cup \{\gamma : (\alpha{:}M\beta \; / \; \gamma) \in D, \; \alpha \in E_i, \text{ and } \neg\beta \notin E\} \; \cup$$
$$\cup \; \{\gamma : (\alpha{:}M\beta \; / \; \gamma) \in D, \; \alpha \in E_i, \text{ and } \models \neg(\alpha \wedge \beta) \supset \gamma\}$$

Given only the intuitive motivation behind default logic, I don't think that one can prefer the original formulation over this one or vice versa. True, the original formulation is a little more concise, but this formulation has the nice property that every default theory has an extension (though, it must be said, some extensions are inconsistent). And again, it seems a bit misguided to adopt a logic on the basis of such partial considerations. It is preferable to base the decision on the desired model-theoretic semantics, and deciding on the preference criterion for models seems a good way to do so. However, more work needs to be done in this area before definite conclusions can be drawn.

Chapter 4

Chronological Ignorance

In the introductory chapter it was explained why a temporal logic alone does not yield a method for reasoning about change. In particular, two problems were shown to arise: the *qualification* problem and the problem of *extended prediction*. In this chapter I propose a solution to the first of the two.

As explained in the first chapter, the *qualification* problem is essentially that of having to specify too many details in order to make predictions. For example, it is not sufficient to describe the way the ball is rolling right now in order to predict its future behavior; we must explicitly state that there are no other balls in its path, no holes in the table, no explosives in the ball, and so on. It was said in the Introduction that in the absence of all those details, the conclusion that the ball will continue rolling is necessarily defeasible. This suggests that the inference about the ball continuing to roll might be valid in some nonmonotonic logic. The question is what specific nonmonotonic logic is needed here.

In the previous chapter I outlined a semantical approach to constructing nonmonotonic logics. In light of that discussion, the question we are facing now is what monotonic logic $\mathcal{L}$ and what preference criterion on models $\sqsubset$ should be adopted, so that $\mathcal{L}_{\sqsubset}$ will have the right model-theoretic properties. In the language $\mathcal{L}$ the theory consisting of the description of the rolling ball will have many models. One of them is the intended one, in which the ball continues rolling. Another is one in which another ball exists which collides with the first ball, and so on. We would like all preferred models in $\mathcal{L}_{\sqsubset}$ to be like the first one.

In principle we want to capture the implicit assumption that "all the relevant facts have been mentioned explicitly." For example, if there had been a second ball that collided with the first ball then it would have been mentioned. This suggests that we prefer models in which "as little as possible happens." The question is what precise meaning this phrase can be given.

For example, it might seem that we prefer models in which the ball is deflected from its straight-line trajectory as rarely as possible. In the case of a single ball rolling, this preference criterion will indeed exclude models in which any other balls collide with it. However, upon close examination in turns out that it is not exactly the *number* of deflections that we worry about, but the times at which they occur. Consider for example a scenario in which two balls roll towards each other. In the intended model they continue to roll until they collide. In another model a third ball appears out of nowhere and collides with the first ball before the first and second balls have a chance to collide. In both scenarios there is exactly one deflection of balls, so both are equally preferrable under the "minimum number of deflections" criterion.

In looking for an alternative preference criterion, we notice that in the intended model the single deflection occurred later than the single deflection in the other (unwanted) model. This suggests a modification of the defective preference criterion: we prefer models in which deflections occur as *late* as possible, rather than as *rarely* as possible. And in fact, it turns out that this criterion of preference admits only models in which the intended deflections take place. I will call this *chronological minimization* (of deflections, in this case). This will not be the final solution to the qualification problem, but it is a good point at which to start making the discussion more formal.

Both in this chapter and in the next one I will make some simplifying assumptions, which include the following two:

1. Recall that in Chapter 2 I made no assumptions about time, other than its being a partial order. Here I will assume a very specific temporal structure, that of the (positive and negative) integers (that is, a structure which is discrete, linear and unbounded in both directions).

2. I will discuss the propositional case, as opposed to the first-order one.

In Chapter 7 I will briefly discuss what is needed in order remove such limitations.

4.1 Chronological minimization

Rather than introduce the proposed solution directly, let me first in this section introduce a solution that "almost" works. The advantages and disadvantages of this proposal will motivate the final solution.

First we need a language in which to represent temporal information. In chapter 2 two langauges were introduced, a classical one and a modal one. As was explained there, the classical logic subsumes the modal one in its expressiveness, and so from here on I will use the former. Since as I have said I will assume here that the structure of time is that of the integers, I will also assume the standard representation of the integers as the set of time-point symbols. Furthermore, since the interpretation of time will be so standard, I will often write $t_1 \leq t_2$ for time time-point symbols t_1 and t_2, with the understanding that the relation really holds between their semantic counterparts. One other convenient notational convention that I will adopt is to replace a formula TRUE(t,t,p) by the formula TRUE(t,p).

Let me illustrate the proposal through a simple example which involves reasoning about the effect of firing a loaded gun.[1] Consider the following two axioms:

1. TRUE(1,loaded)

2. TRUE(5,pull-trigger)

Suppose we want to be able to infer that a loud noise will take place at time 6, since pulling the trigger of a loaded gun normally results in a loud noise. What do we need to add?

We first notice that the extended-prediction problem (or, in its special form here, the persistence problem) raises its ugly head: our theory does not entail the fact that the gun is loaded at time 5. Since we are not concerned with the extended-prediction problem right now, let us get around it by simply adding the appropriate frame axiom-scheme:

---

[1] One feels the need to apologize for such violent examples (even though no one is about to get hurt). By way of such an apology let me point out that the prototypical examples of causation center either around an application of force which results in movement, or around an action which results in some bodily harm. The current discussion will turn out to be intimately connected to the notion of causation.

3. TRUE(t,loaded) ∧ ¬TRUE(t,pull-trigger) ∧
   ∧ ¬TRUE(t,emptied-manually) ⊃ TRUE(t+1,loaded),
   for all t.

We now add the "physics" rule about firing guns:

4. TRUE(t,loaded) ∧ TRUE(t,pull-trigger) ∧ Φ ⊃ TRUE(t+1,noise),
   for all t.

where the Φ is the conjunction TRUE(t,no-vacuum) ∧ TRUE(t,firing-pin) ∧ TRUE(t,no-marshmallow-bullets) ∧ ..., all those mundane facts that are, "strictly speaking," needed in order to make a sound prediction (the pun wasn't intended, but there you are).

Just as in the rolling balls example, we cannot predict a noise at time 6 within the classical logic, since our axioms have models in which the gun was fired or emptied manually prior to time 6, or in which gnomes conspire to create a vacuum or remove the gun's firing pin. Instead we will define a nonmonotonic logic in which the inference about the noise at time 6 indeed follows from axioms (1)-(4). As was explained in the previous chapter, we will do so by defining a notion of *preferred models* that will exclude all those undesired models.

Definition 4.1 *Let* $S = p_1, \ldots, p_m$ *be a set of primitive propositions, and* M_1 *and* M_2 *two interpretations.* M_2 *is* __chronologically smaller in S__ *than* M_1 *(written* $M_1 \sqsubset_S M_2$*) if there exists a time* t_0 *such that*

1. *for all* $p \in S$ *and all* $t_1, t_2 \leq t_0$ *(w.r.t. the global interpretation of time, remember), if* $M_2 \models$ TRUE(t_1,t_2,p) *then also* $M_1 \models$ TRUE(t_1,t_2,p)*, and*

2. *there exists a* $p \in S$ *and a* $t \leq t_0$ *such that* $M_1 \models$ TRUE(t,t_0,p) *but* $M_2 \not\models$ TRUE(t,t_0,p).[2]

---

[2]The reader may wonder why the preference criterion refers to the ending point of intervals rather than to the beginning point, or for that matter any other point in the interval. The answer is that although in this case it really would make sense to define the logic that way (although the result would be a different logic), in the definition of chronological ignorance, which is the generlization of chronological minimization that will be discussed in the next section, we really need to refer to the end point of intervals.

As explained in the previous chapter, the temporal logic (called, say, $\mathcal{L}$) and a set of propositions S define a nonmonotonic logic $\mathcal{L}_{\sqsubset S}$. Notice that a formula in $\mathcal{L}_{\sqsubset S}$ (or in $\mathcal{L}$, since the formulas of $\mathcal{L}$ and $\mathcal{L}_{\sqsubset S}$ are the same) may have many preferred models, or none at all. For example, for any primitive propositions p and q, *all* models of the formula

$$\forall\, t \leq t' \text{ TRUE}(t,t',p) \equiv \neg\text{TRUE}(t,t',q)$$

are also chronologically minimal in {p,q}. Or, as another extreme example, for any primitive proposition p, the formula

$$\text{TRUE}(t_0,p) \wedge \forall t \ (\text{TRUE}(t,p) \supset (\exists t' \ (t'<t \wedge \text{TRUE}(t',p))))$$

has *no* model that is chronologically minimal in p (although it is does have a model).

However, the logic was not defined in order to investigate such rather extreme cases. Instead, let us apply it to the shooting scenario. We must identify a set of primitive propositions S such that in $\mathcal{L}_{\sqsubset S}$, axioms (1)-(4) entail there being a noise at time 6. To exclude models in which premature trigger-pulling take place, we will chronologically minimize pull-trigger. Since the gun might be emptied also manually, we will simultaneously minimize emptied-manually. This will guarantee that we arrive at time 5 with the gun loaded and the trigger being pulled. We now add the chronological minimization of all the conjuncts of Φ in axiom-scheme 4, that is, of all those "implicit" factors on which the occurrence of the noise depends. We end up selecting models that are chronologically minimal in the set $S_0 = \{$pull-trigger, emptied-manually, vacuum, no-firing-pin, marshmallow-bullets, $\dots\}$. When we examine the models of (1)-(4) that are chronologically minimal in this set, it is not hard to see that in all of them "the right thing happens": they all satisfy the formulas TRUE(1,loaded), TRUE(2,loaded), $\dots$, TRUE(5,loaded), TRUE(5,pull-trigger), and TRUE(6,noise). Furthermore, if we augment the set of axioms (for example) by the axiom TRUE(5,vacuum), the formula TRUE(6,noise) will no longer be satisfied by *any* chronologically minimal model. So far, so good.

One problem that we haven't addressed yet, even if we are satisfied with the new logic, is how it can be used to make inferences mechanically. I have said that it has the right model-theoretic properties, but not how to write algorithms to compute those formulas that are satisfied in the models that are chronologically minimal in S_0. Unfortunately, as it stands, there are severe problems even with the model-theoretic solution.

To begin with, how did I decide to chronologically minimize S_0 specifically and not, say, noises, or the number of guns, or for that matter elections or *nonfirings*? What happens when we move from the domain of guns to the domains of billiards balls or liquids, in which we will clearly need new preference criteria for models? Will there exist in those domains sets of propositions whose chronological minimization will have the right effect? How will we go about finding them?

There is something very dissatisfying about having to construct a new logic for each class of problems. In fact even in our particular domain, the set of propositions that needs to be chronologically minimized depends critically on the kind of information we would like to predict. Chronological minimization of S_0 has the right effect only if what we care about is to make sure we predict a noise if one is going to take place. We cannot predict, for example, that there will be *no* noise at time 7. For that we would have to simultaneously minimize noises. If we do that, it turns out that we no longer need to explicitly minimize trigger-pulling. Again, that is true if all we care about are noises; if we want to measure the amount of exercise the gunman's finger has had, we need to minimize trigger-pulling after all.

In short, although we can identify an instance of the logic that has nice properties as far as some predictions go, the general utility of the logic is unclear. However, the reader was not dragged through this section only for this gloomy conclusion. In the next section I will offer a solution to the qualification problem that can be viewed as a generalization of chronological minimization of particular sets of propositions. What we will do is chronologically minimize *all* propositions: trigger-pulling, noises, rolling of billiard balls, collisions, explosions, elections, and everything else. However, since at any time and for any formula φ, either φ or $\neg\varphi$ must be true, we must change our view of what it is that is being minimized. Rather than think of (chronologically) minimizing those things that actually happen, we will think of (chronologically) minimizing those things that are *known* to have happened. The reason this transition is meaningful is precisely because the logic of knowledge does not have the strong law of excluded middle: it is not the case that for any formula φ, either φ or $\neg\varphi$ are known. Since modal logic captures the distinction between that which is known and that which is merely true, we will end up constructing a nonmonotonic modal logic, called the logic of *chronological ignorance*. It turns out that the logic of chronological ignorance not only has attractive model-theoretic properties, but that, if used judiciously, it also affords a very efficient way of making predictions.

4.2   The logic of chronological ignorance

4.2.1 TK: a monotonic logic of temporal knowledge

The logic of *temporal knowledge* (or the logic TK) is a logic of knowledge of temporal information. By this I mean that what is known has a temporal aspect to it, rather than the fact that knowledge changes over time. The logic is defined as follows.

Syntax.   The syntax of TK is the syntax of the propositional classical interval logic given in Chapter 2, augmented by the modal operator $\Box$.

Specifically, given P: a set of primitive propositions, TV: a set of variables, TC: the set $\{\ldots, -3, -2, -1, 0, 1, 2, \ldots\}$ (i.e., the standard representation of the integers), and U: TC∪TV, the set of well-formed formulas of TK is defined inductively as follows:

1. If $u_1 \in$ U and $u_2 \in$ U then $u_1 = u_2$ and $u_1 \preceq u_2$ are wffs.

2. If $u_1 \in$ U, $u_2 \in$ U, and $p \in$ P then TRUE(u_1, u_2, p) is a wff.

3. If φ_1 and φ_2 are wffs then so are $\varphi_1 \wedge \varphi_2$, $\neg\varphi_1$, and $\Box\varphi_1$.

4. If φ is a wff and $v \in$ V, then $\forall v\ \varphi$ is also a wff.

We assume the usual definitions of $\vee$, $\supset$, $\equiv$, $\exists$, and so on. As usual, $\Diamond$ is defined by $\Diamond\varphi \equiv \neg\Box\neg\varphi$. I will also use some convenient abbreviations. I will replace $\Box$TRUE(t_1, t_2, p) by $\Box(t_1, t_2, p)$, and $\Box\neg$TRUE(t_1, t_2, p) by $\Box(t_1, t_2, \neg p)$. Similarly, $\Diamond$TRUE(t_1, t_2, p) will be replaced by $\Diamond(t_1, t_2, p)$, and $\Diamond\neg$TRUE(t_1, t_2, p) by $\Diamond(t_1, t_2, \neg p)$. Also, since TRUE$(t, p)$ abbreviates TRUE(t, t, p), I will use $\Box(t, p)$ and $\Diamond(t, p)$ with the obvious intended meaning.

Semantics.   In TK, a *Kripke interpretation* is a set of infinite "parallel" time lines, all sharing the same interpretation of time: a "synchronized" copy of the integers. Each world describes an entire possible course of the universe, and so over the same time interval, but in different worlds, different facts are true. This structure is illustarted in Figure 4.1.

More formally we make the following definitions ($\mathcal{N}$ is used to denote the integers with $\leq$). A *Kripke interpretation* is a pair $\langle W, M \rangle$ where W is

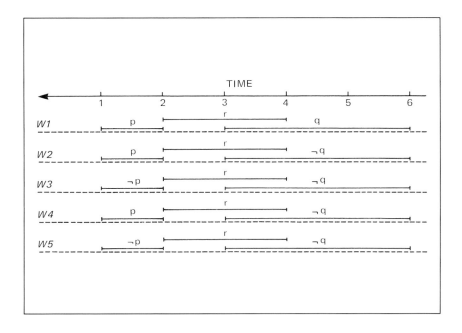

Figure 4.1: A structure consisting of five possible worlds. TRUE(2,4,r) holds in all worlds, and therefore the structure satisfies □(2,4,r). Other sentences are not known; for example, TRUE(1,2,p) is true in some worlds and false in others.

a nonempty universe of *(possible) worlds*, and M is a meaning function M: $P \to 2^{W \times \mathcal{N} \times \mathcal{N}}$. As in the nonmodal case, we require that $\langle w, t_1, t_2 \rangle \in M(p)$ iff $\langle w, t_2, t_1 \rangle \in M(p)$, again reflecting the intuition that a pair of time points denotes a single interval.

(The reader familiar with standard modal logics will notice that no accessibility relation is mentioned. The explanation for this is that, for reasons that will be made clear later, I will want to assume an S_5 structure (with a fixed interpretation of time across worlds). Therefore the possible worlds form one big equivalence class, and since thus the set of all worlds can be equated with the set of accessible ones, explicit mention of an accessibility relation is unnecessary.)

A *variable assignment* is a function VA: TV $\to \mathcal{N}$. Also, we if $u \in U$ then define $VAL(u)$ to be $VA(u)$ if $u \in$ TV, and the standard interpretation of u if $u \in$ TC.

A Kripke interpretation $KI = \langle W, M \rangle$ and a world $w \in W$ satisfy a formula φ under the variable assignment VA (written $KI, w \models \varphi[VA]$) under the following conditions.

- $KI, w \models u_1 = u_2[VA]$ iff $VAL(u_1) = VAL(u_2)$.

- $KI, w \models u_1 \preceq u_2[VA]$ iff $VAL(u_1) \leq VAL(u_2)$.

- $KI, w \models \text{TRUE}(u_1, u_2, p)[VA]$ iff $\langle w, VAL(u_1), VAL(u_2) \rangle \in M(p)$.

- $KI, w \models (\varphi_1 \wedge \varphi_2)[VA]$ iff $KI, w \models \varphi_1[VA]$ and $KI, w \models \varphi_2[VA]$.

- $KI, w \models (\neg\varphi)[VA]$ iff $KI, w \not\models \varphi[VA]$.

- $KI, w \models (\forall v \; \varphi)[VA]$ iff $KI, w \models \varphi[VA']$ for all VA' that agree with VA everywhere except possibly on v.

- $KI, w \models \Box\varphi[VA]$ iff $KI, w' \models \varphi[VA]$ for all $w' \in W$.
  (Therefore we will be able to write $KI \models \Box\varphi[VA]$ and $KI \not\models \Box\varphi[VA]$ without fear of ambiguity.)

(The reader familiar with modal logic will note that from the identity of time across worlds follows the validity of the "Barcan formula," $\Box\forall v \; \varphi \equiv \forall v \; \Box\varphi$.)

With the exception of the special nature of time, the logic TK is a perfectly standard modal logic. Consequently, the following definitions are also standard. A Kripke interpretation $KI = \langle W, M \rangle$ and a world $w \in W$

are a *model* for a formula φ (written $KI, w \models \varphi$) if $KI, w \models \varphi[VA]$ for any variable assignment VA. (As in the classical case, it is easy to see that if φ is a sentence, and $KI, w \models \varphi[VA]$ for *some* VA, then KI and w are a model for φ.) A wff is *satisfiable* if it has a model, and *valid* if its negation has no model. φ_1 *entails* φ_2 iff φ_2 is satisfied by all models of φ_1.

We now deviate more significantly from standard constructions by making the logic nonmonotonic.

4.2.2 CI: a nonmonotonic logic of temporal knowledge

The logic of chronological ignorance (or the logic CI) is a nonmonotonic version of the logic of temporal knowledge TK. As usual, the syntax of the two is identical, and CI is obtained by associating with TK a preference criterion on Kripke structures. We begin with a few preliminary definitions.

Definition 4.2 *Base wffs are those containing no occurrence of the modal operator.*

Definition 4.3 *The latest time point (l.t.p) of a base formula is the latest time point mentioned in it (that is, the latest chronologically, not the last syntactically). Formally, it is defined as follows.*

1. *The l.t.p. of* TRUE(t_1, t_2, p) *is* $max\{t_1, t_2\}$ *(recall that the logic permits* $t_2 < t_1$*).*

2. *The l.t.p. of* $\varphi_1 \wedge \varphi_2$ *is the latest (w.r.t. the standard interpretation of time) between the l.t.p. of* φ_1 *and the l.t.p. of* φ_2.

3. *The l.t.p. of* $\neg\varphi$ *is the l.t.p. of* φ.

4. *The l.t.p. of* $\forall v\, \varphi$ *is the earliest among the l.t.p.'s of all* $\varphi\prime$ *which result from substituting in* φ *a time-point symbol for all free occurrences of* v, *or* $-\infty$ *if there is no such earliest l.t.p.*

This last case requires some explanation, since one might have intuitively expected "latest" and "∞" rather than "earliest" and "$-\infty$." It turns out, however, that we will be interested in formulas with the *earliest* l.t.p.'s. But $\forall v\, \varphi$ entails $\varphi\prime$ for any $\varphi\prime$ which result from the above substitution, and hence the definition.

Definition 4.4 *A Kripke interpretation M_2 is chronologically more ignorant than a Kripke interpretation M_1 (written $M_1 \sqsubset_{ci} M_2$) if there exists a time t_0 such that*

1. *for any base sentence φ whose l.t.p. $\leq t_0$, if $M_2 \models \Box\varphi$ then also $M_1 \models \Box\varphi$, and*

2. *there exists some base sentence φ whose l.t.p. is t_0 such that $M_1 \models \Box\varphi$ but $M_2 \not\models \Box\varphi$.*   .

Definition 4.5 *M is said to be a chronologically maximally ignorant (or c.m.i.) model of φ if $M \models_{\sqsubset_{ci}} \varphi$, that is, if $M \models \varphi$ and there is no other $M\prime$ such that $M\prime \models \varphi$ and $M \sqsubset_{ci} M\prime$.*

Definition 4.6 *The logic of chronological ignorance, CI, is the nonmonotonic logic $TK_{\sqsubset_{ci}}$.*

These definitions may seem undermotivated at this point. In the next sections I will discuss an intuitive interpretation of the logic. First, though, let me illustrate the fact that at least technically the logic CI is well suited for our purposes. As in previous cases, it is possible to construct formulas which have models but no c.m.i. models, or formulas all of whose models are also c.m.i. models. Instead of discussing those, though, let us look at a CI theory which describes the shooting scenario.

4.2.3   The shooting scenario revisited

There is more than one way that the shooting scenario can be represented in the logic of chronological ignorance; I choose the following axioms and axiom schemas for reasons that will become clear soon.

1. $\Box$(1,loaded)

2. $\Box$(5,fire)

3. $\Box$(t,loaded) $\wedge$ $\Diamond$(t,¬fire) $\wedge$ $\Diamond$(t,¬emptied-manually) $\supset$
   $\Box$(t+1,loaded),   for all t

4. □(t,loaded) ∧ □(t,fire) ∧
   ◇(t,air) ∧
   ◇(t,firingpin) ∧
   ◇(t,no-marshmallow-bullets) ∧
   ... ◇ ... other mundane conditions
   ⊃
   □(t+1,noise),   for all t

Axioms 1 and 2 can be thought of the *boundary conditions* of the scenario. Axiom schema 3 is again the frame axiom, which is necessitated by the extended-prediction problem, and which will disappear when we solve the extended-prediction problem in a later chapter. Axiom schema 4 represents "physics," in this case consisting of a single *causal rule*. It says that firing a loaded gun causes a noise, unless certain conditions obtain which "disable" this particular rule. At this point these causal terms are meant to be only suggestive, but in the next section, and especially in Chapter 6, I will motivate them in a more precise manner.

What do c.m.i. models of this theory look like? There are many different such models, but they have one thing in common: in all of them exactly the same base sentences are known. These are TRUE(1,loaded), ..., TRUE(5,loaded), TRUE(5,fire) and TRUE(6,noise) — exactly the ones we would have liked — and their tautological consequences.

In fact, this model-theoretic property is no coincidence, and in the next section I identify a whole class of theories that share it. Furthermore, while I have so far said nothing about algorithms for computing valid wffs, I will show that while the general problem of determining the consequences of a theory in *CI* is very hard, determining the consequences of any theory in this particular class is easy.

4.3   Causal theories: the technicalities

In the previous section I offered a representation of the shooting scenario whose formal properties were "exactly right": the theory had one class of c.m.i. models, in all of which what is known is precisely what one would expect (the persistence of the gun being loaded, the firing, and the subsequent noise). In the next section I will discuss the intuition behind the construction, but first let me define a whole class of theories which share the nice properties of the shooting scenario example.

It may be helpful at this point to provide a glossary of some of the terminology and notation that will be used in this section. The following is meant only as a reminder, the precise definitions having already been given.

- Formulas in the logic of chronological ignorance (CI) are those of the interval logic augmented by the modal operator $\square$.

  We will also adopt the following convetion. Recall that both TRUE(t_1, t_2, p) and TRUE(t_2, t_1, p) are legal sentences. In the following we will want to refer to l.t.p.'s of formulas. To simplify things, we will take the l.t.p. of TRUE(t_1, t_2, p) to be t_2, but it should be understood the one really means $max\{t_1, t_2\}$.

- In CI, A entails B iff B is true in all c.m.i. models of A.

- $\square(t_1, t_2, p)$ is shorthand for $\square$TRUE(t_1, t_2, p), $\square(t_1, t_2, \neg p)$ is shorthand for $\square\neg$TRUE(t_1, t_2, p), and similarly for $\lozenge$.

- *Base sentences* in CI are those sentences not containing any occurrence of the modal operator, i.e., sentences that refer directly to the real world and not to knowledge of it.

  Atomic base sentences are either of the form TRUE(t_1, t_2, p) or of the form $\neg$TRUE(t_1, t_2, p), where p is a primitive proposition. The former are said to be *positive*, and the latter *negative*.

- A *theory* in CI is a collection of sentences in CI.

- The l.t.p. of a base sentence is the latest time point mentioned in it, or, if the sentence contains a quantifier, the earliest among the l.t.p.'s of all sentences resulting from replacing the quantified variable by a constant.

Returning to the theory describing the shooting scenario, we notice that it consists of two kinds of statements. The first two axioms had the structure "it is known that this fact is true at this time," that is, knowledge of an atomic sentence. The last two axioms embodied an implication from knowledge of past atomic sentences and ignorance of past atomic sentences to knowledge of future atomic sentences: "if it is known that these facts are true at these times, and it is not known that these other facts are true at these other times, then it is also known that that fact is true at that *later* time." In fact, the first kind of sentence can be viewed as a special case of the second kind, in which the antecedent is identically true. It turns out that *any* theory consisting of sentences which fit this mold has the same nice model-theoretic property: in all its c.m.i. models the same base sentences are known. In the following definition, Φ will denote the conjunction of those atomic sentences that must be known in order for the prediction to hold (such as the gun being loaded and fired), and Θ will denote the conjunction of the conditions such that prediction depends only on not knowing their negation (such as there being air, the gun being in good working order, and so on).

Definition 4.7 *A causal theory* Ψ *is a theory in* CI, *in which all sentences have the form*

$$\Phi \wedge \Theta \supset \Box\varphi$$

where (in the following, [$\neg$] means that the negation sign may or may not appear)

1. φ *is a (positive or negative) atomic base sentence* TRUE$(t_1, t_2, [\neg]p)$ *(and, by our convention,* $t_1 \leq t_2$.

2. Φ *is a conjunction of sentences* $\Box\varphi_i$, *where* φ_i *is a (positive or negative) atomic base sentence with l.t.p.* t_i *such that* $t_i < t_1$,

3. Θ *is a conjunction of sentences* $\Diamond\varphi_j$, *where* φ_j *is a (positive or negative) atomic base sentence with l.t.p.* t_j *such that* $t_j < t_1$,

4. *Either or both* Φ *and* Θ *may be empty (that is, identically true). A sentence in which* Φ *is empty is called a* boundary condition. *Other sentences are called* causal rules.

5. *There is a time point* t_0 *such that if* $\Theta \supset \Box(t_1, t_2, [\neg]p)$ *is a boundary condition, then* $t_0 < t_1$.

Explanation: I will show that causal theories have unique models. The proof is by induction on time, and the basis of the induction will be this t_0. Indeed, without this condition, causal theories could have multiple models, each having different knowledge extending unboundedly into the past.

6. *There do not exist two sentences in* Ψ *such that one contains* $\Diamond(t_1,t_2,p)$ *on its l.h.s. and the other includes* $\Diamond(t_1,t_2,\neg p)$ *on its l.h.s., for any* p, t_1 *and* t_2,

Explanation: The $\Diamond$-conditions can be thought of as assigning propositions default truth values. For example, the condition $\Diamond(t_1,t_2,\text{air})$ in the shooting example embodies the default assumption that the scenario does not take place in a vacuum. It makes no sense to make both a formula and its negation true by default. From the technical standpoint, without this condition causal theories could again have multiple models. In this connection, see the discussion of *soundness conditions* in Subsection 4.4.2.

7. *If* $\Phi_1 \wedge \Theta_1 \supset \Box(t_1,t_2,p)$ *and* $\Phi_2 \wedge \Theta_2 \supset \Box(t_1,t_2,\neg p)$ *are two sentences in* Ψ, *then* $\Phi_1 \wedge \Theta_1 \wedge \Phi_2 \wedge \Theta_2$ *is inconsistent.*

Explanation: Later on we will see that causal rules can indeed be thought of representing causation, with the $\Box$-conditions on the l.h.s. denoting causes, and the r.h.s. denoting an effect. It makes sense that consistent causes cannot bring about inconsistent effects. And again, without this restriction, some causal theories would have multiple models.

The discussion in this section will still be purely technical, and I will discuss the concept of causation in Chapter 6. Let me, however, digress for a moment, and in two paragraphs motivate the terms "causal rules" and "boundary conditions." In a nutshell, causation we will be viewed as implication from knowledge and ignorance about the past and present to knowledge about the future. I will suggest that when we say "A causes B" then A and B have the form $\text{TRUE}(t_1,t_2,[\neg]p)$, and the statement means that we believe in the validity of the implication $\Box A \wedge \Diamond C \supset \Box B$, for some C. Boundary conditions are those items of knowledge that come into being "for no reason," simply because one posits their truth. All other knowledge must be "justified" by causal rules, as it will turn out in the logic.

At this point the structure of causal rules may seem too restrictive, since it prohibits simultaneous or overlapping cause and effect. For example, one cannot say that pushing the box at a time instant (or over a period of time) causes it to move at that time instant (or over that period). In the last chapter I discuss ways to relax these restrictions.

Let us now continue with the technical analysis of simple causal theories, ignoring for the moment the intuitive motivation behind them. Informally, the content of the remainder of this section can be summarized as follows:

Causal theories are always consistent, and they even have c.m.i. models. In fact, in all c.m.i. models of a given causal theory the same base sentences are known. Furthermore, these known base sentences can be computed efficiently. The basic argument is very simple: since all we have are implication from knowledge and ignorance about the past to knowledge about the future, we can always build a c.m.i. model of a causal theory by going forward in time and adding only knowledge that is implied by what is already known and what is not known about the prior times.

To make the discussion more precise, we proceed as follows.

Definition 4.8 *A time-bounded Kripke interpretation M/t is a structure which can be viewed as an incomplete Kripke interpretation. Like a Kripke interpretation it assigns a truth value to atomic propositions, but only to those whose l.t.p. $\leq t$. The truth value of an arbitrary sentence whose l.t.p. $\leq t$ is also determined in M/t, according to the usual compositional rules. It is easy to see that this is well defined, since, by the semantics of the logic and by the definition of an l.t.p., the truth value of a sentence whose l.t.p. $\leq t$ does not depend on any sentence whose l.t.p. $> t$.*

For such a sentence φ whose l.t.p. $\leq t$, we make the obvious definition of what it means for φ to be satisfied by M/t (written $M/t \models \varphi$).

M/t partially satisfies a theory Ψ if M/t satisfies all members of Ψ whose l.t.p. $\leq t$.

Comment: A full Kripke interpretation M can be viewed as the limiting case M/∞.

It is possible to prove that all simple causal theories are satisfiable, but I will prove directly a much stronger statement. It turns out that a simple causal theory not only has models, but in fact has c.m.i. models. Furthermore, all these c.m.i. models are essentially the same: in all of them exactly the same base sentences are known.

Theorem 4.1 (The "unique c.m.i. model" theorem)
If Ψ is any causal theory, then

1. Ψ *has a c.m.i. model, and*

2. *if M_1 and M_2 are both c.m.i. models of Ψ, and φ any base sentence, then $M_1 \models \Box\varphi$ iff $M_2 \models \Box\varphi$.*

Proof: It is sufficient to construct a model M for Ψ, and show that M is chronologically more ignorant than any model for Ψ which differs from M on the truth value of some sentence $\Box\varphi$, where φ is a base sentence.

The construction starts with some time-bounded interpretation M/t_0, and augments it to later time points iteratively:

1. Let t_0 be time point preceding the l.t.p. of any sentence φ such $\Theta \supset \Box\varphi$ is a boundary condition. (by assumption such a point exists). For any base tautology φ whose l.t.p. $\leq t_0$, let $M/t_0 \models \Box\varphi$. For any other base wff φ whose l.t.p. $\leq t_0$, let $M/t_0 \not\models \Box\varphi$.

   Notice that M/t_0 (partially) satisfies the boundary conditions of Ψ vacuously (since the l.t.p.'s of all boundary conditions are greater than t_0), and (partially) satisfies all the causal rules (since if their l.t.p. is no later than t_0, then their antecedents are falsified).

2. We now specify how to augment M/t to $M/t + 1$ for any t. Let

$$\text{CONSEQUENTS}_{t+1} =$$
$$\{\Box(\text{t'},\text{t+1},\text{x}): \Phi \wedge \Theta \supset \Box(\text{t'},\text{t+1},\text{x}) \in \Psi, \text{ and } M/t \models \Phi \wedge \Theta\}$$

$M/t + 1$ is obtained by making all wffs in CONSEQUENTS_{t+1} and all their tautological consequences true, and for any other base wff $\varphi\prime$ whose l.t.p. is $t + 1$, making $\Box\varphi\prime$ false.

Note that by the assumption about causal theories, CONSEQUENTS_{t+1} does not contain both a $\Box\varphi$ and $\Box\neg\varphi$, and therefore this construction introduces no inconsistency among knowledge of atomic base sentences. But this means that it introduces no inconsistency at all, since the totality of known bases sentences whose l.t.p. is $\leq t + 1$ are the tautological consequences of the atomic ones.

Clearly M/∞ (or simply M) is a model for Ψ. To conclude the proof, it remains to show that if a model M' differs from M on the truth value of $\Box\varphi$ for some base sentence φ, then M' is not a c.m.i. model. To prove that, suppose that some model M' of Ψ indeed differs from M on the truth value of $\Box\varphi$ for some base sentence φ.

1. If $M' \models \Box\varphi$ for some nontautological base sentence φ whose l.t.p. $\leq t_0$, then M' is chronologically less ignorant than M.

2. Otherwise, there is an earliest t such that $t_0 \leq t$, and such that for some base sentence φ whose l.t.p. is $t + 1$, M and M' differ on the truth value of $\Box\varphi$. There are two possible cases:

   (a) $M \models \Box\varphi$ and $M' \not\models \Box\varphi$. By the construction procedure, if $M \models \Box\varphi$ then there exists a sentence $\Phi \wedge \Theta \supset \Box\varphi \in \Psi$, such that the l.t.p.'s of the base sentences in Φ and Θ are $\leq t$, and such that $M \models \Phi \wedge \Theta$. Since M and M' agree on the knowledge of all base sentences whose l.t.p. $\leq t$, it must be the case that also $M' \models \Phi \wedge \Theta$. But since $M' \not\models \Box\varphi$, M' cannot be a model for Ψ; contradiction.

   (b) $M' \models \Box\varphi$ and $M \not\models \Box\varphi$. From the first case it is known that for any φ' whose l.t.p. is $t + 1$, if $M \models \Box\varphi'$ then also $M' \models \Box\varphi'$. But these two facts together imply that M' is chronologically less ignorant than M.

   ∎

From the details of the construction we have also the following

Corollary 4.2 *The (unique) set of base sentences that are known in any c.m.i. model of a simple causal theory is exactly the set of tautological consequences of all (positive and negative) atomic base sentences that are known in that c.m.i. model.*

The proof of the "unique model" theorem actually included an effective procedure for computing the atomic base sentence that are known in any c.m.i. model, namely starting with knowledge of no atomic base sentences prior to l.t.p. of the first boundary condition, and then iteratively progressing in time, adding only knowledge of atomic base sentences that is necessitated by prior knowledge and ignorance. However, while this procedure is effective, it can be very slow. Intuitively speaking, it requires that one "step through" each time point even if knowledge is quite sparse, and most time points are not l.t.p's of any atomic base sentence that is known in the c.m.i. model.

The alternative is to focus the attention on the "interesting" time points, those that are "potentially" l.t.p.'s of known atomic base sentences. It turns out that those can be circumscribed quite tightly, which is a direct consequence of the construction procedure in the proof of the "unique model" theorem:

Corollary 4.3 *If M is a c.m.i. model of a simple causal theory Ψ and φ is an atomic base sentence such that $M \models \Box\varphi$ ($M \models \Box\neg\varphi$), then there exist Φ and Θ such that $\Phi \wedge \Theta \supset \Box\varphi$ (respectively, $\Phi \wedge \Theta \supset \Box\neg\varphi$) is a sentence in Ψ.*

This means that in constructing the c.m.i. model, one can skip the time points which are not the l.t.p. of the r.h.s. in any sentence of the causal theory: at those points no atomic base sentences are known.

In order to analyze the precise complexity of the procedure, let us look at the finite case.

Theorem 4.4 *Let Ψ be a finite causal theory of size n. Then the (unique) set of atomic base sentences that are known in any c.m.i. model of Ψ is of size $O(n)$, and can be computed in time $O(n \log n)$.*

Proof:
Intuitively, the following algorithm organizes all atomic base subformulas of Ψ in ascending order of l.t.p., and then steps through those one at a time, determining for each one whether either it or its negation must be known. The details of the algorithm are given below. (In the following, [¬] means that negation sign may or may not appear.)

1. Let T be the lists of all sentences in Ψ. (Whereas the sentences in Ψ are implicitly conjoined and therefore Ψ is a formula, T is merely a collection of sentences.)

   Gather all atomic base sentence appearing in T into a list S, dropping negation signs and removing duplicates. In other words, if $\Phi \wedge \Theta \supset \Box(t_1, t_2, [\neg]p) \in T$ then TRUE$(t_1, t_2, p) \in S$, and furthermore if either $\Box(t_3, t_4, [\neg]q)$ is a conjunct of Φ or $\Diamond(t_3, t_4, [\neg]q)$ is a conjunct of Θ, then TRUE$(t_3, t_4, q) \in S$.

2. Sort T by the l.t.p. the consequent (that is, by t_2 in $\Phi \wedge \Theta \supset \Box(t_1, t_2, p)$, given our convention stated at the beginning of the section).

   Sort S by l.t.p. (that is, by t_2 in TRUE(t_1, t_2, p)). Mark all members of S UNMARKED.

3. If T is empty then halt. The (positive and negative) atomic base sentences that are known in the c.m.i. models of Ψ are exactly those marked YES in S, and the negation of those marked NO in S.

4. Remove the first element of T, say $\Phi \wedge \Theta \supset \Box(\mathtt{t}_1, \mathtt{t}_2, [\neg]\mathtt{p})$. For each conjunct $\Box(\mathtt{t}_{i_1}, \mathtt{t}_{i_2}, [\neg]\mathtt{p}_i)$ of Φ and each conjunct $\Diamond(\mathtt{t}_{i_1}, \mathtt{t}_{i_2}, [\neg]\mathtt{p}_i)$ of Θ, determine how $\mathtt{TRUE}(\mathtt{t}_{i_1}, \mathtt{t}_{i_2}, \mathtt{p}_i)$ is marked in S, performing binary search on S. If one of the following conditions is true:

   (a) $\Box(\mathtt{t}_{i_1}, \mathtt{t}_{i_2}, \mathtt{p}_i)$ is a conjunct of Φ and $\mathtt{TRUE}(\mathtt{t}_{i_1}, \mathtt{t}_{i_2}, \mathtt{p}_i)$ is not marked YES in S

   (b) $\Box(\mathtt{t}_{i_1}, \mathtt{t}_{i_2}, \neg\mathtt{p}_i)$ is a conjunct of Φ and $\mathtt{TRUE}(\mathtt{t}_{i_1}, \mathtt{t}_{i_2}, \mathtt{p}_i)$ is not marked NO in S

   (c) $\Diamond(\mathtt{t}_{i_1}, \mathtt{t}_{i_2}, \mathtt{p}_i)$ is a conjunct of Θ and $\mathtt{TRUE}(\mathtt{t}_{i_1}, \mathtt{t}_{i_2}, \mathtt{p}_i)$ is marked NO in S,

   (d) $\Diamond(\mathtt{t}_{i_1}, \mathtt{t}_{i_2}, \neg\mathtt{p}_i)$ is a conjunct of Θ and $\mathtt{TRUE}(\mathtt{t}_{i_1}, \mathtt{t}_{i_2}, \mathtt{p}_i)$ is marked YES in S

   then go to 3.

   Otherwise, label $\mathtt{TRUE}(\mathtt{t}_1, \mathtt{t}_2, \mathtt{p})$ in S with YES or NO, depending on whether the consequent is $\Box(\mathtt{t}_1, \mathtt{t}_2, \mathtt{p})$ or $\Box(\mathtt{t}_1, \mathtt{t}_2, \neg\mathtt{p})$. Go to 3.

Complexity analysis:
since T is finite, the algorithm clearly must halt. Its time complexity is as follows.

Step 1: $O(n)$.

Step 2: $O(n \log n)$ (sorting).

Step 3: $O(1)$.

Step 4: Checking the existing labeling is done at most n times during the entire execution of the algorithm, and every individual checking is done in time $O(\log n)$ (binary search). Similarly, at most n new labels are made throughout the algorithm, and again each labeling can be done in time $O(\log n)$. Total complexity: $O(n \log n)$.

Thus the total running time of the algorithm is $O(n \log n)$.

Having discussed some of the technical aspects of causal theories, let us now step back and gain a global perspective of when and why one constructs causal theories.

4.4   Causal theories: a global perspective

In Section 4.2 it was shown that in the logic of chronological ignorance, the theory describing the shooting scenario had essentially a unique model, and that this model happened to be the "right" one according to our intuition. In Section 4.3 it was shown that *any* simple causal theory has this "unique model" property, and that knowledge in that model can be computed efficiently. Yet I have given no explicit motivation for constructing the theory describing the shooting scenario in the particular way that I did. Let us now look more closely at that example and understand the general phenomenon.

4.4.1   Causal rules and the ostrich principle

Recall the discussion in Chapter 3, Section2 about the computational motivation for adopting a nonmonotonic logic, in which I called the principle underlying any nonmonotonic logic *the ostrich principle*, or the *what-you-don't-know-won't-hurt-you* principle. It was said that when we bias the models of our theories in a certain way (here, by preferring chronologically most ignorant models), we do so in order to save computational resources in the long run. For example, when we prefer models in which birds can fly to those in which they cannot, we do not have to specify the flying capabilities of most birds; their ability to fly will follow "automatically." The price we pay is when reasoning about "abnormal" birds such as penguins: if we do not specify their (nonexistent) flying capabilities then we will erroneously infer that they can fly (whereas in an ordinary monotonic logic, in the absence of explicit information about it, we would neither infer that they can fly nor that they cannot). When the frequency of flying birds overwhelms the expected danger of making wrong predictions about penguins, we assume that birds fly by default.

The same tradeoff underlies causal theories. For example, the last causal rule in the theory describing the shooting scenario was the formula:

```
□(t,loaded) ∧ □(t,fire) ∧
   ◇(t,air) ∧
   ◇(t,firingpin) ∧
   ◇(t,no-marshmallow-bullets) ∧
   ...◇...other mundane conditions
⊃
□(t+1,noise),          for all t
```

Consider the conjunct ◇(t,air). We could replace this conjunct by a conjunct □(t,air), but the result would be slightly different. In the theory as we have it above, we need not say anything about there being air in order to be able to infer that there will be a noise after the firing (since ◇(t,air) ≡ ¬□(t,¬air), and we minimize knowledge). On the other hand, if there is *no* air we had better state that fact explicitly in the initial conditions, otherwise we will erroneously conclude that there will be a loud noise. If we changed the ◇ to a □, we would be in the exact opposite situation: although we would never conclude that a loud noise took place in a vacuum, we would fail to predict a noise if we neglected to state explicitly that air was present. Which alternative is better depends on what happens more often. If shooting scenarios rarely take place in a vacuum, as indeed is the case in everyday life, then we are better off sticking with the original theory; we will not need to mention the atmospheric conditions, except in those unusual occasions when things indeed take place in a vacuum. One can imagine other circumstances, say of creatures living in outer space, in which it would be more economical to adopt the alternative formulation, since then you would have to explicitly describe the atmospheric conditions only in those rare cases in which air were present.

4.4.2   Causal rules and "real" physics

The explanation just given of the role played by causal rules relied on the principle of minimal knowledge, and thus on the contrapositive reading ¬□(t,¬p) of the conjunct on the l.h.s. of causal rules (¬□(t,¬air) in the particular causal rule used as an example). Another way to understand causal rules is by their relation to "real" rules of lawful change, and this relies on the original form of the causal rules (in the particular example, ◇(t,air)).

Rules of lawful change are believed to be universally true, and therefore one could expect them to hold in every possible world. Correspondingly, the causal rule under discussion might have been expected to be:

□ [
    TRUE(t,loaded) ∧ TRUE(t,fire) ∧
    TRUE(t,air) ∧
    TRUE(t,firingpin) ∧
    TRUE(t,no-marshmallow-bullets) ∧
    ... TRUE ... other mundane conditions
    ⊃
    TRUE(t+1,noise)
    ]

As defined, causal rules have a different structure. Indeed, according to the particular causal rule being discussed, there is a possible world in which a loaded a gun is fired in a vacuum, and nevertheless a loud noise follows. Does that mean that the physics embodied in the causal rule is unsound?

The answer is no, and the trick is to make sure that such a world which violates true physics is not the "real world."

Definition 4.9 *The* <u>*soundness conditions*</u> *of a causal theory* Ψ *are the set of sentences* $\Diamond(t_1,t_2,p) \supset \text{TRUE}(t_1,t_2,p)$ *such that* $\Diamond(t_1,t_2,p)$ *appears on the l.h.s. of some sentence in* Ψ.

Notice that from the restriction on simple causal theories, namely that there do not exist two sentences in a causal theory such that one contains $\Diamond(t_1,t_2,p)$ on its l.h.s. and the other includes $\Diamond(t_1,t_2,\neg p)$ on its l.h.s., it follows that the soundness conditions introduce no inconsistency into the c.m.i. models.

We now assume that the soundness conditions are implicitly part of the causal theory itself, and are omitted simply for reasons of economy of expression. In our particular example, we get (among other sentences) the sentence $\Diamond(t,air) \supset \text{TRUE}(t,air)$, which reads "if there exists a world in which TRUE(t,air) holds, then TRUE(t,air) is true in our world." This means that if we ever use this causal rule, we might be making wrong predictions about *some* possible worlds, but never about the "real" one. This is why "what you don't know won't hurt you": anything potentially harmful is guaranteed to happen in a different world from your own.

Chapter 5

Potential Histories

In the introductory chapter two problems were shown to arise in temporal reasoning, the *qualification problem* and the *extended prediction problem*. So far I have concentrated on the former, which is the problem of having to specify too many conditions in order to make even a single prediction about the future. To summarize the discussion in previous chapters, I have shown that one can get around the problem by adopting a specific nonmonotonic logic, and that in that logic, *causal theories* have attractive properties. In this chapter I address the second problem, the extended prediction problem. Fortunately, the discussion here will be much shorter, since we will be able to use the machinery developed at some length in the previous chapters.[1]

The reader is reminded that the extended prediction problem is the difficulty of predicting things about extended periods of time in the future (as opposed to predicting things about intervals of infinitesimal duration). The example used in Chapter 1 referred to two billiard balls heading towards a collision point; although physics gives the instantaneous acceleration of each ball at every moment in time, actually predicting that the two balls will collide is problematic. Similarly, when representing the initial conditions as two `rolling` histories, it is unclear how to achieve the effect of having two new rolling histories end precisely at the collision point. As was explained in Chapter 1, a special case of the extended prediction problem is the *persistence* problem, which is the difficulty in inferring that things remain unchanged until perturbed.

---

[1] The reader is reminded that the discussion of causation in the next chapter does not depend in any crucial way on this chapter.

The flavor of the solution to the extended prediction problem will be the same as that of the solution to the qualification problem, in that I will invoke a nonmonotonic logic. In fact, we will not need any new machinery. I will continue to use the logic of *chronological ignorance*, although in a slightly more sophisticated way than before. Before descending into technicalities, however, let me explain the intuition behind the formal construction.

5.1 The intuition behind potential histories

The solution I will propose to the extended prediction problem will be to grab the bull by the horns and make bold predictions about the distant future, predictions that are based on only the past and present. As a result, these sweeping predictions will necessarily be defeasible. More specifically, I will propose talking of "the way things would turn out naturally, if nothing interfered with the course of events." The defeasibility comes from assuming by default that the "natural" thing indeed happens, but as soon as some interfering factor is detected, the part of the "natural" course of events that succeeds it is no longer held to be true. This gives rise to the notion of *potential histories*.

Imagine that our world — past, present and future — is inhabited by *potential histories* which try to manifest themselves, as it were. For example, consider again the familiar "concurrent billiards" scenario. We begin with a simple scenario in which a single ball is rolling (Figure 5.1). In this case there is a single potential `rolling` history (that ends when the ball hits the edge of the table) which "succeeded" in manifesting all of itself. Now consider the original scenario with two rolling balls. We first consider how each ball would have behaved in the absence of other balls. In this case we have two potential `rolling` histories with intersecting trajectories (see Figure 5.2): the one from the previous, simple scenario, and a new one. Of course, the laws of physics tell us that when two balls collide they both stop rolling in the "expected" direction. In the new terminology this means that each of the two potential histories managed to manifest only an initial segment of itself (see Figure 5.3). This is the general nature of potential histories: they start out as histories, but due to interaction with other potential histories become counterfactual histories.

Physics tells us that not only will the two colliding balls stop rolling in the "expected" direction, but in fact they will both start rolling in new specified directions. In the new terminology this means that not only do we have the original potential histories with their manifested initial segments, but we also have two *new* potential histories — from the moment of collision onwards — which in this case both manifest all of themselves (Figure 5.4).

Contrary to Hayes' histories, potential histories need not have a spatial dimension, although it is convenient to continue to use the terminology from the spatial case. For example, we may have a `loaded-gun` history extending from t_1 to ∞, and another one, `unloaded-gun`, extending from t_2 to ∞, such that $t_1 < t_2$. Using the spatial metaphor,

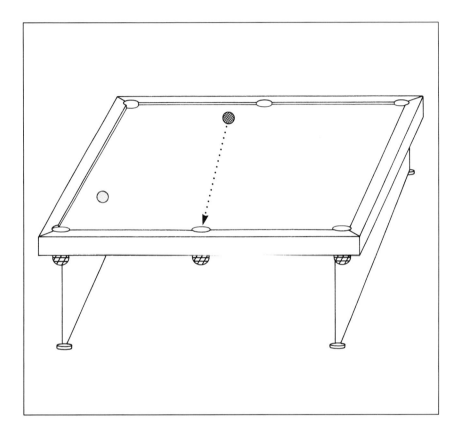

Figure 5.1: A single potential history

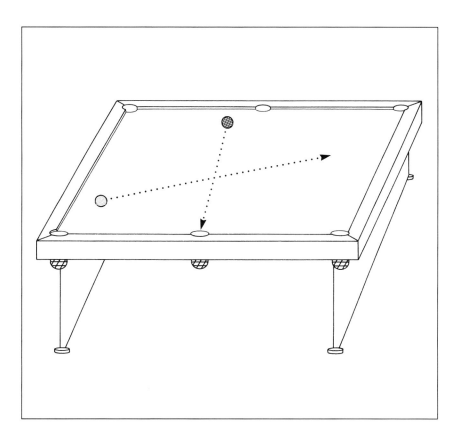

Figure 5.2: Two potential histories

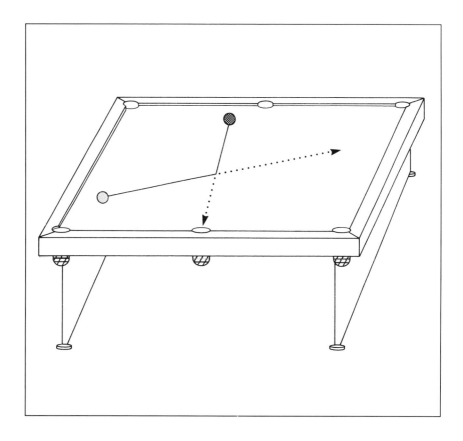

Figure 5.3: Manifested parts of the two potential histories

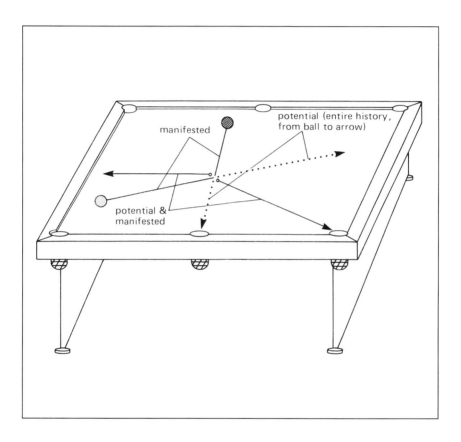

Figure 5.4: Four potential histories and their manifestations

we can say that these two gun histories "collided" at time t_2. The result of this collision is that the loaded-gun history was truncated at that point, and that the unloaded-gun history continued unperturbed. The case of histories involving physical objects is simply a special case in which the collision between potential histories is determined completely by their contiguity in spacetime. In fact, even the two gun histories in the example just used are a special case, since they involve exactly two potential histories colliding. In the general case, I will allow a collision between a set of histories of any size, even though none of its proper subsets yield a collision. For example, the set {substance-1-present, substance-2-present, substance-3-present} may yield a dramatic collision (say, a chemical reaction that truncated the existences of the three substances after some time), although none of its proper subsets does.

Practically all the details of the theory are yet to be given, but the the reader should already have an image in mind. It is an image of a world full of potential histories fighting for existence, each one manifesting only a small initial segment of itself which is determined by some central arbiter; reality is but the tip of an iceberg.

In the next sections I anchor this intuitive image in a precise formalism, but let me first acknowledge the intellectual origins of the concept of potential histories.

The notion of something happening "for as long as possible" was introduced already in McDermott's temporal logic [59]. To use a version of McDermott's own example, when we perceive a boulder lying beside the highway, we believe that it will be there for the next twenty years; this is an "immobile boulder" persistence. Persistences represent unchanging facts, and are nonmonotonic predictions. For example, if we drive by the same spot a year later and see a new MacDonald's restaurant where the boulder used to be, we modify the previous prediction, and "clip" the persistence at that point in time. McDermott's notion of persistence was adopted by Tom Dean and given an operational role in his *time maps* [14]. I too have adopted McDermott's basic idea of assigning "inertia" to propositions, but ended up with a notion that is slightly different from his.

A purely technical comparison between the two notions is impossible, since the notion of persistence was never anchored in a formal system. (In his original writing McDermott voiced a hope that formal semantics could be achieved using the M operator of his nonmonotonic logic, but, together with S. Hanks, later showed that such hopes were unfounded [28]). One way to view the notion of potential histories is as a formalization of the intuitive notion of persistences. However, the difference between the two formulations is not only in their degree of rigor. Technical considerations aside, there are also some philosophical differences between the two approaches.

First, potential histories are a broader notion than persistences. A potential history represents an arbitrary course of events which is "the way things would happen naturally," whereas a persistence is the special case of a fact that tends to remain unchanged. This is really not an overwhelming difference, since, as we shall see, I will in a certain sense "reduce" the more general notion to the special case.

The second distinction is more significant. Potential histories are determined completely by the rules that govern the world, "causal forces" if you will, whereas persistences reflect in addition degrees of confidence in knowledge. This difference is manifested in the upper bounds on the intervals of prediction, which exist both in potential histories and in persistences.

In potential histories, such upper bounds reflect the fact that what gave rise to the predicted potential history is a mechanism that does not "cause" the occurrence of the potential history beyond that particular interval. For example, when you press a button on the electric dryer in many public bathrooms, the device emits hot air for the next thirty seconds (potentially, since it may, e.g., break down in midst operation). In the potential histories framework, the reason we do not predict the emission of hot air beyond that time period is not because we know it to be false — someone might press the button repeatedly and cause the device to emit air continuously — but because the particular act of our pushing the button once "caused" the emission of hot air for only thirty seconds. For a similar reason, if we learn of a boulder lying beside the road, we predict that it will continue to lie there forever, potentially — since its being there now is sufficient to "cause" its presence there forever.

Upper bounds on persistences, on the other hand, reflect in addition the deterioration of knowledge. For example, the reason we predict that the boulder will persist in being immobile for twenty years and not any longer is that, after all, things do move in the world, and we're sufficiently unsure that the boulder will remain unmoved for much longer to avoid making that prediction. It is therefore the case that, unlike potential histories, persistences embody two distinct sources of defeasibility: information specific to the particular case (such as the existence of a new MacDonald's), or "causal" information, and statistical data (such as the fact that with high probability boulders move after 20 years). The former is taken into account by allowing clipping of persistence, the latter by being conservative about the initial prediction.[2]

I want to separate these two considerations, and will ignore the "statistical" component: if the boulder moved at any point in time, something must have caused it. Consequently, I would have the potential boulder-at-rest history extend infinitely into the future, and have its manifested part be finite only if there is definite information that it has moved.

---

[2]This dual purpose of McDermott's persistences was noted by Reid Simmons in [89].

5.2 The main technical idea behind potential histories

I will now embody the intuitive notion of potential histories in a precise formalism. As in the previous chapters, I will limit the discussion to the propositional case, and will continue to assume that the structure of time is that of the integers.

How do we represent a notion of something happening "for as long as possible, but at most until time t, unless there is another reason to believe that it extends beyond t"? There are more that one way this particular cat can be skinned; I choose the following one since on the one hand it is faithful to the intuitive image created in the previous section, and on the other hand it requires no new machinery beyond that which was already developed in previous chapters.

The key to capturing the property of "maximal extension" of potential histories is the fact that in the logic of chronological ignorance we prefer delaying knowledge of base sentences whose *latest* time point is maximal. A potential history will therefore be represented by an atomic sentence whose second temporal argument is quantified over. To use the other canonical example of this dissertation, we will represent a potential loaded-gun history that took place from time t_1 to time t_2 by $\exists v$ $(t_1 \leq v \leq t_2 \land \Box(t_1, v, \text{loaded}))$; this formula has the effect that loaded must hold from t_1 for as long as possible, but not beyond t_2. It does not *prohibit* the gun from being loaded beyond t_2, but such a prediction must be justified by other evidence. If we do not wish to bound the duration of the potential history, as is probably the case in the loaded-gun example (since guns don't unload spontaneously), we need not do so. In this case we could write simply $\exists v$ $(t_1 \leq v \land \Box(t_1, v, \text{loaded}))$, but it will be convenient to add to time-point symbols (i.e., the integers) the symbol ∞, with the obvious interpretation.

Actually, this basic construction requires some modifications. I have already mentioned that potential histories are a somewhat broader notion than persistences. In this loaded-gun example, the potential history really denotes a fact persisting over time. In more complex cases that will not be the case. For example, one might say that pressing the START button on the washing machine results in a sequence of events — such as pre-washing, washing, rinsing and spinning. Of course, this sequence of events can be truncated at any point (e.g., by unplugging the washing machine).

Therefore this sequence too is a potential history, and although it cannot be represented directly as a fact persisting over time, it can be reduced to that case. Intuitively, we postulate a potential p-machine-in-operation history, and decompose it to its various subcomponents. We do so by stating that if the potential history actually persisted for long enough, then the particular component indeed took place. For example, in the washing machine case we might postulate the sentence:

$\Box(t_1,t_2,\text{p-machine-in-operation}) \equiv$
$\quad \Box(t_1,t_1,\text{start}) \land$
$\quad (t_2 \geq t_1 + 5_{min} \supset \Box(t_1,t_1+5_{min},\text{prewash})) \land$
$\quad (t_2 \geq t_1 + 15_{min} \supset \Box(t_1+5_{min},t_1+15_{min},\text{wash})) \land$
$\quad (t_2 \geq t_1 + 20_{min} \supset \Box(t_1+15_{min},t_1+20_{min},\text{rinse})) \land$
$\quad \ldots$

In general, whenever we have a feeling that a particular course of events is the "natural one," we also have a notion of some underlying mechanism that tends to steer the world in that particular direction. Potential histories such as p-machine-in-operation can be thought of as that mechanism. Similarly, in the gun example will have a p-loaded potential history, in addition to the loaded proposition. The two will have the same technical status (i.e., "proposition types"), but conceptually the p-loaded proposition will represent the underlying mechanism (in this case, kinematic properties of rigid objects) which propagates the loaded property forward in time.

In general, to emphasize the special conceptual status of propositions denoting potential histories, I will prefix each one with a p-, as I have done above.

To see why this construction solves the extended prediction problem, let us reconsider the shooting scenario. Recall that the causal theory describing the scenario consisted of the following four axioms and axiom schemes:

1. $\Box(1,\text{loaded})$

2. $\Box(5,\text{fire})$

3. $\Box(t,\text{loaded}) \land \Diamond(t,\neg\text{fire}) \land \Diamond(t,\neg\text{emptied-manually})$
   $\supset \Box(t+1,\text{loaded}),\qquad$ for all t

4. $\Box(t,\text{loaded}) \land \Box(t,\text{fire}) \land$
   $\quad \Diamond(t,\text{air}) \land$
   $\quad \Diamond(t,\text{firingpin}) \land$
   $\quad \Diamond(t,\text{no-marshmallow-bullets}) \land$
   $\quad \ldots \Diamond \ldots \text{other mundane conditions}$
   $\quad \supset \Box(t+1,\text{noise}),\qquad$ for all t

The third axiom schema was the frame axiom, which was needed in order to ensure that the gun remained loaded at time $t = 5$. Now we can finally get rid of it, simply by making Axiom 1 a potential history. Specifically, we can have the following theory:

1. $(\exists v \ (\Box(t_1,v,\text{p-loaded}) \land t \leq v)) \supset \Box(t,\text{loaded})$,
   for all t_1 and t such that $t_1 \leq t$.

2. $\exists v \ (1 \leq v \leq \infty \ \land$
   $(\not\exists v' \ 1 \leq v' < v \land \Box(v',\text{fire})) \ \land$
   $(\not\exists v' \ 1 \leq v' < v \land \Box(v',\text{emptied-manually}))) \ \land$
   $\Box(1,v,\text{p-loaded}))$

3. $\Box(5,\text{fire})$

4. $\Box(t,\text{loaded}) \land \Box(t,\text{fire}) \land$
   $\Diamond(t,\text{air}) \ \land$
   $\Diamond(t,\text{firingpin}) \ \land$
   $\Diamond(t,\text{no-marshmallow-bullets}) \ \land$
   $\ldots \Diamond \ldots$ other mundane conditions
   $\supset \Box(t+1,\text{noise})$,   for all t

It is not hard to see that this new theory has a "unique" c.m.i. model (again, in the sense that in all c.m.i. models of the theory the same base sentences are known), and that this c.m.i. model is essentially identical to that of the original theory: in both the gun remains loaded until $t = 5$, at which time it is fired, and a noise follows. The only difference is that in the new formulation we have the extra knowledge about the the the proposition TRUE(1,5,p-loaded). Notice also the convenience of having ∞ as an explicit time-point symbol: in a scenario in which the gun was never fired we would have $\Box(1,\infty,\text{p-loaded})$, and hence $\Box(t,\text{loaded})$ for all $t_1 \leq t$.

Actually, this new theory too can be improved on. The second axiom, describing the potential p-loaded history, mentioned explicitly the conditions under which the prediction about the gun being loaded is no longer justified. The alternative is to say that the gun will remain loaded *until it is known to have been unloaded*. We can achieve that by replacing Axiom 2 by the following axioms:

2a. $\exists v \ (1 \leq v \leq \infty \land \Box(1,v,\text{p-loaded}))$

2b. $\Box(t,\text{fire}) \supset \Box(t+1,\neg\text{loaded})$ for all t

2c. $\Box$(t,emptied-manually) $\supset$ $\Box$(t+1,$\neg$loaded)   for all t

These more elegant theories, which eliminate the need for explicit "frame axioms," are no longer in the form of simple causal theories. Although the reader can verify that they indeed have "unique" c.m.i. models, it is no longer clear what the general phenomenon is. In particular, it isn't clear that there is a class of theories which include the ones presented above, to which the simple model-theoretic and complexity results explained in Section 3 of Chapter 4 (e.g., "unique" c.m.i. model, $O(n \log n)$ computability) apply. In the next section I show that such a class of theories (called *inertial theories*) in fact exists.

5.3 Inertial theories

The previous section offered a new way of describing the shooting scenario which eliminated the need for explicit "frame axioms," but, as was said, the resulting theory did not fit the mold of "causal theories." It is the case, though, that the nice properties of causal theories can be retained even if the restrictions on such theories are somewhat relaxed. Intuitively, all we need to ensure is the "autonomy of the past," according to which the bounded model M/t can be computed independently of the bounded model M/t', for any $t < t'$. The strict restrictions on causal theories guaranteed these properties, but weaker ones will too. In this section I introduce one such weakening which allows the new formulations discussed in the previous section.

The last theory that was discussed included two axioms that are disallowed in causal theories. Axiom 1 contained implication from knowledge that a potential history extended to at least certain point, to knowledge about that point. Axiom 2a (like Axiom 2 before it) contained knowledge about a potential history whose end point was quantified over existentially. *Inertial theories* will generalize causal theories to allow those two kinds of statements. In fact, it will allow more than having points inherit knowledge about intervals, as in Axiom 1: knowledge that a potential history lasted at least until a certain point may imply knowledge about *any* subinterval ending at that point. Intuitively, this general case will allow us to reason about arbitrary potential histories, whereas restricted axioms such as Axiom 1 will allow us to reason about the special case of simple persistences.

This departure from causal theories is quite radical, since, unless one is careful, it admits a certain form of "backwards causation." In causal theories one can determine knowledge of the past with total disregard of the future, and, conversely, one can determine the future uniquely on the basis of the past. In inertial theories, on the other hand, the endpoints of potential histories which did not completely manifest themselves are determined by the fact that extending the potential histories beyond that point would yield a contradiction *in the future*. But now suppose that one has two potential histories, p-1 and p-2, and that they imply contradictory facts. For example, suppose one has the following axioms:

$$\exists v \ t_1 {\leq} v \ \wedge \ \Box(t_1,v,\text{p-1})$$
$$\exists v \ t_2 {\leq} v \ \wedge \ \Box(t_2,v,\text{p-2})$$
$$\forall v \ \Box(t_1,v,\text{p-1}) \ \wedge \ t_3 {\leq} v \ \supset \ \Box(t_3,\text{fact})$$
$$\forall v \ \Box(t_2,v,\text{p-2}) \ \wedge \ t_3 {\leq} v \ \supset \ \Box(t_3,\neg\text{fact})$$

where $t_1 < t_2 \leq t_3$. What do the c.m.i. models of this minitheory look like?
If $t_3 = t_2$ then there is a unique answer: p-1 will terminate at $t_2 - 1$, and
p-2 will end at ∞. If on the other hand $t_3 \neq t_2$ then we no longer have
a unique model. Clearly one of p-1 and p-2 will end exactly at $t_3 - 1$
and the other will persist to ∞, but the theory does not favor one over the
other.

In principle there is nothing wrong with theories that have more than
one c.m.i. model — they simply do not contain enough information to
predict the future uniquely. Still, it certainly would be nice to have the
past uniquely determine the future, both for computational reasons and
so that the theories correspond to our intuition. And in fact, there is a
natural way to restrict potential histories so that their deterministic nature
is preserved.

Consider the above example involving p-1 and p-2. The two potential
histories are meant to represent on-going processes that were brought about
somehow. As I have said, the axioms of the theories do not contain the
explicit information about either process being truncated, just the implicit
information that at least one of them had to be. The solution will be to
simply disallow such theories — if two potential histories contradict one
another at some point, the theory must make sure that if both of them
take place, then at least one of them has to be truncated explicitly prior
to the point of contradiction. This is similar to the restriction that was
imposed on causal theories: recall that if both $\Phi_1 \wedge \Theta_1 \supset \Box(t_1, t_2, p)$ and
$\Phi_2 \wedge \Theta_2 \supset \Box(t_1, t_3, \neg p)$ were causal rules, then $\Phi_1 \wedge \Theta_1 \wedge \Phi_2 \wedge \Theta_2$ had
to be inconsistent.

5.3.1   Formal definition of inertial theories

After this long introduction and motivation, let me proceed with the precise
definition of inertial theories.

Definition 5.1 *An* inertial theory *is a collection of sentences* $\Psi_1 \cup \Psi_2 \cup \Psi_3$
*such that (as usual, [¬] means that the negation sign may or may not
appear,* p, q *are primitive propositions, and all the* t_i*'s are time point
symbols, i.e., constants):*

I. Ψ_1 *is a causal theory, as defined in Chapter 4.*

II. Ψ_2 *is a collection of sentences of the form*

$\Phi \wedge \Theta \supset \text{POTEN}(t_1,t_2,\text{p-i})$ $=_{def}$

$\Phi \wedge \Theta \supset \exists v \ (t_1 \leq v \leq t_2 \wedge \Box(t_1,v,\text{p-i}))$,
such that

1. *If* $\Phi \wedge \Theta \supset \text{POTEN}(t_1,t_2,\text{p-i})$ *is in* Ψ_2, *then* p-i *may appear only on the r.h.s. of sentences in* Ψ_2 *(or in* Ψ_3 *as explained below).*

   (Explanation: The symbol p-i is said to denote a potential history. The symbols denoting potential histories are distinct from those that do not, and will be distinguished by the 'p-' prefix.)   .

2. Φ *is a conjunction of sentences* $\Box\varphi_i$, *where* φ_i *is a (positive or negative) atomic base sentence with l.t.p.* t_i *such that* $t_i < t_1$.

3. Θ *is a conjunction of sentences* $\Diamond\varphi_j$, *where* φ_j *is a (positive or negative) atomic base sentence with l.t.p.* t_j *such that* $t_j < t_1$.

4. *Either or both of* Φ *and* Θ *may be empty (that is, identically true). A sentence in which* Φ *is empty is called an* inertial boundary condition. *Other sentences are called* inertial causal rules.

5. *There is a time point* t_0 *such that if* $\Theta \supset \text{POTEN}(t_1,t_2,\text{poten})$ *is an inertial boundary condition, then* $t_0 < t_1$.

   (Explanation: As in the case of causal theories, we will want to exclude knowledge about an arbitrarily distant past.)

6. *There do not exist two sentences in* $\Psi_1 \cup \Psi_2$ *such that one contains* $\Diamond\varphi$ *on its l.h.s. and the other contains* $\Diamond\neg\varphi$ *on its l.h.s.*

   (Explanation: Again, one can view the $\Diamond$-conditions as the 'biases' of the theory, an assume implicit 'soundness conditions,' as defined in Subsection 4.4.2. In particular, we can assume that if $\Diamond\varphi$ oppears in the theory then $\Diamond\varphi \supset \varphi$ holds, which explains the need for this last restriction.)

III. Ψ_3 *is a collection of sentences of the form*

$\text{PROJECT}(t_1,\text{p-i},t_2,t_3,[\neg]\text{p}) =_{def}$

$(\ \exists v \ (t_3 \leq v \wedge \Box(t_1,v,\text{p-i}))) \supset \Box(t_2,t_3,[\neg]\text{p})$

such that

1. $t_1 \leq t_2 \leq t_3$.

2. p-i *is a proposition denoting a potential history.*

3. *If* X $\supset$ POTEN(t_1,t_4,p-1) *is a sentence in* Ψ_2,
PROJECT(t_1,p-1,t_1,t_1,p) *is in* Ψ_3, *and* Y $\supset$ $\square$(t_1,t_1,¬p) *is
in* Ψ_1, *then* X $\wedge$ Y *is inconsistent.*

(Explanation: This is analogous to the restriction on causal rules
whose 'effects' (i.e., r.h.s.'s) were contradictory. Without this
restriction one does not get determinism, or independence of
the past from the future.)

4. *If* X_1 $\supset$ POTEN(t_1,t_4,p-1) *and* X_2 $\supset$ POTEN(t_5,t_6,p-2) *are
sentences in* Ψ_2, PROJECT(t_1,p-1,t_2,t_3,p) *and*
PROJECT(t_5,p-2,t_2,t_3,¬p) *are sentences in* Ψ_3 *such that* $t_1 \leq t_5$,
and X_1 $\wedge$ X_2 *is consistent, then the following must hold:*

(a) *If* $t_5 = t_2 = t_3$ *then* $t_1 < t_5$.

(b) *Otherwise, for some* $t_8 \leq t_3$ *and some* q,
PROJECT(t_5,p-i,t_7,t_8,q) *is in* Ψ_3 *and* X_j $\supset$ $\square$(7,8,¬q)
is in Ψ_1, *for* $i = 1, j = 2$ *or vice versa.*

(Explanation: This too is analogous to the restriction on causal
theories discussed above. If two potential histories are contradictory, then of two cases must take place. The first possibility
is that the conflict occurs at the first instant of one of the potential histories, which implies that the other potential history
must end (and therefore also begin no later than) at the previous time point (a). Otherwise, it must be that the cause of
one potential history is also an independent cause of the other
potential history's ending no later than at the endpoint of the
interval of contradiction (b). Either way, the "autonomy of the
past" will be guaranteed.)

5.3.2   The "unique"-model property

The first property of causal theories is shared by inertial theories, and it is
the fact that they have "unique" c.m.i. models. I mean this in the same
sense that was used in Chapter 4: any two c.m.i. models of an inertial
theory agree on the truth value of all sentences $\square\varphi$, where φ is a base
sentence.

Theorem 5.1
If $\Psi = \Psi_1 \cup \Psi_2 \cup \Psi_3$ *is any inertial theory as above, then*

1. Ψ *has a c.m.i. model, and*

2. *if M_1 and M_2 are both c.m.i. models of Ψ, and φ any base sentence,*
   then $M_1 \models \Box\varphi$ iff $M_2 \models \Box\varphi$.

Proof: The flavor of the proof is identical to that of the proof of the analogous theorem for causal theories. We will construct a model M for Ψ, and show that M is chronologically more ignorant than any model for Ψ which differs from M on the truth value of some sentence $\Box\varphi$, where φ is a base sentence. Again, the construction starts with some time-bounded interpretation M/t_0, and augments it to later time points iteratively. The difference between the two proofs will be in the inductive construction step. Intuitively, at each point we will determine not only what effects are caused by earlier occurrences, but also what potential effects are actually still manifested at that time. We will therefore compute not only the CONSEQUENTS$_t$ set at each time point, the "effects" which terminate at t, but also the POTENTIALS$_t$ set, which will identify the potential histories which are still active at time t. More precisely, $\langle t_1, t_2, p \rangle$ will be in POTENTIALS$_t$ just in case there is a potential history POTEN(t_1, t_2, p) such that $t_1 \leq t \leq t_2$, and that potential history in fact does not terminate before t. Of the potential histories in POTENTIALS$_t$, some will actually terminate at t. This might be because t is the upper bound on the duration of the potential (the NATURAL-DEATH$_t$ set), or because extending it to $t + 1$ causes a contradiction (the CLIPPED$_t$ set).

Since the identity of the potential histories ending at time t depends in part on known propositions whose l.t.p. is $t + 1$, determining them will "lag" one time instant behind determining the other known propositions. In other words, strictly speaking we will not simply extend M/t to $M/t+1$ in each iteration. Rather, at that stage we will determine the known temporal propositions whose l.t.p. is no later that $t + 1$ *except for the propositions denoting potential histories, or the p- propositions.* In addition, at this stage we will complete the M/t model constructed in the previous iteration by determining the known p- propositions that ended at time t. Thus when in the following I speak of the partial model M/t, it should be taken to mean the partial interpretation which determines knowledge of all non-p-wffs whose l.t.p. is no later than t, and of all p- wffs whose l.t.p. is no later than $t - 1$.

The precise construction is as follows.

1. Let t_0 be some point that precedes any point t_1 such that either $\Theta \supset \Box(t_1, t_2, p)$ is a boundary condition, or else $\Theta \supset$ POTEN(t_1, t_2, p) is an inertial boundary condition (from the restriction on Ψ_2, and a similar restriction on Ψ_1 due to its being a causal theory, it follows

that such a point exists). For any base tautology φ whose l.t.p. $\leq t_0$, let $M/t_0 \models \Box\varphi$. For any other base wff φ whose l.t.p. $\leq t_0$, let $M/t_0 \not\models \Box\varphi$.

Notice that M/t_0 (partially) satisfies the boundary conditions of Ψ_1 vacuously (since the l.t.p.'s of all boundary conditions are greater than t_0), and (partially) satisfies all the causal rules (since if their l.t.p. is no later than t_0, then their antecedents are falsified). For a similar reason M/t_0 satisfies also all sentences in Ψ_2. Finally, M/t_0 (partially) satisfies also all sentences in Ψ_3 since it falsifies all their antecedents.

Let $\text{POTENTIALS}_{t_0} = \emptyset$, the empty set.

2. We now specify how to augment M/t to $M/t + 1$ for any t. Let
   $\text{NEW-POTENTIALS}_{t+1} =$
   $\{\langle\texttt{t+1},\texttt{t}_1,\texttt{p-i}\rangle:$
   $\Phi \wedge \Theta \supset \texttt{POTEN}(\texttt{t+1},\texttt{t}_1,\texttt{p}) \in \Psi_2$ and $M/t \models \Phi \wedge \Theta\}$

   Explanation: $\text{NEW-POTENTIALS}_{t+1}$ contains the potential histories whose beginning point is $t + 1$. At this point their ending point is not determined.

   $\text{PARTIAL-CONSEQUENTS}_{t+1} =$
   $\{\Box\varphi: \text{the l.t.p. of } \varphi \text{ is } \texttt{t+1}, \Phi\wedge\Theta \supset \Box\varphi \in \Psi_1, \text{ and } M/t \models \Phi\wedge\Theta\}$
   $\cup$
   $\{\Box(\texttt{t+1},[\neg]\texttt{p}):$
   $\langle\texttt{t+1},\texttt{t}_1,\texttt{p-i}\rangle \in \text{NEW-POTENTIALS}_{t+1}, \text{ and}$
   $\texttt{PROJECT}(\texttt{t+1},\texttt{p-i},\texttt{t+1},\texttt{t+1},[\neg]\texttt{p}) \in \Psi_3\}$

   Explanation: $\text{PARTIAL-CONSEQUENTS}_{t+1}$ contains the known atomic base sentences with l.t.p. $t + 1$, knowledge of which does not depend on the fact that certain potential histories persisting long enough (those will be computed momentarily). These known base sentences are either r.h.s.'s of ordinary causal rules, or else they refer to the single time point $t + 1$ (i.e., they are of the form $\texttt{TRUE}(\texttt{t+1},\texttt{t+1},[\neg]\texttt{p})$), and their is a potential history starting at $t + 1$ which implies knowledge of that base sentence. In either case knowledge of the base sentence can be safely added to the model.

$\text{NATURAL-DEATH}_t = \{\Box(\texttt{t}_1,\texttt{t},\texttt{p-i}): \langle\texttt{t}_1,\texttt{t},\texttt{p-i}\rangle \in \text{POTENTIALS}_t\}$

Explanation: NATURAL-DEATH$_t$ contains the potential histories that were never cliped, and which ended at t simply because t was their upper bound.

CLIPPED$_t$ =
$\quad$ {□(t₁,t,p-i):
$\quad\quad$ ⟨t₁,t₂,p-i⟩∈ POTENTIALS$_t$,
$\quad\quad$ PROJECT(t₁,p-i,t₃,t+1,[¬]p) ∈ Ψ₃, and
$\quad\quad$ □(t₃,t+1,¬[¬]p) ∈ PARTIAL-CONSEQUENTS$_{t+1}$}

Explanation: CLIPPED$_t$ contains the remainder of the potential histories which ended at t. They were clipped at that point because extending them to $t + 1$ would cause a contradiction. This means that if they extended beyond t they would imply knowledge of an atomic base sentence whose l.t.p. is $t + 1$, and whose negation is known in $M/t+1$. But the last restriction on inertial theories guarantees that this negated base sentence must be in PARTIAL-CONSEQUENTS$_{t+1}$.

POTENTIALS$_{t+1}$ =
$\quad$ (NEW-POTENTIALS$_{t+1}$ ∪ POTENTIALS$_t$) −
$\quad$ {⟨t₁,t₂,p-i⟩:
$\quad\quad$ □(t₁,t,p-i) ∈ (NATURAL-DEATH$_t$ ∪ CLIPPED$_t$)}

Explanation: The potential histories persisting at least until $t + 1$ are those who start at $t + 1$, and those which persisted until t and did not end there.

CONSEQUENTS$_{t+1}$ =
$\quad$ PARTIAL-CONSEQUENTS$_{t+1}$ ∪
$\quad$ {□(t₃,t+1,[¬]p):
$\quad\quad$ ⟨t₁,t₂,p-i⟩∈ POTENTIALS$_{t+1}$, and
$\quad\quad$ PROJECT(t₁,p-i,t₃,t+1,[¬]p) ∈ Ψ₃}

Explanation: CONSEQUENTS$_{t+1}$ contains the known atomic base sentences whose l.t.p. is $t + 1$. Beside the sentences in PARTIAL-CONSEQUENTS$_{t+1}$ computed above, it contains sentences whose knowledge follows from potential histories persisting at least until $t + 1$.

$M/t + 1$ is obtained by making all wffs in CONSEQUENTS$_{t+1}$ and all their tautological consequents true, and for any other base wff φ whose l.t.p. is $t + 1$ (other than p- wffs), making □φ false.

As I have said earlier, $M/t + 1$ determines which base sentences are known whose l.t.p. is $\leq t+1$ – except for containing p- propositions. However, at this time one can determine all the known p- sentences with l.t.p. t. The known atomic p- sentences whose l.t.p. is t are exactly those in NATURAL-DEATH$_t$ $\cup$ CLIPPED$_t$, which, together with closure of knowledge under tautological consequence, completely determines *all* the base sentences which are known in M/t.

As in the case of causal theories, here too it can be seen that the construction of $M/t + 1$ introduces no inconsistency. The key observation is again that the various assumptions on inertial theories guarantee that CONSEQUENTS$_{t+1}$ does not contain both a $\Box\varphi$ and $\Box\neg\varphi$, and that therefore the construction introduces no inconsistency among knowledge of non-p- atomic base sentences. Clearly knowledge of p- atomic base sentences is consistent, since no negative such sentence is known. This means that the construction introduces no inconsistency at all, since the totality of known bases sentences whose l.t.p. is $\leq t+1$ are the tautological consequences of the atomic ones.

Since the construction of $M/t + 1$ never violates any sentence in Ψ, it follows that M/∞ (or simply M) is a model for Ψ. To conclude the proof, it remains to show that if a model M' differs from M on the truth value of $\Box\varphi$ for some base sentence φ, then M' is chronologically less ignorant than M. Since this part of the proof is even more tedious and unilluminating than the first part of the proof, it is relegated to Appendix B. ∎

5.3.3   Computability

Just as in the case of causal theories, the constructive proof of the fact that inertial theories have "unique" models suggests natural way for reasoning about those models. Again, the technique is to "move forward in time," adding knowledge that is necessitated by the model constructed so far and by the inertial theory. In particular, at each iteration one computes the NEW-POTENTIALS$_{t+1}$, PARTIAL-CONSEQUENTS$_{t+1}$, NATURAL-DEATH$_t$, CLIPPED$_t$, POTENTIALS$_{t+1}$, and CONSEQUENTS$_{t+1}$ sets in that order, and adds exactly knowledge of the atomic sentences in the CONSEQUENTS$_{t+1}$, NATURAL-DEATH$_t$ and CLIPPED$_t$ sets.

Here too, this procedure can be improved on, since it requires that one step through every time point, even through points which do not appear in the inertial theory itself, and thus its time complexity is not a function only of the size of the theory but also of its total "time-span." In a way that is completely analogous to the causal theories case, it is possible to construct an $O(n \log n)$ algorithm to compute all the known atomic sentences, which "skips over" the uninteresting points in time (the details of such an algorithm are easy to reconstruct, given the algorithm for causal theories, and are omitted). It must be said, though, that the theoretical advantage of the $O(n \log n)$ algorithm over the naive one will, in practice, be less than earth shattering. As in the case of causal theories, the problem is that a typical inertial theory will contain axiom schemas, which essentially will cover all the time points in the interval under consideration. Here these will be not only schemas of causal rules, but also schemas of inertial causal rules and of "projection" rules (by which I mean the third kind of sentences in inertial theories, according to which knowledge of a potential history implies knowledge of certain facts during it).

Chapter 6

Causation

In the previous chapter I used terms such as "causal theories" and "causal rules" in specific technical senses. I did not motivate the particular names except in passing, but, of course, the choice of terminology was not accidental. I believe that the discussion in the previous chapter can be instrumental in clarifying the meaning of 'causation,' a concept to which the current chapter is devoted.

It's not without a certain amount of trepidation that I approach the topic, being well aware of the vast amount of work done on it in different disciplines, most notably in philosophy. Although I will say a few words on the philosophical literature on causation, and especially on three of the more influential among the recent theories, I cannot hope to cover the evolution of approaches over the centuries. For that let me refer the reader to the relatively recent book by Mackey [49], which includes, besides his own contribution, a survey of accounts of causation in the past. The reader interested in rigorous mathematical investigations may find the discussion there rather loose, as he would the discussion in an earlier book by Bunge [7]. Indeed, much of past discussion of causation has been held at the informal, intuitive level (witness, for example, the presence of Humean terminology even in the most recent literature). With exact philosophy having gained influence in recent years, however, one finds new attempts to define causation quite precisely. For a collection of accounts of causation by many of the outstanding contemporary philosophers, the reader is referred to the book edited by Sosa [93]. One of the major trends that is absent from that collection is that which ties causation to probabilistic notions, and one fine exemplar of that approach is the book by Suppes [96].

It might seem a bit ambitious for a computer scientist with no formal education in philosophy to address a philosophical problem with which so many emminent philosophers have been occupied over the years, without their ever quite laying it to rest. Indeed it is ambitious, but there is at least one justification for the computer scientist's *hutzpah*, and that is simply the different perspective he brings with him. His scientific goals, ways of asking questions, kinds of answers he accepts, conceptual and technical tools — are for the most part different from those of the philosopher. This means that at the very least he might be able to ask new questions about the old problem, if not actually come up with solutions. I think it's fair to say that in its relatively short history, computer science has had a tremendous impact on other fields. I don't mean only by providing new technical gadgets, but also by exporting conceptual frameworks, and in particular the precise notions of processes, resource-bounded computation, and computational complexity. In many other disciplines, such as cognitive psychology, psychiatry, linguistics and neurobiology, one finds new work of the form "a computational theory of X," which addresses the old problem X using the new conceptual apparatus. I will suggest that causation is also a case in which the analysis can benefit from taking into account considerations that are typically those of computer scientists.

The key observation about causal terminology is the high frequency with which it appears in our thinking and speech. It's true that there have been some statements in the past which exhibited a certain amount of scorn for the very concept of causation. The most famous one is due to B. Russell, which appeared in [85] and which is quoted in most texts on causation. Let me too fulfill this pleasant duty (and I am actually reproducing the quotation given by Suppes in [96]):

> All philosophers, of every school, imagine that causation is one
> of the fundamental axioms or postulates of science, yet, oddly
> enough, in advanced sciences such as gravitational astronomy,
> the word 'cause' never occurs ... The law of causality, I believe,
> like much that passes muster among philosophers, is a relic of
> a bygone age, surviving, like the monarchy, only because it is
> erroneously supposed to do no harm ...

Nevertheless, and despite the wit of the statement and the great intellect of its author, it is clear that causation *does* play a role in science. While it may be true that Newton's laws and Schrödinger's equation are mathematical formulations that make no mention of causation, causal reasoning is an important part of scientific reasoning. Suppes shows several publications in modern physics itself that deal directly with causation. Or, in a book edited by D. Lerner [44], one can find discussions by eminent scientists from disciplines as diverse as political science and biology of the role played by causation in their fields. Another example is the book by Susser [97], in which he discusses causal reasoning in epidemiology. Another example, perhaps slightly outside the realm of science, is the book by Hart and Honoré [30], which investigates the role of causation in legal reasoning.

If causal reasoning is common in scientific thinking, it is downright dominant in everyday commonsense thinking. All one needs to do is scan his favorite popular publication, and verify that causal terms — causing, preventing, enabling, bringing about, invoking, resulting in, instigating, affecting, putting an end to, etcetera — appear throughout it. In fact, the sole meaning of many verbs and verb phrases is the description of an effect of some unspecified cause: making, breaking, killing, chilling, lightening, frightening, soothing, smoothing, fattening, flattening, and so on and so forth. To quote Hume (or, actually, Mackey's quotation of him in [49]),

> ...and as these [*resemblence, contiguity* and *causation*] are the only ties of our thoughts, they are really *to us* the cement of the universe, and all the operations of the mind must, in a great measure, depend on them.

Causal terminology is so ingrained into our thinking that psychologists seem to take the meaning of causation for granted, and in their investigations concentrate on how well and how early people make use of this supposedly well-defined concept, and on how causal reasoning interacts with other cognitive mechanisms (see, e.g., the work of Piaget [71,72], although he construes the term 'causal reasoning' rather broadly).

Since causal reasoning appears to be an important component of intelligent human behavior, it stands to reason that researchers in AI should strive to understand it and make use of it in their theories. Indeed, in recent years there has been a growing interest in causation. Medical diagnosis systems stress the "causal reasoning" component of their systems. For example, in his discussion of one of the Internist/Caduceus programs [76], H. Pople talks of the "causal network," one of the two main structures imposed on the medical database:

> In a typical pathophysiological model, manifestations of disease are organized on the basis of pathological states giving rise to such observations, and these rules are in turn organized into a

> causal network. [...] In this graph, arcs are marked by arrow-
> heads in the "caused-by" direction ... Nodes in the network
> having no successor links in the caused-by relation represent
> specific disease entities ...; Those having no predecessors stand
> for possible findings ... ([76], p. 151)

The relation of causation, according to Pople, organizes medical information in a way that helps guide the heuristic search through it for a diagnosis.

Similar sentiments, still in the medical domain, are expressed by Patil et al. in [70] and by Weiss et al. in [99]. Going outside the medical domain, we find de Kleer and Brown talk of "mythical causality" in reasoning about device behavior, and Forbus about "direct-" and "indirect-influence" [11]. There are many other examples of using causal notions in almost all areas of AI. It is the case, though, that most theories of causation in AI are informal, the approach being that we understand intuitively what causation is, and therefore rather than waste time defining it, one should embody it in a program, or possibly in a slightly more abstract computational framework. There are several exceptions in which attempts are made at more or less rigorous definitions of the concept (I have in mind in particular H. Simon's original work on *causal ordering* and some of the more recent formulations in qualitative physics), and I will discuss them briefly towards the end of this chapter.

The rest of this chapter is organized as follows. First I briefly survey what I believe are three of the most influential and technically advanced modern philosophical treatments of causation, due to J. L. Mackey, D. Lewis and P. Suppes. Then, in order to focus the discussion somewhat, I enumerate several properties of causation, with the intention that this list serve at least as partial benchmarks for any proposed account of causation. I then make explicit my own account of the concept, test it against these benchmarks, and relate my account to the philosophical accounts discussed earlier. I end by discussing what role I think causation should play in AI, and briefly relate these ideas to previous work on causation within the field.

6.1 Three philosophical accounts of causation

> *Anaximander used to assert that the primary cause of all things was the infinite - not defining exactly whether he meant air or water or anything else.*
> – Diogenes Laertius
>
> *Nature is but an effect / Whose cause is God.*
> – William Cowper
>
> *Nothing exists from whose nature some effect does not follow.*
> – Baruch Spinoza
>
> *I assert that nothing ever comes to pass without a cause.*
> – Jonathan Edwards
>
> (All quotations reproduced from an article by Sosa in [93].)

As I have said, it is not possible for me to give anything resembling a complete survey of the philosophical literature on causation. Let me instead briefly discuss three specific modern proposals. Unlike many other treatments, these three are characterized by their relative precision and technical sophistication, and by their influence in philosophy which appears to have been quite substantial. This is despite the fact that each has obvious drawbacks, some of which have been pointed out in the philosophical literature itself. I am not, however, setting them up as straw men. Although my account of causation will be different, I think that it is in fact compatible with the spirit of all three, and I will therefore return to them after introducing my own proposal.

6.1.1 J. L. Mackey

The least formal of the three treatments, though still one that has some intuitive appeal, is due to J. L. Mackey, and it appears both in his book [49] and in the collection edited by E. Sosa [93]. Mackey's motivation is to escape the problems that arise from defining causes as necessary and/or sufficient conditions. Instead, he defines C to be a cause of E just in case $(C \wedge X) \vee Y$ is a necessary and sufficient condition for E, for some X and Y. In other words, C is an Insufficient but Necessary condition of an Unnecessary but Sufficient condition for E, and hence the term *INUS condition.*[1] For example, striking a match is a cause (or an INUS condition) of its lighting, since striking a match that is dry against a matchbox that is not worn out results in the match lighting, although there are other conditions that are sufficient for a match to light (such as holding it against a hot surface).

This definition is clearly not strong enough. In fact, if taken literally, it is quite meaningless: according to it, for every E and C, C is a cause of E, since $C \lor E$ is a necessary and sufficient condition for E. Mackey tries to prohibit this by requiring that none of conditions mentioned (C, X, Y) be *redundant*. Unfortunately, I don't believe that he gives a formal definition of this condition. Beside that problem, there are other more minor ones. For example, Mackey's definition does not require that causes precede their effects, and it allows circular and reflexive causation. Mackey himself recognizes some of these difficulties, and the reader is referred to the above-mentioned texts for further details on his proposal.

6.1.2 D. Lewis

In [45] D. Lewis proposed an account of causation based on his theory of counterfactuals. This account was offered as one way of making precise D. Hume's somewhat underspecified but very influential discussion of causation in [38], where in Section VII he says (the following text was actually reproduced from Lewis' article):

> We may define a cause to be an object followed by another, and where all the objects, similar to the first, are followed by objects similar to the second. Or, in other words where, if the first object had not been, the second never had existed.

The fact that this passage actually contains two distinct accounts of causation has been discussed at some length by philosophers. Lewis claims to be adopting the second one, although it seems to me that in fact he gives a precise interpretation to *both* conditions, and takes their conjunction as a definition of causation.

Briefly, Lewis adds to the notions of possible worlds and the accessibility relation between them, the notion of how *similar* worlds are to one another. For any two worlds $W1$ and $W2$, the similarity (or closeness) measure

---

[1]Sometimes one can't help feeling it fortunate that English uses certain prefixes for adjectives and not others.

determines the "distance" from $W1$ to $W2$. The intuitive intention is that
the distance between worlds reflect the amount of perturbation needed to
turn the one world into the other.

The purpose of this construction is to give meaning to counterfactual
statements, such as "if I had struck the match five minutes ago then it
would have lit." The problem in giving meaning to such statements is that
their antecedents are false, which, depending on the formulation, tends
in ordinary logic to make them either identically true or identically false:
the match was in fact not struck five minutes ago, and so adding that
condition to our world simply introduces an inconsistency. Merely replacing
the one fact by the other isn't sufficient either, since the result would be a
violation of the laws of physics (a match was struck but did not light). This
inconsistency too can be removed, by perturbing the world even more. In
this example, the obvious choice is to change the fact that the match did
not light to the fact that it did. But, it has been suggested, the world can be
made consistent in other ways, for example by making the match wet at the
time it was struck (and keeping the fact that it did not light unchanged).
In other words, the argument goes, on ordinary logical grounds alone, the
statement "if I had struck the match five minutes ago then it would have
been wet at that time" makes as good sense as the previous sentence.

Lewis' proposal is very simple. According to it, A *counterfactually*
implies B (written $A \square\!\!\rightarrow B$) in a world W just in case among all the
worlds accessible from W which satisfy A, all the ones *closest* to W also
satisfy B (this includes the case that there are *no* worlds accessible from W
which satisfy A, in which case the counterfactual implication is vacuously
true). To use the same match example, the statement "if I had struck the
match five minutes ago then it would have lit" is true in this world because
the world in which it lights resembles our world more than the world in
which the match becomes wet.

Lewis' counterfactual treatment of causation is also very simple. He
first defines the notion of *causal dependence* between events. An event E
is causally dependent on an event C just in case whether E happened or
not depends counterfactually on whether C happened or not. Formally,
E depends causally on C iff $O(E) \square\!\!\rightarrow O(C) \wedge \neg O(E) \square\!\!\rightarrow \neg O(C)$ holds,
where $O(x)$ represents the fact that event x occurred. Causation is then
defined to be the transitive closure of causal dependence. One can now
verify that by this definition, and assuming a commonsensical similarity
measure, striking a dry match indeed causes it to light.

There are many problems with this account of causation. The first
possible objection is that reducing the notion of causation to the notion

of similarity between possible worlds amounts to reducing a hard problem to an even harder one. Other objections are more technical. For example, according to this definition of causation, every event causes itself, and in general there is nothing to exclude circular causation. Or, as another example, nothing in the theory precludes the possibility of an effect preceding its cause (more on this in the next section). Even if we somehow manage to add those extra conditions to Lewis' definition, we still end up with something that seems too weak. For example, by the resulting definition it would still be the case that John's being born caused him to die later on. Further discussion of the problems with Lewis' account can be found in an article by B. Abbott [1].

Nevertheless, I find Lewis' account admirable because of its clarity and relative precision. Underspecified, ambiguous and suggestive theories have their place along the road to understanding complex phenomena, but real progress will never be made without anchoring the discussion in some firm foundations. I believe that Lewis has helped move towards attaining such a steady basis, even if the details of his construction require change.

6.1.3 P. Suppes

In [96], P. Suppes proposed a most elegant probabilistic account of causation. The feature distinguishing Suppes' treatment from most others is the fact that he ties causation to the notion of *uncertainty* (allowing the special case in which all probabilities are either 0 or 1). The basis of the formulation is a probability space, whose members are called *events*. One property of each event is its time of occurrence, which is assumed to be a time point rather than a time interval. (Suppes himself is not happy with this choice, and at some point states that his formulation should be modified to allow time intervals, or "chunks," as he calls them.) Although Suppes does not discuss the issue explicitly, it's clear that he takes time to be an unbounded linear order. His treatment appears to be independent of further properties of time, such as its being dense or discrete.

Notation: The occurrence of an event A at time t is denoted by A_t, and its probability by $P(A_t)$. $P(XY)$ is the joint probability of X and Y, and $P(X|Y)$ is the conditional probability of X, given Y.

Suppes first defines the notion of *prima facie* causes. Event C_t is said to be a prima facie cause of event $E_{t'}$ just in case

1. $t < t'$, where $<$ is the ordering on time points,

2. $P(C_t) > 0$, and

3. $P(E_{t'}|C_t) > P(E_{t'})$.

In other words, the prima facie causes of an event (the "effect") is the set of possible events which precede the effect, and whose occurrence enables one to predict the occurrence of the effect with higher probability than its given, unconditional one.

Prima facie causes are the pool of candidates among which the *genuine* causes are identified. Those are defined by their complement, the set of *spurious* causes. Suppes gives two alternative definitions for those. I will discuss the first, weaker one (Definition 2, p.23 in [96]), which I find better motivated than the second one. According to this definition, a prima facie cause $B_{t'}$ of an effect E_t is spurious if, intuitively speaking, there is an *earlier* prima facie cause of E_t which allows predicting E_t at least as well as $B_{t'}$. More precisely, $B_{t'}$ is spurious just in case there is a $t'' < t'$ and another prima facie cause $C_{t''}$ such that

1. $P(B_{t'}C_{t''}) > 0$,

2. $P(E_t|B_{t'}C_{t''}) = P(E_t|C_{t''})$, and

3. $P(E_t|B_{t'}C_{t''}) \geq P(E_t|B_{t'})$.

These definitions constitute a small part of Suppes' entire treatment of causation. Among other things, he discusses notions such as *direct* and *indirect* causes and their relation to spurious and genuine causes, *supplementary* causes, *sufficient* causes and *negative* causes. However, since the essential ideas behind the constructions are those I have discussed, let me halt the description of the Suppes' account at this point.

I think it is possible to show that Suppes' account too is somewhat too weak. For example, it appears that by his definition being born is a genuine cause of being dead 200 years later. In general, it is problematic to always equate genuine causes with the earliest strong predictors of the effect. For example, the fact the president of IBM is getting rid of IBM stocks is probably the best indication that IBM stocks are about to drop (since you trust him to have reliable inside information), but in fact the actual cause of the drop is the fact that a month later Apple Computers announce a new PC that renders the IBM PC obsolete (which need not enhance your already strong belief in the plunge). Much depends on what are construed to be events. Does anything that corresponds to what is usually called a 'proposition' qualify as an event, or are events a different sort of thing? The formal definition of events as members of the sample space[2] is neutral on this issue, and discussion about the metaphysics of events (Chapter 6 in [96]) does not seem to resolve it either. I will return to this in the next section.

Again, despite these possible shortcomings, I find Suppes' account quite beautiful. Beside the fact that it is most elegant technically, it has many intuitively correct properties: causes precede their effects, there is a distinction between a causal relation and mere regular succession in time, causation is antisymmetric and antireflexitve, and so on. In particular I believe Suppes is correct in tying causation to the notion of uncertainty. Although the details of my proposal will be quite different from those given by Suppes (in particular, I will rest the account on the notion of ignorance rather than probability), I think the two are compatible, and will discuss the connection between them later.

---

[2]That is, sets of outcomes of an experiment. For example, in a series of two coin tosses, the event "at least one *head*" corresponds to $\{ht, th, hh\}$ (where *ht* designates a *head* followed by a *tail*, and so on).

6.2   Properties of causation

In order to focus the discussion on causation, let me enumerate several
of its properties. It is intended primarily to sharpen the intuition of that
reader who has not given much thought to the topic until now, and possibly
also to bring up some new points for the reader who has. This is not an
exhaustive list; if it were then it would constitute a definition. It is the
case, however, that most past accounts of causation fail on more than one
count in this partial list. The list reads as follows.

1. Causation is not material implication; it is both stronger and weaker.
   It is stronger because, for example, the fact that Old Ebenezer's knees
   hurt implies that it is about to rain, but does not cause the rain. The
   fact that causation is more restrictive than material implication has,
   of course, been taken into account by all philosophers interested in
   the subject (see, e.g., the trouble D. Lewis takes to distinguish real
   causes from *epiphenomena*, or Suppes' distinction between *spurious*
   and *genuine* prima facie causes).

   In a different sense, however, causation is weaker than material implication. We say that firing the gun causes a loud noise, but it of
   course does not imply it; the loud noise depends on other "factors",
   such as there being air to carry the sound, the gun being loaded, and
   so on. To a certain degree, this aspect of causation too has been
   recognized by philosophers. It certainly has by the three philosophers discussed here: Mackey allows for it through the definition of
   INUS conditions, and Suppes through the use of probabilities rather
   than logical connectives, and Lewis by having the similarity between
   worlds be independent from any other properties.

2. Closely related to this last property of causation is its property of
   being *nonmonotonic*. Striking a match causes it to light, but striking
   it simultaneously with soaking it in water does not. Again, all three
   philosophers allow for this property: Mackey by allowing C to be an
   INUS condition of E by virtue of $(C \wedge \neg C' \wedge X) \vee Y \supset E$ (so that
   $C \wedge C'$ is not an INUS condition), Lewis by allowing the closest C-
   worlds to differ from the closest $C \wedge C'$-worlds, Suppes by allowing
   $P(E|C) > P(E|C \wedge C'))$.

3. Still related to the first property is the fact that causation is *context-
   sensitive* (or, as this property is sometimes called, *indexical*). For
   example, we usually say that it is the turning of the ignition key that

causes the engine to start. But consider a slightly unusual situation in which the key is stuck in the 'on' position, and we operate the car by connecting and disconnecting the battery. It now seems natural to say the connecting of the battery caused the car to start. In short, causation seems to take place against the backdrop of a theory about "what things usually take place," or "what happens naturally."

In fact, the concept of a "causal field," the background against which causation is perceived to exist, was introduced already in the 1930's, although it's definition was left at the informal and intuitive level [4]. Mackey makes explicit use of it, having INUS conditions hold relative to some causal field. (Actually, it seems to me that, given his definition of an INUS condition, there is no technical need for a causal field separate from the other conditions in the definition. Rather than say that C is an INUS condition of E in a field F by virtue of $C \wedge X \vee Y \supset E$, one can have the same INUS condition simply hold by virtue of $C \wedge X \wedge F \vee Y \supset E$. There may be other reasons for wanting an explicit causal field, but Mackey does not state them.) Suppes' account embodies the "field" in the explicit enumeration of all the members of the probability space (i.e., the random variables). Lewis, on the other hand, seems to reject the "relativization" of causation:

> We sometimes single out one among all the causes of some event and call it 'the' cause ... or we single out a few as the 'causes', calling the rest mere 'causal factors' or 'causal conditions' ... We may select the abnormal or extraordinary cause, or those under human control, or those we deem good or bad, or just those we want to talk about. I have nothing to say about these principles of invidious discrimination ... [45], p. 182.

Tempting as it is to ignore these "principles of discrimination", I feel that by doing so, Lewis, and many other philosophers, have thrown out much of the baby with the bath water; these "preference criteria" are a crucial component of causation.

4. Causation is antisymmetric and antireflexive. Of the above three, only Suppes' treatment has either of these properties.

5. Causes cannot succeed their effects in time. I am surprised to see that this is in fact not universally accepted. Again, among the three philosphers, only Suppes' account has this property. Lewis explicitly rejects it:

I reject [stipulating that a cause must always precede its
effect] ... [since] it rejects *a priori* certain legitimate physical hypotheses that posit backwards or simultaneous causation.

I identify with the desire to maintain as general a theory as possible, but our intuitions about causation seem intimately bound to
temporal precedence. Science fiction stories about "backward causation" are amusing precisely because we have such conflicting intuitions about what the concept might mean. We should be wary of
philosophical theories which flatly contradict human intuition, especially when dealing with concepts which we use regularly in everyday
life. I believe this is Heidegger's criterion of respecting the house-
wife's intuition (with apologies for the sexism present in this original
phrasing) [33]. Lewis himself says,

I shall not discuss [the case in which] two overdetermining
factors have equal claim to count as causes. For me these
are useless as test cases because I lack firm naive opinions
about them ([45], footnote on p. 191).

Does Professor Lewis have better intuitions about backward causation?[3]

6. Even less controversial than the previous property, is the fact that
the entities participating in the causal relation have a temporal dimension. Often they are called 'events.' Says Lewis,

I shall confine myself to causation among *events*, in the
everyday sense of the word: flashes, battles, conversations,
impacts, strolls, deaths, touchdowns, falls, kisses, and the
like. Not that events are the only things that cause or can
be caused; but I have no full list of the others, and no good
umbrella-term to cover them all ([45], p. 182).

As was said in the previous section, Suppes too speaks of causation
among events, but says nothing about them except that they have
a temporal dimension. While technically the definition is precise, I
find that it does not reflect my full intuition about those entities that
cause and are caused. I believe that pinning down the nature of the
participants in the causal relation, in a way that is both rigorous

---

[3]Although I reject Professor Lewis' dissociation of causation from temporal precedence, I agree with him that making that association does not on its own solve the
problem of epiphenomena, discussion of which is the context of the quoted text.

and intuitive, is a prerequisite for a satisfactory account of causation. J. Kim seems to agree with me on this point. At the beginning of his article [40], in which he pronounces Mackey's theory of causation unacceptable on account of its shaky ontological foundations, he says the following:

> Any discussion of causation must presuppose an ontological framework of entities among which causal relations are to hold, and also an accompanying logical and semantical framework in which these entities can be talked about. We often take *events* as causes and also as effects; but entities of other sorts (if indeed they are 'other sorts'[4]), such as *conditions, states, phenomena, processes*, and sometimes even *facts*, are also pressed into service when we engage in causal talk . . . .

7. Causal terminology consists of other verbs besides the actual 'cause,' such as 'enable' and 'prevent.' The meaning of those does not follow obviously from the meaning of 'cause.' In particular, enabling seems to play an auxiliary role to causation, and, although I've had arguments on this point, it seems to me that preventing E is not the same as causing the absence of E (for example, they differ counterfactually: 'P prevented E' implies that if P had not taken place then X would have, but this is not true for 'C caused $\neg E$'). It would be nice to have a theory of causation sort out the subtle differences between such terms, and yet I can't think of one that has (Suppes does speak of *negative causation*, but, as I have just said, in my opinion that is a notion distinct from 'preventing').

8. The last property of causation is of a different kind, since it is Darwinian rather than technical. The observation is simply that causal reasoning is amazingly ubiquitous in everyday life. As was discussed at the beginning of the chapter, people resort to causal terminology given half a chance. A plausible conclusion is that there is some advantage to causal reasoning, and therefore it is reasonable to expect a good theory of causation to tell us what that advantage is. I have not seen explicit discussion of this consideration *anywhere* in the philosophical literature, but the computational role of causation will in fact be the foundation of my own account of the concept.

---

[4]I will claim that, for the purpose of discussing causation, they are not - Y.S.

6.3   A computational account of causation

Let me now offer a new account of causation which appears to explain all
the properties of the concept that were enumerated in the previous section.
My starting point will be its last property, the ubiquity of causal reasoning in commonsense reasoning. In light of the discussion in Chapters 1, 3
and 4, the reader will probably not be surprised by my approach: I will
claim the concept of causation was invented by the man-in-the-street in
order to reconcile his information-processing limitations with his desire for
structured thinking about the world. The demands of the world force him
to predict the future both reliably and fast, and causation is a mechanism
for accommodating these conflicting requirements. This mechanism dic-
tates the form in which knowledge about the world is represented, what
meaning is assigned to this representation, and how inferences are drawn.
Specifically, I will suggest that the mechanism of causal reasoning consists
of representing the world in a temporal framework such as I have outlined,
interpreting the representation according to the rules of *chronological ignorance* defined in Chapter 3, and attempting to keep the theories in the form
of *causal theories* so that, as shown in Chapter 4, predicting the future can
be done very efficiently. Let me now go into the details.

6.3.1   Two kinds of causal statements

There are two kinds of statements that I would like to account for: 'x causes
y', and 'x (actually) caused y'. A third kind of statement, 'x's cause y's',
is the result of quantifying over time in statements of the first kind, and
will not be dealt with separately.

6.3.2   The participants in the causal relation

The first issue to settle is the nature of the x and the y just mentioned. As
we have seen, both Lewis and Suppes take them to be events. Indeed, some
causal relations hold between objects that we tend to call 'events,' as in "the
tackle by the defensive lineman caused the breaking of the quarterback's
leg"; both "the lineman tackled" and "the leg broke" can be said to be
'events.' But, as Kim says in the passage quoted earlier, often effects do
not correspond to what we ordinarily call 'events.' For example, we say
"spilling the water caused the floor to be wet," but "the floor is wet" is

usually said to be a 'fact' (or a 'proposition,' or a 'property'), not an event. Causes too can be made up of propositions, as in "the fact that there were both an acid and a base in the plate caused salt to be in the plate a little later."

Clearly, the distinction between events and propositions becomes blurred very fast. One difference that might seem to hold is that whereas events are objects isolated from one another, propositions can be combined (using logical connectives) to form new propositions. But surely this is also a property we would want of events: shouldn't we be able to combine two 'person playing chess' events to one 'chess match' event? If we do, what distinguishes events from propositions?

I argue that nothing does, or at least nothing that is relevant in this context, and that if the theory of events were developed to a degree comparable with the theory of propositions (i.e., logic), the two would become indistinguishable.

I suggest that the fundamental concept should be that of a *temporal proposition*, which in the particular logic of time intervals used here is the construct $TRUE(t_1,t_2,p)$.[5] Recall the discussion in Section 4 of Chapter 2 where it was said that, depending on the circumstances, a temporal proposition corresponds to what is usually called a 'fact,' an 'event,' a 'process,' and so on. In particular, *liquid* temporal propositions corresponded to facts, and *solid* temporal propositions corresponded to events. Other temporal propositions correspond to neither, such as temporal propositions that are *upward-hereditary* but not *downward-hereditary*.

Temporal propositions, I suggest, are precisely the umbrella-term that Lewis, according to his own words, lacked. I know of no established term for the semantic counterpart of these syntactic entities, and so I will make one up: let us call the object in the real world which is denoted by a temporal proposition (be it a fact, event, process, or whatever) a *happening*. I will define causal statements over temporal propositions, and thus have what are perceived as causal relations hold between happenings in the world.

---

[5]In Chapter 2 I gave the reasons for the constructing a temporal logic in the particular way that I did. I will indeed use that logic of time intervals, but the discussion here does not depend on its details in any important way; a similar analysis could be given for any standard temporal logic.

6.3.3   'x *causes* y'

Causal statements refer, then, to sentences in the temporal logic. I argue further that these statements involve the concept of knowledge, and that in fact the underlying semantics assume chronological minimization of knowledge. In other words, causal statements are based on the logic of chronological ignorance. Furthermore, any causal statement is made and is understood relative to some causal theory (I am using the term 'causal theory' in the technical sense defined in the Chapter 4). This is true even though we never mention the causal theory explicitly; that is always understood implicitly from the context (for example, commonsense theories of the world that are shared among people in everyday conversation).

Let us first look at the first kind of statement, 'x causes y,' whose simple analysis will be somewhat anticlimactic. I will look at "direct causation," i.e., the nontransitive relation. The general concept can be taken as its transitive closure. First, since the x and y are temporal propositions, we are really looking at a sentence 'TRUE(t_1, t_2, p) causes TRUE(t_3, t_4, q).' I suggest that the truth of this sentence is judged relative to some causal theory Ψ, and it is true just in case Ψ contains a causal rule $\Box(t_1, t_2, p) \wedge \Theta \supset \Box(t_3, t_4, q)$, where Θ is some conjunction $\bigwedge_{i=1}^{n} \Diamond(t_{i,1}, t_{i,2}, r_i)$.

For example, when we say that pulling the trigger of the gun at time 5 causes noise at time 6, it is because the background causal theory contains the causal rule

$$\Box(5,5,\texttt{pulltrigger}) \wedge \Diamond(5,5,\texttt{air}) \wedge \Diamond(5,5,\texttt{firingpin}) \wedge \ldots \supset$$
$$\Box(6,6,\texttt{noise}).$$

(Here I have simplified the causal rule by omitting the condition about the gun being loaded, but see the discussion below on *conjunctive* causation.) More generally, when we say that pulling the trigger of a gun causes a noise at the next time instant, it is because the background causal theory contains the causal rules

$$\Box(t,t,\texttt{pulltrigger}) \wedge \Diamond(t,t,\texttt{air}) \wedge \Diamond(t,t,\texttt{firingpin}) \wedge \ldots \supset$$
$$\Box(t+1,t+1,\texttt{noise}),$$

for all t. This is also the source of general causal statements of the form 'x's cause y's.'

I must confess that, although this definition turns out to have the right technical properties, its strong syntactic nature is dissatisfying. This is somewhat mitigated by the fact that causal rules are not arbitrary, and the motivation behind the division between □-conditions and and ◇-conditions is semantic (in particular, it is based on statistical facts about the domain). Another consolation is the fact that the definition of 'actual' causation, given below, is heavily semantic. Still, in future research I hope to be able to rest the definition of causation on a purely semantic basis, making the connection to syntactic objects a theorem rather than a definition.

6.3.4 'x *(actually) caused* y'

The analysis of the other kind of causal statement will be only slightly more complex. Contrary to the first statement which was analyzed on purely syntactical grounds, analysis of this one relies on semantical notions. Again, the statement 'TRUE(t_1,t_2,p) (actually) caused TRUE(t_3,t_4,q)' will be judged relative to some causal theory Ψ. Specifically, we say that TRUE(t_1,t_2,p) is an *actual cause* of TRUE(t_3,t_4,q) with respect to the theory Ψ just in case the following properties hold (in the following, let M be the "unique" c.m.i. model of Ψ):

1. Ψ contains a causal rule □(t_1,t_2,p) $\wedge$ Θ $\supset$ □(t_3,t_4,q) , where Θ is some conjunction $\bigwedge_{i=1}^{n}$ ◇($t_{i,1}$,$t_{i,2}$,r_i),

2. $M \models$ □(t_1,t_2,p), and

3. $M \models$ ◇($t_{i,1}$,$t_{i,2}$,r_i), for $i = 1, \ldots, n$.

We will now say that TRUE(t_1,t_2,p) (actually) caused TRUE(t_3,t_4,q) just in case TRUE(t_1,t_2,p) is the *only* actual cause of TRUE(t_3,t_4,q).

For example, we say that pulling the gun's trigger at time 5 caused a noise at time 6 since the background causal theory contains the causal rule

$$\text{□(5,5,pulltrigger)} \wedge \text{◇(5,5,air)} \wedge \text{◇(5,5,firingpin)} \wedge \ldots \supset$$
$$\text{□(6,6,noise)},$$

its c.m.i. models satisfies the l.h.s. of this causal rule, and there is no other causal rule in the theory with the same property.

This definition of causation has obvious extensions. First, we can take its transitive closure to be *indirect* causation. We can also generalize the definitions to the notions of *conjunctive* (or *joint*) *causation* and *disjunctive causation*. The former are cases in which the l.h.s. in the causal rule has more than one □-conjunct, and the latter cases in which causal rules with distinct □-conjuncts on the l.h.s. share the same r.h.s. The formal definitions are straightforward and I will leave them to the reader.

6.3.5   Properties of the new definition of causation

I obviously cannot "prove" that this account of causation is correct in any sense. What I can do is point to some of its attractive properties, and I will do so by testing it against the "benchmarks" listed in Section 6.2.

1.   (Relation to material implication.) Clearly, by definition we can have TRUE(t_1,t_2,p) cause TRUE(t_3,t_4,q) without implying it, and vice-versa. In particular, the requirement that the causal rule be a member of the causal theory makes causation stronger than material implication, and the existence of the ◇-conjuncts on the l.h.s. of the causal rule makes it weaker.

2.   (Nonmonotonicity.) ◇-conjuncts on the l.h.s. of causal rules also make causation nonmonotonic: TRUE(t_1,t_2,p) may actually cause TRUE(t_3,t_4,q) by virtue of □(t_1,t_2,p) ∧ ◇(t_5,t_6,r) ⊃ □(t_3,t_4,q), which means that this causal connection would no longer exist if □(t_5,t_6,¬r) were to hold.

3.   (Indexicality.) I was very explicit about the indexicality of causation: the "causal field" is the causal theory, relative to which causal relations either do or do not hold.

4+5.   (Temporal precedence, antisymmetry, antireflexivity.) From the definition of causal theories it follows that causes strictly precede their effects, and therefore that causation is antisymmetric and antireflexive. It was already mentioned that prohibiting simultaneity of cause and effect is too strong a restriction. In the last chapter I briefly discuss ways to list this restriction.

6.   (Temporal dimension.) As was discussed at some length, the participants in the causal relation are temporal propositions, which by definition have a a temporal dimension.

7.   (Enabling, preventing.) The setting in which causation was defined suggests natural definitions of causal verbs other than 'cause.' Let me discuss two such verbs, 'prevent' and 'enable.' I suggest that

the meaning of those centers around exactly those objects that were ignored in the definition of 'cause': the $\Diamond$-conjuncts on the l.h.s. of causal rules.

Preventing and causing are not symmetric notions: 'x prevented y' is not quite the same as 'x caused ¬y.' For example, they differ counterfactually, since in the first case if x hadn't been true then y would have, but in the second case that's false. This motivates the following definition of *direct prevention*, which will then be extended to a more general notion.

Again, the statements 'x prevents y' and 'x (actually) prevented y' are made relative to some causal theory Ψ. We will say that TRUE(t_1,t_2,p) prevents TRUE(t_3,t_4,q) just in case Ψ contains a sentence (either a causal rule or a boundary condition) $\Phi \wedge \Theta \supset$ TRUE(t_3,t_4,q), and $\Diamond(t_1,t_2,\neg p)$ is a conjunct of Θ.

Similarly, we will say that TRUE(t_1,t_2,p) is an (actual) direct preventing condition of TRUE(t_3,t_4,q) if the following is true (in the following, again let M be the "unique" c.m.i. model of Ψ):

1. Ψ contains a causal rule $\Phi \wedge \Theta \supset \Box(t_3,t_4,q)$,

2. $\Diamond(t_1,t_2,\neg p)$ is a conjunct of Θ,

3. $M \models \Phi$,

4. $M \not\models \Box(t_3,t_4,q)$, and

5. $M \models \Box(t_1,t_2,p)$.

Finally, we say that TRUE(t_1,t_2,p) (actually) directly prevented TRUE(t_3,t_4,q) just in case TRUE(t_1,t_2,p) is the only (actual) direct preventing condition of TRUE(t_3,t_4,q). For example, if in the shooting scenario an extra condition is added about the gun having no firing pin, then this extra fact will be said to directly prevent a noise following the pulling of the trigger.

This definition too has obvious extensions to *conjunctive* prevention (where several conditions "block" different causal rules with the same r.h.s.) and *disjunctive* causation (where several $\Diamond$-conditions on the l.h.s. of the same causal rule are violated). The precise definitions are omitted.

We can now define a more general notion of prevention, *indirect* prevention. According to it, TRUE(t_1,t_2,p) indirectly prevented TRUE(t_3,t_4,q) just in case TRUE(t_1,t_2,p) indirectly caused TRUE(t_5,t_6,r), and TRUE(t_5,t_6,r) (directly) prevented TRUE(t_3,t_4,q). For example, in firing-pin-less gun case, we can say that removing the firing pin from the gun indirectly prevented the fact of noise following the pulling of the trigger.

Finally, we notice that 'enabling' is the dual to 'preventing' in the following sense: TRUE(t_1,t_2,p) enables TRUE(t_3,t_4,q) just in case TRUE(t_1,t_2,¬p) prevents TRUE(t_3,t_4,q). This directly yields definitions of enabling conditions, direct and indirect, and so on. For example, we have that the gun's having a firing pin enabled the fact of the noise following the pulling of the trigger.

8. (Computational utility.) As I said early on, the most striking feature of causal reasoning is its ubiquity, and it is therefore this property that I'm most anxious to account for. I believe I am now in a position to do so, and in fact the utility of causal reasoning has been the subject of Chapter 4. The logic of chronological ignorance was proposed as a solution to very real problems in temporal reasoning, including the *qualification problem*. The solution to the problem enables one to represent temporal information in a way that on the one hand does not require explicit storage of overwhelming amounts of data (in the gun example – the atmospheric conditions, the fact that the gun has a firing pin, etcetera), and on the other hand does not require overidealization of the world (e.g., occasionally guns indeed do not have firing pins.) Furthermore, it is not only storage space that is saved: the particular form of causal theories enables one to predict the future *efficiently*, as shown in the previous chapter.

   Since predicting the future efficiently and reliably is a crucial ability in our world, these properties of causal reasoning are of tremendous value to us. I think it is reasonable to argue that very early on (both evolutionarily and developmentally) people learned these advantages of causal reasoning, which accounts for the fact that causation is ingrained so deeply into our everyday thinking.

6.3.6   Comparison with the three philosophical accounts

The details of my proposal are quite different from those in the three philosophical accounts discussed earlier, and for that matter from any other account of causation with which I am familiar. Still, I share many of the intuitions behind the three philosophical theories, and so let me briefly point out some commonalities.

As was discussed, Mackey's motivation for defining INUS conditions was to escape the problems that arise when one tries the obvious definitions of causation in terms of necessary and sufficient conditions. For that reason he requires that there be other conditions that, together with the cause, are sufficient to guarantee the effect. I had the same intuition in defining causal rules, the difference being that, through the use of modal logic, I made those other conditions secondary: whereas causes need to be known (i.e. they are $\Box$-conditions), it is sufficient that the "enabling" conditions not be known to be false (i.e., they are $\Diamond$-conditions). Then, by employing a nonmonotonic underlying logic, I was able to avoid the problems that were discussed in connection with Mackey's treatment.

With Lewis I share the intuition that causation is related to a certain kind of conditional statements, but I reverse the perspective. I suggest reducing the notion of (causal) counterfactual implication to the notion of causation, rather than vice versa. It is, admittedly, tempting to take the similarity measure between worlds as a basic notion, since answers to the question "what would (have) happen(ed) if" seem very immediate on introspective grounds. The problem is that introspection can be very misleading. In particular, I believe that our answers to such counterfactual statements rely on other mechanisms, most notably causal reasoning. The reason these answers seem so effortless is precisely because causal reasoning is so basic. In fact, when you think of counterfactual conditions that are *not* causal, such as "if 1 were equal to 2 then ...," the answers seem much slower in arriving, which strengthens the case for the primacy of causation over counterfactual implication.

Certainly the reduction of causation to similarity between worlds is not on its own satisfying from a computational point of view, since it leaves open the question of how one constructs good similarity measures. As I have said, in my opinion this measure is the outcome of the more basic process of causal reasoning. Those who disagree are presumably under the obligation to produce a similarity measure that accounts for the sorts of reasoning which we usually view as causal. I do not believe such a measure has been offered, although M. Ginsberg has argued very eloquently on behalf of the computational utility of Lewis' theory of counterfactuals. His approach is explained in [21], where the theory is applied to diagnosing malfunctions of electronic circuits.

I am particularly in sympathy with Suppes in his account of causation. In particular, I share with him the view that causation is intimately bound to uncertainty, and that its definition relies on the prior notion of temporal precedence (although, while he seems almost apologetic about the latter assumption, I take definite pride in it). The fundamental difference between the two formulations is in how the notion of uncertainty is incorporated. Suppes embodies it in the language itself through the use of probabilities. I elect to capture it by talking directly about knowledge and ignorance. For example, Suppes would say that pulling the gun's trigger causes a noise since the conditional probability of a noise given the trigger-pulling is greater than the unconditional probability of noise. I, on the other hand, postulate a logical sentence, in which knowledge of a trigger-pulling and ignorance of a host of other conditions together imply knowledge of noise.

There is nevertheless a close connection between my account and probabilistic information, and therefore between my account and Suppes'. Recall the earlier discussion of the extra-logical probabilistic reasons for adopting nonmonotonic theories in general (Chapter 3, Section 2), and causal rules in particular (Chapter 4, Section 4). For example, the reason for adopting the rule

$$\Box(t,t,\text{pulltrigger}) \land \Box(t,t,\text{loaded}) \land \Diamond(t,t,\text{air})$$
$$\land \Diamond(t,t,\text{firingpin}) \land \dots \supset \Box(t+1,t+1,\text{noise})$$

rather than the "true" rule

$$\Box(\ \text{TRUE}(t,t,\text{pulltrigger}) \land \text{TRUE}(t,t,\text{loaded}) \land \text{TRUE}(t,t,\text{air})$$
$$\land \text{TRUE}(t,t,\text{firingpin}) \land \dots \supset \text{TRUE}(t+1,t+1,\text{noise}))$$

is that the conditions $\text{TRUE}(t,t,\text{air}) \land \text{TRUE}(t,t,\text{firingpin}) \land \dots$ are highly likely, and therefore, since we assume minimal knowledge, the first formulation allows us in most cases to omit explicit mention of those mundane conditions. But since mundane conditions are by definition highly probable, it follows that conditional probability of $\Box(t+1,t+1,\text{noise})$ given $\Box(t,t,\text{pulltrigger}) \land \Box(t,t,\text{loaded})$ will be higher than the unconditional probability of $\Box(t+1,t+1,\text{noise})$. In other words, not only is Suppes' treatment compatible with mine, but it actually follows from it.

6.4   Causation in AI, revisited

At the beginning of the chapter I discussed the fact that causal terminology appears very frequently in AI. Let me end the chapter with an informal discussion of the role causation might be expected to play in AI, this time in light of the foregoing analysis of the concept.

I have argued that causal reasoning is a mechanism for predicting the future both efficiently and reliably. It requires one to organize temporal knowledge in the form of causal theories and to interpret those according to the logic of chronological ignorance, and enables him to compute the consequences of this body of knowledge efficiently. This form of representation – implication from knowledge and ignorance about the past to knowledge about the future – is very intuitive, and the style of reasoning – propagation of effects into the future – is a natural one too. The claim is that this is no accident, since we all employ the same technique in our everyday thinking.

Consider, for example, Pople's "causal networks" that were mentioned at the beginning of the chapter. Those were graphs whose nodes were symptoms and diseases, and whose directed edges meant intuitively "is caused by." We can now give a precise meaning to such a graph. The nodes really have a hidden temporal dimension (i.e., symptoms and diseases that took place at particular times), and the "caused by" connection is indeed the causal connection that was defined earlier: "influenza at time t_2" is caused by "exposure to cold weather at time t_1" (to use a simplistic example) not because the latter implies the former, but because the statement represents some causal rule such as $\Box(t_1,t_1,\texttt{exposure}) \wedge \Theta \supset \Box(t_2,t_2,\texttt{influenza})$, where Θ is some conjunction of $\Diamond$-conditions.

This means that the causal network loses part of the causal information, namely the $\Diamond$-conditions, which in turn suggests a slight modification of causal networks: edges could be annotated by "exceptions," which would recapture the information present in the $\Diamond$-conditions. For example, the edge connecting "influenza at time t_2" and "exposure to cold weather at time t_1" may be annotated by "wearing warm clothes at t_1" and "high tolerance to cold weather at t_1." These annotations are pointers to other nodes, which themselves may participate in causal relations. For example, "high tolerance to cold weather at t_1" can be caused by "living in an arctic climate for 20 years prior to t_1." Of course, the hard question is what specific causal rules and annotations should be present (for example, the exposure-influenza rule used as an example seems very unlikely), and this is where the insight of knowledgeable people such as Pople becomes crucial. All I have suggested is the *form* such knowledge should take, its associated semantics, and an algorithm for propagating information forward in time.

Causal theories have another benefit, beside being rigorous, natural, and supporting efficient inferences. This added benefit is their *modularity*, which makes them convenient to use in a dynamic setting, one in which new rules are learned and old ones modified as new knowledge is added. This property is an important one to have, if we expect our theories of lawful change to be anything other than toy theories. Constructing rich theories will be a long process in which formulations will require constant modification. In fact, it has been argued that we will never be able to explicitly teach our programs all they need to know. Just as people learn on their own (again, I mean this both developmentally and evolutionarily), our programs will have to be able to construct theories which account for the data they already have. In this case it will certainly be true that as new data become available, old theories will have to be revised. Either way, whether the updating of the theories is done manually or mechanically, it will be most advantageous to keep the required revision down to a minimum, and for this a modular representation is needed.

Causal theories are modular in the sense that one can alter the predictions of a causal theory by adding causal rules, without modifying existing ones (since old predictions rely on some ◇-conditions, which may be vio lated by the new causal rules). In fact, causal theories can be made even more modular. Consider, for example, someone (a person, a program) learning about the effect of firing a gun.[6] She might start out with a hypothesis that pulling the trigger always produces noise. She might then modify that, and condition the prediction on the gun's being loaded. Then, in time, she might learn about the other necessary conditions, such as there being air, the gun having a firing pin, and so on and so forth. Depending on the likelihood of each of these conditions and on the gravity of making wrong default assumptions, they will become either □-conditions or ◇-conditions. After a short while the theory will become sufficiently stable so that, unless that someone were fed seriously biased data, any new modifications will require adding only ◇-conditions. For example, in the gun example one might settle on two □-conditions – the gun being fired and being loaded – but add more and more ◇-conditions, such as there being air, there being a firing pin, the gun not having a silencer, and so on.

---

[6]My point here will be not to discuss the process of inductive inference, a topic worth more than such a passing comment, but only the representation from which such a process might benefit.

Since after a while the □-conditions of the causal rule become relatively stable, it would be nice to be able to treat the rule as essentially unchanged from then on, while at the same time registering the added qualifications of its efficacy. Fortunately, it is possible to achieve that, using a trick similar to the "abnormality" trick used by McCarthy in [53]. What we we will do is replace all the ◇-conditions with a single ◇-condition which states that it is possible that things are normal as far as this rule goes. Specifically, we replace the sentence

$$\Phi \wedge \bigwedge_{i=1}^{n} \diamond(\mathtt{t}_{i_1}, \mathtt{t}_{i_2}, \mathtt{p}_i) \supset \square(\mathtt{t}_1, \mathtt{t}_2, \mathtt{p})$$

by the sentences

$$\Phi \wedge \diamond(\mathtt{t}_1, \mathtt{t}_1, \mathtt{normalconditions17}) \supset \square(\mathtt{t}_1, \mathtt{t}_2, \mathtt{p})$$
$$\square(\mathtt{t}_{1_1}, \mathtt{t}_{1_2}, \mathtt{p}_1) \supset \square(\mathtt{t}_1, \mathtt{t}_1, \neg\mathtt{normalconditions17})$$
$$\square(\mathtt{t}_{2_1}, \mathtt{t}_{2_2}, \mathtt{p}_2) \supset \square(\mathtt{t}_1, \mathtt{t}_1, \neg\mathtt{normalconditions17})$$
$$\cdots$$
$$\square(\mathtt{t}_{n_1}, \mathtt{t}_{n_2}, \mathtt{p}_n) \supset \square(\mathtt{t}_1, \mathtt{t}_1, \neg\mathtt{normalconditions17}).$$

We now still minimize knowledge chronologically, except that at each time point we first minimize knowledge of abnormal conditions (such as ¬normalconditions17 at time $\mathtt{t}_1$), and only then minimize other knowledge. Let us called models that are minimal according to this new criterion *normal* c.m.i. models. It is not hard to see that the c.m.i. models of the original causal theory and the normal c.m.i. models of the transformed causal theory agree on the knowledge of all base sentences other than those denoting normality conditions. But if in the original causal theory each new qualification of the causal rule

$$\Phi \wedge \bigwedge_{i=1}^{n} \diamond(\mathtt{t}_{i_1}, \mathtt{t}_{i_2}, \mathtt{p}_i) \supset \square(\mathtt{t}_1, \mathtt{t}_2, \mathtt{p})$$

required modification of this rule, in the transformed causal theory all one needs to do is add more causal rules of the form

$$X \supset \square(\mathtt{t}_1, \mathtt{t}_1, \neg\mathtt{normalconditions17}).$$

These are some of the ways in which causal theories could be put to good use in AI. However, several objections might arise to relying so heavily on causal theories. One such objection might be the fact that causal theories and chronological ignorance are geared towards a very specific kind of inferences, prediction, but predicting the future on the basis of the past is only one kind of interesting temporal reasoning. In the introductory chapter I mentioned several different subareas of temporal reasoning, such as explaining observations, planning to achieve goals, and learning new rules of lawful change. In fact, in the domain of medical diagnosis that was mentioned earlier, it is indeed the process of explanation (or, as it is sometimes, called, the process of *abductive reasoning*) that is needed. This process, which involves reasoning from effects to possible causes, might put into question the wisdom of adopting a representation that supports exactly the opposite inference. Indeed, there is no "unique explanation" theorem that corresponds to the "unique c.m.i. model" theorem, and correspondingly no easy algorithm to compute possible explanations that is analogous to the $O(n \log n)$ prediction algorithm. Why then should we stick with causal theories? Why not organize the knowledge differently so that, for example, prediction might become harder, but planning easier?

I'm not sure I have a good answer, but several thoughts do come to mind in this connection, one of which is the following. Predictive capabilities are really indispensible, even if other functionalities are needed in addition to them: we (and our robots and programs) must be able to anticipate the future, if only to jump out of the way of a falling rock, or to to know that if we hit the tennis ball too hard then we not only lose the point, but also have to look for the ball in the field. In other words, we must predict the future in order to know *what* to plan for in the first place. This means that there is really no real tradeoff between predicting and planning, since the former is always needed. It makes sense therefore to cater to that first basic need, and only then worry about other processes.[7]

---

[7]In fact, even if one wanted to make planning easier than predicting, it's not clear to me how he would go about it; planning seems inherently harder. The tasks of predicting and planning are asymmetrical in that planning is much more open-ended: whereas in predicting implicit is the assumption that "all relevant details have been given," that assumption is purposely absent in planning. For example, when we ask "what will happen when the trigger of the loaded gun is pulled," we have given the information necessary to infer that a noise will follow. On the other hand, when we ask "what could explain a noise" (or, equivalently, how could we bring about a noise), we have not given enough information to constrain the past to have had a shooting event. Indeed, noise might come about in any number of other ways, and if all we care about is that there be a noise then it is unnecessary to constrain the past any further. Still, this remark

Another possible objection to putting such an emphasis on causal the-ories might be that even if they are desirable, sometimes we do not have the freedom to choose the form of our theories. The main area in which this arises is the area of naive theories about phenomena usually explained by physics, and in particular the area in AI which has become known as *qualitative physics*. The main constraints in that area are that one *starts out* with a noncausal, scientific formulation (usually a set of linear, differ-ential, or other equations, either quantitative or "qualitative," the latter meaning that numerical values are replaced by their sign), a formulation about which reasoning is to proceed in a way that corresponds to the way people reason in that domain. Since typically people reason about it using causal notions, most formulations bring in causation in one way or another when reasoning about the given, noncausally-formulated problem.

It is not my intention to speak about qualitative physics at any length. For details of the proposals by people such as de Kleer and Brown, Forbus, Kuipers, Genesereth, Williams and others, the reader is referred to [11]. Rather than discuss any of those, let briefly discuss previous work by H. Simon on *causal ordering*, which appeared in [91] and later also in [92]. I discuss this formulation not only because Professor Simon later became one of the foremost figures in AI, but also because his formulation bears a resemblance to more recent theories in qualitative physics. Indeed, his formulation was resurrected in a recent article coauthored with Y. Iwasaki [39], and compared to the more recent work by de Kleer and Brown [13]. I specifically do not wish to engage in the dispute between de Kleer and Brown on the one hand, and Iwasaki and Simon on the other, over the relative merits of (and magnitude of difference between) the two proposals. As far as evaluating the causal notions in the two systems, my remarks will apply almost equally to both.

In Simon's formulation, one identifies causality within a set of equations (which in the original publications were required to be linear, but really for no good reason), and the entities participating in the causal relation are the variables appearing in the equations. Certain restrictions apply to the set of equations, and causation is defined essentially by the effect of perturbing one variable on other variables. For example, the set of equations might be the triple

---

is put into a footnote since I'm not convinced that it is not merely a reflection of my own biases as a human being who's perception of reality happens to be causal. It could be that a cleverer God would have designed us differently, in which case we might have been able to design our robots differently. As things stand now, however, it seems that these will have to inherit some of our own myopic views.

$$F = M \times A$$
$$F = f$$
$$M = m$$

The variables are partitioned into *layers*, such that the values of variables at layer i can be computed from the values of variables at layers $< i$, but not from values of variables at layers $< i - 1$ alone. In this example the two quantities F and M are placed at layer 0, since they can be determined independently from any other quantities. A is placed at layer 1, since it can be determined by the quantities in layer 0. Essentially, the layer in which a variable is placed is the stage at which it is computed when using Gaussian elimination (at least in the case of linear equations). This relation between quantities is called *causal ordering*, where a variable x is less than y in this (partial) order just in case x is placed at a layer lower than y.

In this particular example causal ordering indeed corresponds to causal dependence, in the sense that a quantity in layer i can be said to be causally dependent on quantities in layer $i - 1$. In particular, it seems natural to say that acceleration is causally dependent on force. However, it is obvious that in other examples the connection between causal ordering and causal dependence breaks down. For example, if the above three equations were instead

$$F = M \times A$$
$$A = a$$
$$M = m$$

then we would have that "acceleration caused force." The notion of causal ordering is really that of "information-theoretic dependence," and to make it into a theory of causation more needs to be said about what quantities are allowed to be manipulated externally, such as F and M in the original example, and which are to be derived from those, such as A in that example (the former are said to be *exogenous*, the latter *endogenous*). These considerations lie outside the theory as laid out by Simon. Also, more needs to be said about the temporal aspect of things, in order to ensure that effects do not precede their causes.

To the extent that Iwasaki and Simon aim to explain the concept of causation (and it seems that they do: "It is the purpose of this paper to show what [statements of the form 'A causes B'] might mean, and how they can be useful in describing the behavior of physical devices," p.3 in [39]), I'm not convinced that they have met their goal. This applies equally well to de Kleer and Brown, who talk about "mythical causality" in devices whose behavior is captured by differential equations. In both cases the authors try to define the notion of causation in the narrow context of a mathematical formulation,[8] rather than relate the noncausal formulation to an independently-defined causal one. I'm sure all four researchers will agree that causation transcends the particular realm of physical devices. Therefore, if the intention is to emulate human understanding of physical devices (and both pairs of authors imply that it is), it seems reasonable to first understand how people comprehend causation (independently of the particular domain), and only then figure out how people apply that notion to the particular domain.

I think what people do in this context is reduce the functional, noncausal formulation to a weaker causal one, trying to make sure that no important information is lost along the way. In the language of causal ordering, people decide what variables are to be exogenous, and then define causal rules correspondingly. In general, given an equation with n variables, the person reasoning about it selects m exogenous ones for some $1 \leq m \leq n$, and constructs causal rules whose l.h.s.'s are made up of the first m and r.h.s.'s of the remaining $n - m$. In the $F = M \times A$ example we have $n = 3$ and $m = 2$ (the exogenous variables are F and M). The causal rules that are constructed depend on the specific theory. For example, in Forbus' theory of qualitative processes one constructs exactly two rules, the one describing the influence of M on A, and the other describing the influence of F on A.[9] In no case, however, is there a causal rule describing the effect of A on F, although that information *is* present in the original formulation.

This means that there are questions that can be answered easily in the original framework but not in the causal one, such as "how hard do you need to push on a block weighing x in order for it to accelerate at rate y?". The transition to a causal theory traded in this information for the ability to make other inferences efficiently. This is somewhat different from Simon's approach: whereas he would have the selection of exogenous variables be inherent in the original formulation itself, I suggest that it has to do with external considerations such as what uses are intended for the theory, which in turn depend on question such as "what variables do not depend on any others" (force is one because we can set it to any reasonable

---

[8]And I tend to agree with Simon and Iwasaki that the apparent differences between their representation and that of de Kleer and Brown are just that, and that the notion of a "device" as used by de Kleer and Brown really carries no more information than is already present in the partial differential equations.

[9]The reader may note that here we have simultaneous cause and effect, which are disallowed in causal theories. For possible ways to remove this restriction see the discussion in Chapter 7.

amount by merely exercising our free will, mass is another since there is nothing *anyone* can do to change it). This theory of "directly manipulable variables" is an independent theory of the capabilities of agents to intervene in the world, and is the source, rather than the outcome, of equations such as $F = f$. Among the theories in qualitative physics, only the one due to Forbus, called *Qualitative Process Theory* [19], imports causal notions from outside the mathematical formulation. In this respect my approach is close in spirit to Forbus', although otherwise the two approaches to reasoning about change are quite different.

All this, however, does not directly address the second possible complaint against causal theories, namely the fact that they are not as expressive as general laws. All I have said that general laws can be weakened and made into causal theories in a way that yields easy reasoning methods. It is true, however, that while causal reasoning is a good rough-and-ready tool, it is also fairly crude. As de Kleer and Brown point out in [13], other forms of reasoning, such as *reductio ad absurdum*, very much enhance the reasoning power. In fact, when one looks at the developmental stages in reasoning about the physical world as laid out by J. Piaget in [71] (and one need not accept his theories in order to accept his data), it is clear that "true" causal reasoning, which develops around the ages of 7-8, is a significant improvement upon previous motivational, magical, moral and animistic explanations of physical phenomena. Later developments, however, such as the ability to employ conservation laws around the age of 11, improve the child's abilities even further. As far as AI programs go, the obvious conclusion from all this is that causal reasoning will have to be augmented by other mechanisms. Unfortunately, these other mechanisms, and their relation to causal reasoning, lie beyond the scope of this dissertation.

Chapter 7

A Final Perspective

The main message of this book has been that mechanical reasoning about the real world can be done in a manner that is both efficient and rigorous. In particular, I have argued that efficiency in the process of predicting the future does not have to come at the expense of reliability. Let me briefly summarize the argument, and then go on to discuss what has *not* been accomplished here.

7.1   Summary of the book

In the first chapter I identified two problems that arise from the conflict between the goals of efficiency and rigor in the particular context of the prediction task, the *qualification problem* and the *extended-prediction problem* (and, incidentally, argued that the latter subsumes the infamous but underdefined *frame problem*). I then proceeded to make the discussion more precise.

In Chapter 2 I defined a language for representing temporal information. In fact, I gave two related logics of time intervals – a classical one and a modal one. Neither one resolves the conflict between the need for efficiency and the need for reliability, since straightforward use of the logics would require compromising one goal or the other – but they form a setting in which a solution can be given.

The solution takes the form of nonmonotonic reasoning. In Chapter 3 I proposed a somewhat new, semantical approach to nonmonotonic reasoning.

Then, in Chapter 4, I defined a particular new nonmonotonic logic, the logic of *chronological ignorance*. I demonstrated that this logic solves the first problem mentioned, the qualification problem, since it allows one to omit "obvious" facts, and still be able to deduce the desired facts about the future. Abstracting away from the particular example (the shooting scenario), I identified a whole class of theories, called *causal theories*, which have nice formal properties in the logic of chronological ignorance (a "unique" c.m.i. model, which can be computed efficiently). I also gave an intuitive motivation for employing theories that have that particular form.

Chapter 5 showed that a slightly more sophisticated use of the logic of chronological ignorance yields a solution also to the second problem, the extended prediction problem. The intuitive concept of *potential histories*, which are ways the world tends to behave in the absence of interference, was embodied in the class of theories called *inertial theories*. It was shown that, although the restrictions on these theories are weaker than those on causal theories, inertial theories share some of the elegant formal properties of causal theories.

Finally, in Chapter 6 it was argued that the solutions offered are more than a mere technical hack. It was suggested that the proposed mechanism corresponds very closely to the commonsense mechanism of causal reasoning, as used by all of us in our everyday thinking. I outlined a new theory of causation, compared it to some previous accounts, and put it in a context of causal reasoning in AI.

7.2   Technical limitations

To be sure, the discussion in this dissertation has been far from complete. To begin with, there are some glaring technical limitations that call for further treatment. These include limiting the discussion to the propositional case, assuming discrete time, and prohibiting simultaneity of cause and effect, so to speak. In this section I discuss each of these in turn.

7.2.1   The first-order case

Generalizing the discussion from the propositional case to the first-order case is completely straightforward. The definition of chronological ignorance can remain unchanged: one prefers delaying knowledge of base sentences, or sentences containing no modal operator. The difference is that the set of base sentences is now the set of sentences in the first-order interval logic discussed in Chapter 2, rather than the those of the propositional logic (and the definition of the "last time point," or l.t.p., of a formula has to be modified accordingly).

The treatment of causal theories and inertial theories also remains intact, if one understands atomic base sentences to mean ground sentences of the form $\texttt{TRUE}(t_1, t_2, [\neg]R(d_1, \ldots, d_n))$, where R is a relation symbol, and the d_i's are ground (i.e., variable-free) terms. This ground nature of the theories essentially reduces them to the propositional case. In particular, inertial theories (and therefore also causal theories, their special case) will have "unique" models. In those models the known base sentences will be the tautological closure of the atomic ones, and the set of the atomic ones will be computable exactly as in the propositional case.

7.2.2   Continuous time

It is less straightforward to relax the discreteness requirement for time. The reader may recall that although the interval logics that were introduced in Chapter 2 made no commitment to any specific underlying structure of time, subsequent discussion in Chapters 4 and 5 assumed a very particular structure, that of the (positive and negative) integers.

This assumption about time made it easier to perform the analyses in Chapters 4 and 5, but it is clear that for many purposes, viewing time in this way is a severe handicap. In particular, when reasoning commonsensically about the physical world, the natural view of time seems to be that of the real numbers. For example, this is true of the "concurrent billiards" scenario which was used in Chapter 1 to illustrate the problems in temporal reasoning, in which billiard balls rolled continuously until a collision point.

The analyses in Chapters 4 and 5 does not hold if we simply switch the model of time to be that of the reals. For finite causal theories, of course, such a transition makes no difference. In this case only a finite number of time points are mentioned, and those can mapped onto the integer line while preserving the order between points.

The problem arises in the context of infinite causal theories, which, due to the presence of axiom schemas, will be the usual case. Here the mapping onto the integer line will not be possible, since the time points mentioned in the infinite causal theory might (and, typically, will) be dense. For this reason the techniques used in the integer case will cease to apply directly.

Indeed, in general the results are simply wrong for the continuous case. For example, the "unique"-model property does not hold. Recall that one restriction on causal theories (as well as inertial theories) was that boundary conditions could not extend infinitely into the past: there was a t_0 such that if $\Theta \supset \Box\varphi$ was a boundary condition, then the l.t.p. of φ could not precede t_0. This condition was necessary in order to prohibit competing c.m.i. models, in which different sets of base sentences were known, each with l.t.p.'s extending infinitely into the past. This restriction is insufficient when one has a dense structure such as the reals, since then these infinite sets of l.t.p.'s can "telescope" to the left. For example, consider the causal theory consisting of the following single causal rule:

$$\Diamond(1/(t+1),1/(t+1),\neg p) \supset \Box(1/t,1/t,p), \text{ for all } t \geq 1$$

This theory has two c.m.i. models. In one $\Box(1/t,1/t,p)$ holds for all even t's, in the other for all odd t's.

This is certainly an artificial-looking theory. The question is whether the multiple-c.m.i.-model phenomenon can be shown to arise *only* in such uninteresting, pathological theories. Although I do not pursue this much further here, I think the answer is yes. The basic property one needs to guarantee, in addition to other properties of causal theories, is that there is no infinite set of time points $\{\ldots t_3, t_2, t_1\}$ such that a) $t_{i+1} < t_i$, and b) for all t_i there is a base sentence φ whose l.t.p. is t_i, such that φ is known in some c.m.i. model of the causal theory. It seems that there exist several sensible restrictions on boundary conditions and causal rules that could guarantee this property.

However, even if causal (or inertial) theories were constrained so as to make the "unique"-model theorem true, the proof of the theorem would have to change, since the inductive construction would make no sense. Instead, one would presumably have to give a proof by contradiction. One would assume that two models differ on knowledge of base sentences. Then, one would have to look for an earliest point which is the l.t.p. of a base sentence on whose knowledge the models differ. Actually, this is not quite right, since such a point might not exist. However, given that the l.t.p.'s of known base sentences are bounded from below (a fact that will require proof), and given that the real numbers are complete (i.e., each descending sequence with a lower bound also has a greatest lower bound), it is guaranteed that there is a time point which is the earliest greatest lower bound of l.t.p.'s of known base sentences, on whose knowledge the two models differ. Based on this fact it seems that a contradiction could be shown, but, as I have said, I have not worked out the details of this argument.

It does not seem necessary from the technical point of view to require that there be no "rightward telescoping" sequence of points $\{t_1, t_2, t_3, \ldots\}$ such that $t_i < t_{i+1}$ and that all the t_i's are l.t.p.'s of some known base sentence. Interestingly, this also corresponds to intuition. Consider a light billiard ball bouncing between massive parallel walls which are moving towards each other (see Figure 7.1). Reasoning about this scenario seems quite intuitive: the ball will hit alternate walls an infinite number of times but with increasing frequency, so that after a finite amount of time it will have touched both walls an infinite number of times. This means that there is a sequence of "rightward telescoping" points at which the ball hit a wall. On the other hand, it seems quite unintuitive to think of the reverse occurrence, in which the ball initiates "spontaneous" oscillations between the two very close but gradually separating walls, hitting the two walls infinitely often in a finite amount of time, until the oscillations are lengthy enough to become observable stretches during which the ball rolls from one wall to the other. This is slightly paradoxical since physics is totally symmetrical in this respect, and it is reassuring to see that the intuitively baffling situations correspond exactly to conditions prohibited for technical reasons.

Notice that even if a proof of the "unique"-model theorem were successful, its nonconstructive nature would yield no algorithm for computing what is known in that model. In fact, since the set of points is uncountable, it needs to be made clear what is meant by "computing the model." This too is work that is yet to be done.

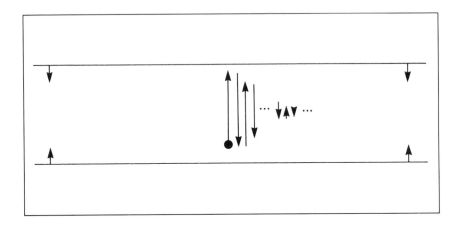

Figure 7.1: An infinite number of collisions in a finite amount of time

7.2.3   Simultaneity of cause and effect

In both causal theories and inertial theories it was assumed that, intuitively speaking, causes strictly precede their effects. In the case of causal theories, for example, for any sentence $\Phi \wedge \Theta \supset \Box(t_1, t_2, \varphi)$ in a causal theory it was required that if either $\Box(t_3, t_4, \vartheta)$ was a conjunct of Φ or $\Diamond(t_3, t_4, \vartheta)$ was a conjunct of Θ, then $t_4 < t_1$. Similar constraints applied to inertial theories.

To see why this can be too restrictive, consider a scenario in which a block is pushed slowly along a rough surface, so that it keeps sliding as long as the force is applied. Intuitively, it seems that the 'cause' (the pushing, or the existence of the force) coincides with the 'effect' (the moving), rather than preceding it. How do we reason about this scenario formally?

The first question is whether time is viewed as discrete or dense. One *could* "digitize" the domain, and state that applying a certain amount of force to an object causes it to move "one distance unit" at the next tick of the clock, but this is quite problematic. For example, two different applications of this rule may predict that two distinct objects will occupy the same space at the same time. Or, what happens if at the time the force is applied, the location to which the block is supposed to slide is occupied? Will the block push it out of the way? Or, if the force on the block is not sufficient, perhaps there are independent forces on this second object that will cause it to move, and thus vacate the spot for the first object? Such concerns were raised by Matt Ginsberg and Dave Smith in [22], whose solution was to leave the world "digitized," but have a mechanism which resolves the conflict between all the possible next states of the world.

I consider it unnatural to view time as the integers in this case, and in particular think it wrong to temporally separate the cause and the effect. What is really going on here is that applying the force at a certain time causes the block to move *at that time*. I'm deliberately being vague here: it isn't important whether one takes the underlying physics to be Newtonian (i.e., $F(t) = A(t)$), Aristotelian, or any other more naive theory of motion. What is important is that the cause and the effect coincide in time.

Suppose one wanted to capture this in a causal theory. A natural causal rule would be something like $\Box$(t,t,strongforce) $\land \Diamond$(t,t,¬blocked) $\supset \Box$(t,t,move).[1] Presumably in this case one would want to add rules such as $\Box$(t$_1$,t$_2$,move) $\equiv \forall t_1 < t < t_2 \ \Box$(t,t,move) and $\Box$(t$_1$,t$_1$,inlocation1) $\land \Box$(t$_1$,t$_2$,move) $\supset \Box$(t$_2$,t$_2$,inlocation2). However, the proposed causal rule alone is already problematic, and so let me concentrate on it.

As I have said, this rule is forbidden in causal theories. The reason for this restriction is to avoid peculiar situations that might otherwise arise. For example, permitting simultaneous temporal propositions on both side of causal rules might permit circular causation: It would allow a set of sentences $\Box$(t,t,p$_i$) $\supset \Box$(t,t,p$_{i+1}$), $i = 1 \ldots n - 1$, p$_n$ = p$_1$. This on its own wouldn't be devastating, but other possibilities would be less benign. For example, one might have a set of sentences $\Box$(t,t,p$_i$) $\supset \Box$(t,t,p$_{i+1}$), $i = 1 \ldots n - 1$, p$_n$ = ¬p$_1$; This would destroy the independence of the past from the future in general, and the "unique"-model property in particular. Or, as another example, one might have have sentences of the form $\Diamond$(t,t,p) $\supset \Box$(t,t,¬p), which would have a similarly detrimental effects on the properties of causal and inertial theories.

Restricting causal theories so that causes strictly precede their effects, as I have done, avoids these problems, but it may be argued that this is an overkill. It is easy to come up with weaker restrictions that are nonetheless sufficient to guarantee the nice properties of causal and inertial theories (for example, requiring for each t a partial order on the propositions p,q for which there exists a causal rule $\Box$(t,t,q) $\supset \Box$(t,t,p)). Indeed, all the examples brought up in the previous paragragh seem contrived, and one can imagine various reasonable restrictions on causal theories which

---

[1]To simplify things, I am suppressing the direction and magnitude aspects here.

would exclude them, but which would still permit forms of simultaneity. Again, although the direction in which to go from here seems clear, I have not worked out the details, and therefore do not understand the issues as well as I would like to.

7.3 What else is missing?

Even if the three particular technical limitations discussed in the previous section were removed, the discussion in this dissertation would still be incomplete. First, several more technical questions may be raised. One such question has to do with the use of axiom schemas in both causal theories and inertial theories. Usually sentences in such theories will indeed be schemas, with the time arguments being the variables (e.g., the effect of firing a gun is the same, regardless of when it happens). Still, the complexity analysis of causal theories referred only to *finite* theories. It seems clear that further analysis is needed, which investigates the complexity of computing c.m.i. models of causal theories containing axiom schemas. Can one do no better than is suggested by the construction procedure in the proof of the "unique"-model theorem in Chapter 4, or perhaps an algorithm can be devised for such theories whose complexity depends solely on the size of the theory?[2]

A related technical question is whether better algorithms are possible for special cases of causal or inertial theories. What about causal theories whose l.h.s. always refers to time points, and never to extended intervals (a "triggering" physics)? Inertial theories that contain no noninertial rules (that is, Ψ_1 in the definition of inertial theories contains no causal rules)? Inertial theories in which the only potential histories are persistences (that is, all sentences in Ψ_3 have r.h.s.'s that refer to time points, rather than extended intervals)? And so on.

This leads to what is probably the main limitation of this dissertation, which is the extreme levels of discussion: I oscillated between concrete, trivial examples such as the shooting scenario, and very abstract, high-level constructs such as causal theories. The idea was that the concrete cases bring out the problems, which are then given a very general solution. The problem with this approach is that it leaves much work to be done when one descends from the high-level solution to intermediate-level classes of problems. For example, in my account of causation given in Chapter 6, I said little about what actual causal theories are employed by human beings. The closest I got to that was to say that the $\diamond$-conditions of a causal rule are those that are typically true in the particular context of reasoning.

---

[2]Here I mean that the size of the theory is its size in written form, with axiom schemas considered on an equal basis with ground axioms of the same length. This is in contrast with the analysis in Chapter 4, where an axiom schema was considered to stand for an infinite set of ground axioms.

I certainly had nothing to say about how such causal rules are acquired and modified, or about the nature of specific causal rules common to most people.

By way of contrast, most of the work in the so-called area of qualitative reasoning is concerned primarily with such "intermediate-level" issues [11]. This area of research aims at determining the behavior of a system specified by "qualitative" differential equations, or differential equations in which absolute values rae replaced by their signs. For example, rather than represent the level of the liquid in a container and its exact rate of change, one represents the fact that there is (say) a nonzero amount of liquid present, and that the container is filling. The particular context of problems representable by partial differential equations is on the one hand special enough to allow special inference techniques, and on the other hand general enough to include many problems of interest. For example, in the simple container scenario just sketched, one would like to predict that either the level of water will stop increasing eventually, or else the container will overflow. Many programs and articles have been written on the subject, for example by de Kleer and Brown [13], Forbus [19], Kuipers [43], Genesereth [20], Simmons [90], Williams [101], Davis [12], Weld [100], and many others. The flavor of the treatment is usually on the informal side (Williams' and (especially) Davis' treatments are exceptions), but the specific properties of the domain are explored in great detail. High-level analyses such as I have undertaken cannot replace these detailed investigations. In future work I intend to give high priority to applying the formulations given in this dissertation to problems such as those raised in qualitative physics.

Yet I do not regret the tack I have taken. As was said in the introductory chapter, we cannot hope for significant and durable advances in AI without resting our theories on some firm foundations. This dissertation is offered as a step towards attaining such a steady basis, so that our theories of time and causation may be well-defined and evaluable. In particular, I have demonstrated that the reassuring presence of logical foundations can be achieved without giving up the ability to make fast and intuitive inferences.

Undoubtedly, further investigations in temporal reasoning will suggest changes in the proposed framework. Temporal reasoning, in both theoretical and applied forms, is a very active area of research nowadays.[3] I have not addressed several recent proposals which relate to the issues raised here, simply because of their fluid status and early stage of development. I expect this trend to gather even greater momentum as we become more

---

[3] Witness the number of articles on the topic which appeared in the recent (August '86) annual conference of the American Association for Artificial Intelligence.

ambitious in our programs which reason about the real world, and more demanding of our robots. And if this prediction about the course of science is at all correct, then the coming years promise to be a lot of fun.

Appendix A

As was said in Chapter 2, detailed discussion of the complexity of the interval logics lies outside the scope of this dissertation. In [25] the complexity of the validity problem for the modal logic is investigated. Here I reproduce the main results, with little explanation and no proofs.

The degree to which the complexity of the validity problem depends on the underlying temporal structure is striking; depending on the class of temporal models being considered, the validity problem ranges from being decidable to being Π_1^1-hard (correspondingly, the satisfiability problem ranges from being decidable to being Σ_1^1-hard.) Actually, for most interesting classes of temporal models, validity and satisfiability are undecidable. One gets decidability only in very restricted cases, such as when the set of temporal models considered is a finite collection of models, each consisting of a finite set of integers (since in this case one can simply perform an exhaustive check on all models). Furthermore, the various hardness properties hold even if we weaken the logic by restricting it to the B, E and A operators.

To make our results precise, we need a few brief definitions. A temporal structure is said to contain an *infinitely ascending sequence* if it contains an infinite sequence of points $t_0, t_1, t_2, \ldots$ such that $t_i < t_{i+1}$. Note that any unbounded structure contains an infinite ascending sequence. A *class* of temporal structures contains an infinitely ascending sequence if *at least one* of the structures in it does. *Complete* temporal structures are those in which any sequence with an upper bound has a least upper bound. A class of temporal structures is said to be complete if *all* structures in the class are complete. A class $\mathcal{A}$ of structures is said to have *unboundedly ascending sequences* if for any integer n there is a structure in $\mathcal{A}$ which contains a sequence $t_1, t_2, \ldots, t_n$ such that $t_i < t_{i+1}$, $0 < i < n$.

The lower bounds can be summarized as follows (in the following, $\mathcal{N}$, $\mathcal{Q}$ and $\mathcal{R}$ stand for (respectively) the integers, the rationals, and the real numbers).

Theorem A.1 *The validity problem for any class of temporal structures that contains an infinitely ascending sequence is r.e.-hard.*

Corollary A.2 *The validity problem for $\mathcal{N}$, $\mathcal{Q}$ and $\mathcal{R}$ is r.e.-hard.*

In fact, Theorem A.1 tells us that the validity problem for almost any interesting class of temporal structures will be r.e.-hard. For example, we have:

Corollary A.3 *The validity problem for each of the following classes of temporal structures is r.e.-hard:*

1. *The class of all temporal structures.*

2. *The class of all linear temporal structures.*

3. *The class of all discrete temporal structures.*

4. *The class of all dense temporal structures.*

In the case of classes that are complete as well as containing an infinitely ascending sequence, we can show that the validity problem is even harder.

Theorem A.4 *The validity problem for complete classes of temporal structures which contain an infinitely ascending sequence is Π_1^1-hard.*

Corollary A.5 *The validity problem for $\mathcal{R}$ and for $\mathcal{N}$ is Π_1^1-hard.*

Even for classes of structures which contain no infinitely ascending sequence we can often get undecidability results:

Theorem A.6 *The validity problem for any complete class of temporal structures which has unboundedly ascending sequences is co-r.e.-hard.*

Let $\mathcal{K}$ be the set of all finite initial segments of the integers:

$$\mathcal{K} \ = \ \{ \langle \ [1..n], \leq \rangle : \ n = 1, 2, \ldots \},$$

$\mathcal{K}$ is useful, for example, when reasoning about possible computations of a program, knowing that the computation is finite but having no bound on its length.

Corollary A.7 *The validity problem for $\mathcal{K}$ is co-r.e.-hard.*

Notice that all hardness results for validity that are at least co-r.e.-hard, in our case co-r.e. and Π_1^1, imply the impossibility of a complete finite axiomatization for the logic.

Appendix B

In this appendix we complete the proof of the "unique"-model theorem for inertial theories, Theorem 5.1, from Chapter 5. It remains to show that if a model M' differs from M on the truth value of $\Box\varphi$ for some base sentence φ, then M' is not a c.m.i. model of Ψ. To prove that, suppose that some model M' of Ψ indeed differs from M on the truth value of $\Box\varphi$ for some base sentence φ.

If $M' \models \Box\varphi$ for some nontautological base sentence φ whose l.t.p. $\leq t_0$, then necessarily M' is chronologically less ignorant than M. It must therefore be the case that there is an "earliest point of discrepancy" between the two models. Specifically, there is an earliest t_2 such that $t_0 \leq t_2$, and such that for some base sentence φ whose l.t.p. is t_2, M and M' differ on the truth value of $\Box\varphi$. It is sufficient to show that for any such φ, if $M \models \Box\varphi$ then also $M' \models \Box\varphi$ (since that will imply that M' is chronologically less ignorant than M).

The proof is by contradiction. Suppose $M \models \Box\varphi$ and $M' \not\models \Box\varphi$, for some φ whose l.t.p. is t_2. Since the base sentences known in M are the tautological closure of the atomic ones, it is sufficient to show that this case is impossible for any *atomic* $\varphi = \text{TRUE}(t_1, t_2, x)$ (x is either a p or a ¬p).

By the construction procedure, if $M \models \Box\varphi$ then either $\Box\varphi \in$ CONSEQUENTS$_{t_2}$, or else $\Box\varphi \in$ NATURAL-DEATH$_{t_2}$ $\cup$ CLIPPED$_{t_2}$. We investigate each case in turn.

1. ($\Box\varphi \in$ CONSEQUENTS$_{t_2}$) Again, by the construction procedure we know that if $\Box\varphi \in$ CONSEQUENTS$_{t_2}$, then either $\Box\varphi \in$ PARTIAL-CONSEQUENTS$_{t_2}$, or else $\Box\varphi$ was added at the last step of the construction interation, as a result of some potential histories lasting at least until t_2. In the former case, two subcases are possible –

either $\Box\varphi$ is the l.h.s. of some causal rule, or else φ refers to a single time point (i.e., $t_1=t_2$, and its knowledge is the result of some new potential history starting at t_1. These three possible case are investigated below.

(a) ($\Box\varphi \in$ PARTIAL-CONSEQUENTS$_{t_2}$, case I) In this case there exists a sentence $\Phi \wedge \Theta \supset \Box\varphi \in \Psi_1$, such that the l.t.p.'s of the base sentences in Φ and Θ are $\leq t_2 - 1$, and such that $M \models \Phi \wedge \Theta$. In this case the argument proceeds as in the proof for causal theories: Since M and M' agree on the knowledge of all base sentences whose l.t.p. $\leq t_2 - 1$, it must be the case that also $M' \models \Phi \wedge \Theta$. But since $M' \not\models \Box\varphi$, M' cannot be a model for Ψ_1, and therefore not of Ψ; contradiction.

(b) ($\Box\varphi \in$ PARTIAL-CONSEQUENTS$_{t_2}$, case II) In this case $t_1 = t_2$, there exists a sentence PROJECT(t_1,p-i,t_1,t_1,x) $\in \Psi_3$, and $M \models \Box(t_1,t_3,$p-i$)$ for some $t_3 \geq t_1$. If $M \models \Box(t_1,t_3,$p-i$)$ then there has to be a sentence $\Phi \wedge \Theta \supset$ POTEN(t_1,t_4,p-i) $\in \Psi_2$, for some $t_4 \geq t_3$, such that the l.t.p. of the base sentences in Φ and Θ are $\leq t_2 - 1$, and such that $M \models \Phi \wedge \Theta$. But this means that also $M' \models \Phi \wedge \Theta$, and therefore also $M' \models$ POTEN(t_1,t_4,p-i), and therefore $M' \models \Box(t_1,t_5,$p-i$)$ for some $t_1 \leq t_5 \leq t_4$. But if $M' \models \Box(t_1,t_5,$p-i$)$ and PROJECT(t_1,p-i,t_1,t_1,x) $\in \Psi_3$, then it must be the case that $M' \models \Box(t_1,t_1,$x$)$; contradiction.

(c) ($\Box\varphi \notin$ PARTIAL-CONSEQUENTS$_{t_2}$) In this case there exists a sentence PROJECT(t_3,p-i,t_1,t_2,x) $\in \Psi_3$, and $M \models \Box(t_3,t_4,$p-i$)$ for some $t_2 \leq t_4$. If $M \models \Box(t_3,t_4,$p-i$)$ then there has to be a sentence $\Phi \wedge \Theta \supset$ POTEN(t_3,t_5,p-i) $\in \Psi_2$, for some $t_4 \leq t_5$, such that the l.t.p. of the base sentences in Φ and Θ are $\leq t_3 - 1$, and such that $M \models \Phi \wedge \Theta$. But this means that also $M' \models \Phi \wedge \Theta$, and therefore also $M' \models$ POTEN(t_3,t_5,p-i), and therefore $M' \models$ POTEN(t_3,t_6,p-i) for some $t_3 \leq t_6 \leq t_5$. However, since M and M' agree on knowledge of all base sentences ending before t_2, it must be the case that $t_2 \leq t_6$. But if $M' \models$ POTEN(t_3,t_6,p-i) and PROJECT(t_3,p-i,t_1,t_2,x) $\in \Psi_3$, then it must be the case that $M' \models \Box(t_1,t_2,$x$)$; contradiction.

From these three cases it follows that $\Box(t_1,t_2,$x$) \notin$ CONSEQUENTS$_{t_2}$. In other words, any non-p-i sentence whose l.t.p. is $\leq t_2$ which is known in M is known also in M'. This leaves us with the possibility that TRUE(t_1,t_2,x) is a p-i sentence, to which now turn.

2. $(\square(t_1,t_2,x) \in \text{NATURAL-DEATH}_{t_2} \cup \text{CLIPPED}_{t_2})$ In this case x must be of the form p-i, $\square(t_1,t_2,\text{p-i})$ denoting the manifestation of some potential history. p-i sentences are known in M only by virtue of being included in either the NATURAL-DEATH set or the CLIPPED set. We examine both cases below.

   (a) $(\square(t_1,t_2,x) \in \text{NATURAL-DEATH}_{t_2})$ By the construction procedure there must be a sentence $\Phi \wedge \Theta \supset \text{POTEN}(t_1,t_2,x) \in \Psi_2$, such that the l.t.p. of the base sentences in Φ and Θ are $\leq t_1 - 1$, and such that $M \models \Phi \wedge \Theta$. But this means that also $M' \models \Phi \wedge \Theta$, and therefore also $M' \models \text{POTEN}(t_1,t_2,\text{p-i})$, and therefore $M' \models \square(t_1,t_4,\text{p-i})$ for some $t_1 \leq t_4 \leq t_2$. However, since M and M' agree on knowledge of all base sentences ending before t_2, it must be the case that $t_4 = t_2$; contradiction.

   (b) $(\square(t_1,t_2,x) \in \text{CLIPPED}_{t_2})$ This is the case whose analysis is the most complex. By the construction procedure there must be a sentence $\Phi \wedge \Theta \supset \text{POTEN}(t_1,t_3,\text{p-i}) \in \Psi_2$, for some $t_2 < t_3$, such that the l.t.p. of the base sentences in Φ and Θ are $\leq t_1 - 1$, and such that $M \models \Phi \wedge \Theta$. But this means that also $M' \models \Phi \wedge \Theta$, and therefore also $M' \models \text{POTEN}(t_1,t_3,\text{p-i})$, and therefore $M' \models \square(t_1,t_4,\text{p-i})$ for some $t_1 \leq t_4 \leq t_3$. By assumption we have that $t_4 \neq t_2$, and since M and M' agree on wffs whose l.t.p. $< t_2$, we also cannot have that $t_4 < t_2$. Therefore $t_2 < t_4$.

   (We are now in a situation where a potential history lasted longer in M' than in M. We now show that this is impossible, since whatever caused the potential history to end in M must have done so also in M'.)

   Since $M \models \square(t_1,t_2,\text{p-i})$, even though the sentence $\Phi \wedge \Theta \supset \text{POTEN}(t_1,t_3,\text{p-i}) \in \Psi_2$ allows the potential history to extend beyond t_2, there must be a sentence $\text{PROJECT}(t_1,\text{p-i},t_5,t_2 + 1,y) \in \Psi_3$ such that $M \models \square(t_5,t_2 + 1,\neg y)$. But why is it the case that $M \models \square(t_5,t_2 + 1,\neg y)$? Since y is a non-p-i proposition, we again have exactly the three possibilities that were explored in part (1) of this proof. In other words, the construction procedure guarantees that one of the following must be the case:

   i. $(\square(t_5,t_2+1,\neg y) \in \text{PARTIAL-CONSEQUENTS}_{t_2 \mid 1}$, case I) In this case there is a sentence $\Phi' \wedge \Theta' \supset \square(t_5,t_2+1,\neg y) \in \Psi_1$, where the l.t.p. of $\Phi' \wedge \Theta'$ is $\leq t_2$, such that $M \models$

$\Phi' \wedge \Theta'$. But from part (1) of the proof we know that all non-p-i sentences with l.t.p. $\leq t_2$ known in M are known also in M'. Thus we have that $M' \models \Phi' \wedge \Theta'$ (since the sentence contains no p-propositions), and therefore it must be that $M' \models \Box(t_5, t_2 + 1, \neg y)$. However, together with the fact that $M' \models \Box(t_1, t_4, \text{p-i})$ for some $t_2 < t_4$, this implies that $M' \not\models \text{PROJECT}(t_1, \text{p-i}, t_5, t_2 + 1, y)$, and therefore $M' \not\models \Psi_3$, and therefore $M' \not\models \Psi$; contradiction.

ii. $(\Box(t_5, t_2+1, \neg y) \in \text{PARTIAL-CONSEQUENTS}_{t_2+1}$, case II) In this case $t_5 = t_2 + 1$, and there is a sentence $\Phi' \wedge \Theta' \supset \text{POTEN}(t_2 + 1, t_6, \text{p-j}) \in \Psi_2$, whre the l.t.p. of $\Phi' \wedge \Theta'$ is $\leq t_2$, such that $M \models \Phi' \wedge \Theta'$, and $\text{PROJECT}(t_2 + 1, \text{p-j}, t_2 + 1, t_2 + 1, \neg y) \in \Psi_3$. But again, from part (1) of the proof it follows that also $M' \models \Psi' \wedge \Theta'$, and therefore $M' \models \text{POTEN}(t_2 + 1, t_6, \text{p-j})$, and therefore $M' \models \Box(t_2 + 1, t_7, \text{p-j})$ for some $t_2 + 1 \leq t_7 \leq t_6$, and therefore $M' \models \Box(t_2 + 1, t_2 + 1, \neg y)$; contradiction.

iii. $(\Box(t_5, t_2 + 1, \neg y) \notin \text{PARTIAL-CONSEQUENTS}_{t_2+1})$ In this case there must be some other potential history p-j, such that $M \models \Box(t_6, t_7, \text{p-j})$, $t_6 \leq t_5 \leq t_2 + 1 \leq t_7$, and $\text{PROJECT}(t_6, \text{p-j}, t_5, t_2+1, \neg y)$. But if $M \models \Box(t_6, t_7, \text{p-j})$, then by the construction procedure there exists a sentence $\Phi' \wedge \Theta' \supset \text{POTEN}(t_6, t_8, \text{p-j}) \in \Psi_2$, for some $t_7 \leq t_8$, where the l.t.p. of $\Phi' \wedge \Theta'$ is $\leq t_2$, and such that $M \models \Phi' \wedge \Theta'$. Notice that we have two potential histories, $\text{POTEN}(t_1, t_3, \text{p-i})$ and $\text{POTEN}(t_6, t_8, \text{p-j})$, which "contradict" one another due to the sentences $\text{PROJECT}(t_1, \text{p-i}, t_5, t_2 + 1, y)$ and $\text{PROJECT}(t_6, \text{p-j}, t_5, t_2 + 1, \neg y)$. This is where the last restriction on inertial theories comes in. According to it, either $\Phi \wedge \Theta$ must explicitly truncate p-j no later that t_2, or $\Phi' \wedge \Theta'$ must explicitly truncate p-i no later that t_2. Specifically, there must be sentences $\Phi \wedge \Theta \supset \Box(t_{10}, t_{11}, z) \in \Psi_1$, $t_{11} \leq t_2 + 1$, and $\text{PROJECT}(t_1, \text{p-j}, t_{10}, t_{11}, \neg z) \in \Psi_3$, or else sentences $\Phi' \wedge \Theta' \supset \Box(t_{10}, t_{11}, z) \in \Psi_1$, $t_{11} \leq t_2 + 1$, and $\text{PROJECT}(t_1, \text{p-i}, t_{10}, t_{11}, \neg z) \in \Psi_3$. However, the former is impossible, since $M \models \Box(t_6, t_7, \text{p-j})$, $t_2+1 \leq t_7$. This means that $\Phi \wedge \Theta \supset \Box(t_{10}, t_{11}, z) \in \Phi_1$, and, since $M' \models \Phi \wedge \Theta$, it follows that $M' \models \Box(t_{10}, t_{11}, z)$. This, however, violates the facts that $M' \models \Box(t_1, t_4, \text{p-i})$, $t_2 \leq t_4$, and $\text{PROJECT}(t_1, \text{p-i}, t_{10}, t_{11}, \neg z)$; contradiction.

∎

Bibliography

[1] B. Abbott. Some problems in giving an adequate model-theoretic account of cause. *Berkeley Studies in Syntax and Semantics*, I, November 1974.

[2] J. F. Allen. Towards a general theory of action and time. *Artificial Intelligence*, 23(2):123–154, July 1984.

[3] J. F. Allen and P. J. Hayes. A common-sense theory of time. In *Proc. 9th IJCAI*, pages 528–531, Los Angeles, 1985.

[4] J. Anderson. The problem of causality. *Australian Journal of Philosophy*, 2:127–142, 1938.

[5] H. Barringer and A. Pnueli R. Kuiper. A really abstract concurrent model and its temporal logic. In *Proc. POPL*, pages 173–183, ACM, 1986.

[6] G. Bossu and P. Siegel. Saturation, nonmonotonic reasoning, and the closed-world assumption. *Artificial Intelligence*, 25(1):13–65, January 1985.

[7] M. Bunge. *Causality*. Harvard University Press, Cambridge, MA, 1959.

[8] J. P. Burgess. Axioms for tense logic ii: time periods. *Notre Dame Journal of Formal Logic*, 23(4):375–383, October 1982.

[9] B. F. Chellas. *Modal Logic*. Cambridge University Press, 1980.

[10] K. L. Clark. Negation as failure. In *Logic and Databases*, pages 293–322, Plenum Press, New York, 1978.

[11] D. G. Bobrow, editor. Special volume on qualitative reasoning and physical systems. *Artificial Intelligence*, 24(1-3), December 1984.

[12] E. Davis. *An Ontology of Physical Action*. Technical Report TR 123, NYU, Dept. of Computer Science, June 1984.

[13] J. de Kleer and J. Seely Brown. *A Qualitative Physics Based on Confluences*. Technical Report, Xerox PARC Intelligent Systems Laboratory, January 1984.

[14] T. Dean. *Temporal Imagery: An Approach to Reasoning about Time for Planning and Problem Solving*. PhD thesis, Yale University, Computer Science Department, 1986.

[15] J. Doyle. A truth maintenance system. *Artificial Intelligence*, 12:231–272, 1979.

[16] E. A. Emerson and J. Y. Halpern. "sometimes" and "not never" revisited: on branching versus linear time. In *Proceedings 10th ACM Symposium on Principles of Programming Languages*, pages 127–140, 1983.

[17] D. W. Etherington. *Reasoning with Incomplete Information: Investigations of Non-Monotonic Reasoning*. PhD thesis, Computer Science department, University of British Columbia, 1986.

[18] D. W. Etherington, R. Mercer, and R. Reiter. On the adequacy of predicate circumscription for closed world reasoning. *Computational Intelligence*, 1(1), 1985.

[19] K. D. Forbus. *Qualitative Process Theory*. PhD thesis, Artificial Intelligence Laboratory, M.I.T., 1984.

[20] M. R. Genesereth. The use of design descriptions in automated diagnosis. *Artificial Intelligence*, 24(1-3):411–436, 1984.

[21] M. L. Ginsberg. Counterfactuals. *Artificial Intelligence*, 30(1):35–81, October 1986.

[22] M. L. Ginsberg and D. E. Smith. *Reasoning about Action I: A Possible Worlds Approach*. Technical Report KSL-86-37, Stanford Knowledge Systems Laboratory, 1986.

[23] J. Halpern and Y. Moses. *Towards a Theory of Knowledge and Ignorance: Preliminary Report*. Technical Report RJ 4448 48136, IBM Research Laboratory, San Jose, October 1984.

[24] J.Y. Halpern, Z. Manna, and B. Moszkowski. A high-level semantics based on interval logic. In *Proc. ICALP*, pages 278–291, 1983.

[25] J.Y. Halpern and Y. Shoham. A propositional modal logic of time intervals. In *Proc. Symp. on Logic in Computer Science*, IEEE, Boston, MA, June 1986.

[26] J. Y. Halpern, editor. *Proceedings of the Conference on Theoretical issues in Reasoning about Knowledge.* IEEE, Monterey, CA, 1986.

[27] C. L. Hamblin. Instants and intervals. *Stadium Generale*, 27:127–134, 1971.

[28] S. Hanks and D. V. McDermott. *Temporal Reasoning and Default Logics.* Technical Report YALEU/CSD/RR 430, Yale University, October 1985.

[29] D. Harel, D. Kozen, and R. Parikh. Process logic: expressiveness, decidability, completeness. *JCSS*, 25(2):145–180, October 1982.

[30] H. L. A. Hart and A. M. Honoré. *Causation and the Law.* Oxford University Press, 1959.

[31] P. J. Hayes. In defence of logic. In *Proc. IJCAI 7*, 1977.

[32] P. J. Hayes. Naive physics 1 - ontology for liquids. In *Formal Theories of the Commonsense World*, Ablex, Norwood, New Jersey, 1984.

[33] M. Heidegger. *What is a thing?* Regnary/Gateway, Southbend, Indiana, 1967.

[34] J. Hintikka. *Knowledge and Belief.* Cornell University Press, 1962.

[35] J. R. Hobbs, editor. *Commonsense Summer: a Final Report.* Technical Report, CSLI, Stanford University, Palo Alto, CA, 1985.

[36] G. E. Hughes and M. J. Cresswell. *Introduction to Modal Logic.* Methuen, London, 1969.

[37] I. L. Humberstone. Interval semantics for tense logics: some remarks. *Journal of Philosophical Logic*, 8:171–196, 1979.

[38] D. Hume. *An Enquiry Concerning Human Understanding.* Open Court Publishing Co., Chicago, 1938.

[39] Y. Iwasaki and H. A. Simon. Causality in device behavior. *Artificial Intelligence*, 29(1):3–32, July 1986.

[40] J. Kim. Causes and events: mackey on causation. *Journal of Philosophy*, 68:426–441, 1971.

[41] K. Konolige. Circumscriptive ignorance. In *Proc. 2nd AAAI*, Pittsburgh, PA, 1982.

[42] S. Kripke. Semantical considerations on modal logic. *Acta Philosophica Fennica*, 16:83–94, 1963.

[43] B. Kuipers. Getting the envisionment right. In *Proc. 2nd AAAI*, pages 209–212, 1982.

[44] D. Lerner, editor. *Cause and Effect*. Collier-Macmillan, Toronto, 1965.

[45] D. Lewis. Causation. *Journal of Philosophy*, 70:556–567, 1973.

[46] V. Lifschitz. Computing circumscription. In *Proc. 9th IJCAI*, August 1985.

[47] V. Lifschitz. Pointwise circumscription. In *Proceedings of AAAI*, Philadelphia, PA, August 1986.

[48] V. Lukaszewicz. Considerations on default logic. In *Proceedings of the Workshop on Nonmonotonic Reasoning*, pages 165–193, AAAI, 1984.

[49] J. L. Mackey. *The Cement of the Universe: a Study of Causation*. Oxford University Press, 1974.

[50] D. A. McAllester. *Reasoning Utility Package User's Manual*. Technical Report 667, M.I.T. AI Lab memo, 1982.

[51] J. M. McCarthy. Applications of circumscription to formalizing common sense knowledge. In *Proceedings of the Nonmonotonic Reasoning Workshop*, pages 295–324, AAAI, October 1984.

[52] J. M. McCarthy. Circumscription - a form of non monotonic reasoning. *Artificial Intelligence*, 13:27–39, 1980.

[53] J. M. McCarthy. Circumscription - a form of non monotonic reasoning. In *Readings in Artificial Intelligence*, pages 466–472, Tioga Publishing Co., Palo Alto, CA, 1981.

[54] J. M. McCarthy and P. J. Hayes. Some philosophical problems from the standpoint of artificial intelligence. In *Readings in Artificial Intelligence*, pages 431–450, Tioga Publishing Co., Palo Alto, CA, 1981.

[55] D. V. McDermott. Contexts and data dependencies: a synthesis. *IEEE Trans. on Pattern Analysis and Machine Intelligence*, 5(3):237–246, 1983.

[56] D. V. McDermott. *A Critique of Pure Reason.* Technical Report YALE/DCS/RR-480, Yale University, Computer Science Department, June 1986.

[57] D. V. McDermott. Nonmonotonic logic ii: nonmonotonic modal theories. *JACM*, 29(1):33–57, 1982.

[58] D. V. McDermott. Tarskian semantics or, no notation without denotation! *Cognitive Science*, 2(3), 1978.

[59] D. V. McDermott. A temporal logic for reasoning about processes and plans. *Cognitive Science*, 6:101–155, 1982.

[60] D. V. McDermott and J. Doyle. Nonmonotonic logic i. *Artificial Intelligence*, 13:41–72, 1980.

[61] R. Montague. Deterministic theories. In in R. H. Thomason, editor, *Formal Philosophy: selected papers of Richard Montague*, Yale University Press, 1974.

[62] R. C. Moore. *Reasoning about Knowledge and Action.* PhD thesis, M.I.T. Artificial Intelligence Laboratory, 1975.

[63] R. C. Moore. The role of logic in knowledge representation and commonsense reasoning. In *Proc. AAAI*, Carnegie-Mellon University, Pittsburgh, PA, August 1982.

[64] R. C. Moore. Semantical considerations on nonmonotonic logic. In *Proc. 8th IJCAI*, Germany, 1983.

[65] B. C. Moszkowski. *Executing Temporal Logic Programs.* Technical Report 71, University of Cambridge, Computer Laboratory, Cambridge, England, August 1985.

[66] B. C. Moszkowski. *Reasoning about Digital Circuits.* PhD thesis, Stanford University, Computer Science Department, July 1983.

[67] N. Nilsson. Probabilistic logic. *Artificial Intelligence*, 28(1):71–88, February 1986.

[68] H. Nishimura. Descriptively complete process logic. *Acta Informatica*, 14(4):359–369, 1980.

[69] R. Parikh. A decidability result for second order process logic. In *Proc. 19th FOCS*, IEEE, October 1978.

[70] R. S. Patil, P. Szolovitz, and W. B. Schwartz. Causal understanding of patient illness in patient diagnosis. In *Proc. of AAAI*, 1982.

[71] J. Piaget. *The Child's Conception of Physical Causality*. Humanities Press, 1951.

[72] J. Piaget and R. Garcia. *Understanding Causality*. W.W. Morton, 1974.

[73] D. Plaisted. *A Low-Level Language for Obtaining Decision Procedures for Classes of Temporal Logics*, pages 403–420. Springer-Verlag, 1984.

[74] A. Pnueli. Linear and branching structures in the semantics and logics of reactive systems. In *Proc. 12 Intl. Coll. on Automata, Languages and Programming*, pages 15–32, 1985.

[75] A. Pnueli. A temporal logic of programs. In *Proc. 18th FOCS*, pages 46–57, IEEE, October 1977.

[76] H. E. Pople. Heuristic methods for imposing structure on ill-structured problems: the structuring of medical diagnosis. In P. Szolovits, editor, *Artificial Intelligence in Medicine*, pages 119–190, Westview Press, 1982.

[77] V. R. Pratt. Process logic. In *Proc. 6th POPL*, pages 93–100, ACM, January 1979.

[78] V. R. Pratt. Semantical considerations on floyd-hoare logic. In *Proc. 17th FOCS*, pages 109–121, IEEE, October 1976.

[79] A. N. Prior. *Past, Present and Future*. Clarendon Press, Oxford, 1967.

[80] Z. W. Pylyshyn, editor. *The Robot's Dilemma*. Norwood, New Jersey, 1986.

[81] R. Reiter. A logic for default reasoning. *Artificial Intelligence*, 13:81–132, 1980.

[82] P. Roper. Intervals and tenses. *Journal of Philosophical Logic*, 9, 1980.

[83] E. Rosch and C. B. Mervis. Family resemblences: studies in the internal structure of categories. *Cognitive Psychology*, 7:573–605, 1975.

[84] D. E. Rumelhart and J. L. McClelland. *Parallel Distributed Processing: explorations in the microstructure of cognition.* Bradford Books, Cambridge, MA, 1986.

[85] B. Russell. On the notion of cause. *Proceedings of the Arisotelian Society*, 13:1–26, 1913.

[86] R. L. Schwartz, P. M. Melliar-Smith, and F. H. Vogt. An interval logic for higher-level temporal reasoning. SRI Intenational, Computer Science Laboratory, , 1983.

[87] Y. Shoham. Chronological ignorance: time, nonmonotonicity and necessity. In *Proc. AAAI*, Philadelphia, PA, August 1986.

[88] Y. Shoham. Ten requirements for a theory of change. *New Generation Computing*, 3(4), 1985.

[89] R. Simmons. Temporal representations for planning. 1984. M.I.T. AI Laboratory, unpublished area exam paper.

[90] R. Simmons. The use of qualitative and quantitative simulations. In *Proc. 3rd AAAI*, Washington, D.C., 1983.

[91] H. A. Simon. Causal ordering and identifiability. In *Studies in Econometric Methods*, pages 49–74, Wiley, New York, 1953.

[92] H. A. Simon. Causal ordering and identifiability. In D. Lerner, editor, *Cause and Effect*, Collier-Macmillan, Toronto, 1965.

[93] E. Sosa, editor. *Causation and Conditionals.* Oxford University Press, 1975.

[94] R. Stalnaker. A note on nonmonotonic modal logic. 1982. Cornell University, Department of Philosophy, unpublished manuscript.

[95] R. S. Streett. *Global Process Logic is Π_1^1-complete.* Springer-Verlag.

[96] P. Suppes. *A Probabilistic Theory of Causation.* North Holland, 1970.

[97] M. Susser. *Causal Thinking in the Health Sciences.* Oxford University Press, 1973.

[98] J. F. A. K. van Benthem. *The Logic of Time.* D. Reidel, 1983.

[99] S. M. Weiss, C. A. Kulikowski, S. Amarel, and A. Safir. A model-based method for computer-aided medical decision making. *Artificial Intelligence*, 11:145–172, 1978.

[100] D. S. Weld. The use of aggregation in causal simulation. *Artificial Intelligence*, 30(1):1–34, October 1986.

[101] B. C. Williams. Qualitative analysis of mos circuits. *Artificial Intelligence*, 24(1-3):281–346, 1984.

[102] L. Wittgenstein. *Philosophical Investigations*. Basil, Blackwell & Mott, 1958.

[103] L. A. Zadeh. Fuzzy logic and approximate reasoning. *Synthese*, 30:407–428, 1975.

Index

The MIT Press, with Peter Denning, general consulting editor, and Brian Randell, European consulting editor, publishes computer science books in the following series:

ACM Doctoral Dissertation Award and Distinguished Dissertation Series

Artificial Intelligence, Patrick Winston and Michael Brady, editors

Charles Babbage Institute Reprint Series for the History of Computing, Martin Campbell-Kelly, editor

Computer Systems, Herb Schwetman, editor

Exploring with Logo, E. Paul Goldenberg, editor

Foundations of Computing, Michael Garey, editor

History of Computing, I. Bernard Cohen and William Aspray, editors

Information Systems, Michael Lesk, editor

Logic Programming, Ehud Shapiro, editor; Fernando Pereira, Koichi Furukawa, and D. H. D. Warren, associate editors

The MIT Electrical Engineering and Computer Science Series

Scientific Computation, Dennis Gannon, editor